What people are saying about

Mercy - One Life, Many Stories

There are many reasons I call her Amazing Grace and you will read about them all in Mercy - One Life, Many Stories.

Grace epitomizes the ideas associated with her name; Grace under fire, Grace under pressure and simply Graceful.

Grace's story will touch you and remind you in these times that are so turbulent what it is to be resilient, compassionate and caring and Grace's story will show you how these still remain the most important human traits; truly amazing, Grace.

Dr. Rick Csiernik
School of Social Work
King's University College at Western University
London, Ontario Canada

Grace's story will serve as an inspiration for anyone confronting major life challenges, feeling hopeless and angry, yet hungry to positively shape their future. She is unsparing in her self-examination and her willingness to share the raw truth, feelings and insights. But she is also unnecessarily sparing in sharing the amazing things she did with her life after her rehabilitation and after her husband's death.

Grace - more than anyone I know - has 'given back': sharing, caring, volunteering and otherwise freely giving of herself not only to family and friends, but also to countless others struggling to walk the same rehab journey. This book is only one example of her generosity of spirit. Kudos to an extraordinary woman! It has been an enormous privilege to have had a small place in her life.

Judith Skelton-Green RN, PhD, FCCHL
Former Vice President Patient Services,
Kitchener -Waterloo Hospital

Grace Ibrahima's book MERCY – ONE LIFE, MANY STORIES is the one that many of us would like to write but may not be courageous enough to do so. Grace's telling of her life story resonates with a unique authenticity and a sense of hope even during the most complex and heart wrenching of experiences. Grace brings wisdom and character to her stories and challenges the reader to join her in this thoughtful account of a life lived intensely and fully.

Dr. Lorraine Carter
Director, Centre for Continuing Education
McMaster University

Through her impressive articulated writing style, Grace Ibrahima has shown us how she turned her own personal life of struggles and turbulence into a beautiful story of inspiration and hope.

Tom Gabriel (retired Police Officer)
EFAP Consultant, Crisis and Addiction Counsellor

Grace Ibrahima's memoir took me on an incredible and empowering journey. From her harrowing childhood of abject poverty, isolation and abuse, to her troubled adulthood shattered by destructive addiction, Grace's resiliency never ceases to inspire. Her clear, honest and candid voice will push you, as it did me, to nurture, value and grow from your experiences.

Sarah E. Kidd
Freelance Writer

It is an honour and pleasure to know Grace. She writes a book of journey, and the trials and tribulations of life.

I learned from my teacher many years ago something that I thought at the time was profound. He intimated that he learned more from those he taught than he believed he taught them. He was paraphrasing a statement of King Solomon who said; "from everyone I have learned". Reading Grace's book brings meaning to challenge and faith. Her words are motivational and directional and can give a person an opportunity to be "better", than they think.

I find her book to be a testament to her name Grace.

Rabbi Nathan W. Langer
Mgr. Jewish Hospice Services
VNA Health Group NJ

E. Grace H. Ibrahima has written a beautiful book. Her candid and down to earth style makes you want to read more and more about her journey.

Grace learns the value of community and embraces her struggles as well as the wonders in her life in a "Grace" full manner. She is an inspiration to me and I am happy to know her.

Angela Vieth
Ward 3 Councillor
City of Waterloo
5198072111

Mercy - One Life Many Stories is a heartfelt, raw and emotional read of a life worth living! Grace's ability to endure abuse, trauma and addiction and then to later embrace recovery is inspirational and moving. Her warmth of character was never lost in the eyes of so many who believed in her long before she believed in herself.

Grace's story is one of turning adversity into determination and pain and loss into appreciation and gratitude.

While I met Grace many years post recovery, her strength of character and determination had not wavered and she had a way of ensuring that I always heard what was needed to be said…and things that I needed to hear.

A story of hope that anyone who has had, or is continuing, their struggle with trauma and addiction would appreciate.

Paula Podolski
Administrative Director,
Mental Health & Addictions,
Emergency Department,
Access & Flow/Interprofessional Resource Team, and
Family Medicine, St. Joseph's Health Centre Toronto

Mercy
One Life, Many Stories

Dear Jacqueline,
Thanks so much
for your support
Take care,

Grace Ibrahima

MERCY

One Life,
Many Stories

E. Grace H. Ibrahima

Angel Hope Publishing

Mercy - One Life, Many Stories
© 2016 E. Grace H. Ibrahima

Library and Archives Canada Cataloguing in Publication
Ibrahima, E. Grace H., author
    Mercy : one life, many stories / E. Grace H. Ibrahama.
ISBN 978-1-988155-08-1 (paperback)
    1. Ibrahima, E. Grace H--Biography. 2. Nurses--Canada--Biography. 3. Immigrants--Canada--Biography. I. Title.
RT37.I27A3 2016   610.73092   C2016-906030-6
First Edition.

ISBN: 978-1-988155-08-1

Printed in Canada
Angel Hope Publishing
www.glynisbelec.com

Innovative Print
innovativeprint.ca

Cover Design & Author Photo by T&J Studios Photography
Amanda Belec Newton
www.tandjstudiosphotography.com

This book is dedicated to Issah Ibrahima for showing me how to start to accept my imperfect self.

Contents

Acknowledgments

I feel as though the traditional African proverb— "It takes a village to raise a child"—is speaking directly to me. My village consisted of numerous people who encouraged me through different times and at varying degrees of my life, some more forcibly than others. It started when you believed in me when I was incapable of believing in myself. Others picked me up and walked by my side when I was down and my soul felt too weary to go on. I know you (my readers) will understand that it is virtually impossible for me to include everyone's name in this list. You know who you are.

Health Facilities and Staff
To the Grand River Hospital and the Labour and Delivery staff, especially, Linda Corso, Nancy Cobb, Sylvia Brown, Ann Jose, Virginia Henry and Doris Balcarras. You saw an ill woman who desperately needed help she neither acknowledged nor was financially able to afford. You stepped in and took control until I could do it myself.

Dr. Dan Carruthers, Chief of Obstetrics, for your words of wisdom, "Grace, you got to do what you got to do." It helped my decision to seek treatment.

Dr. Denise Wren, my family physician, you accepted me as your new patient and made me feel like I was worthy of your time.

Judith Skelton-Green, for your ongoing support, understanding and providing me with a safe haven—free access to your office—in emotionally overwhelming times.

Homewood Health Centre, Guelph, your caring and understanding were unlike anything I had experienced. Yes, you broke through my denial barrier, encouraged me to seriously look at my unhealthy lifestyle, and to eventually find myself. You provided the tools to lead a better and more productive life.

To congregation and the Ministers, Brooke and Linda Ashfield of Knox Presbyterian Church, Waterloo, thank you for your love, prayers and uplifting words. What was most meaningful and especially touching, to both Issah and our family were those last special moments of his life.

Friends
John and Rachel Goodall, you have been resolute supporters and friends, first to Issah, then me and now, to a second generation of Ibrahimas.

Heidi and Dave Pedican, those boxes of nursing textbooks helped with my preparation to challenge the Canadian exams.

Debra Hawkins, your letter of gratitude could not have come at a better time, when I needed a "pick-me-upper."

Sandra Bussey and family, I appreciated your unbiased help and support. Sandra, you helped to decipher complex issues and you are still there for us.

Anita Noel, your amazing teaching talent brought out the best in your students, even me. I won't ever forget our tribute at Issah's funeral.

Magdalena Tomsinska, I do appreciate your ongoing support and friendship.

Paul Weatherhead, at Digital Boundary Group, London, I used the computers that you donated throughout this project. Here is the evidence.

Rick Csiernik, my ex-professor, at McMaster University. You made me feel confident and hopeful by your answers from my first to the last question. Here is the result.

Groups
Fellow members of the Rockway "Write Now" writers' group for helping me learn what writing is about.

The 12-Step Groups, you shared experiences that gave me the blueprint to understand the program of continuous recovery.

My Family

My thanks to my parents and family of origin. You did your best with the available resources.

My sister, Norma Garrett, you phoned me almost every day in those uncertain times.

Isif and Halim Ibrahima and Sherry Sheldon (a.k.a. Sherry Ibrahima), your encouragement kept me moving forward from the conception to the conclusion of this manuscript.

I clearly remember when the first dictation software refused to cooperate and the computer system swallowed pages and pages of my work and refused to give it back, and when my emotions got the better of me.

You were never tired of my thousands of questions. Well, I will never tell the world you said, "Mom, you asked too many questions." Now you know why.

I am glad I did not sign any hourly rate contract! Thank you for picking up part of these editing bills. Your assistance was invaluable.

Issah Ibrahima, my late husband. Last, but by no means least. You taught me so much, especially during my first formal educational sessions. I am still amazed by the inspiration, indefatigable support and the unconditional love that you gave to this broken young woman.

Most importantly, you showed me something new: how to start loving, nurturing and respecting myself. I listened attentively to you then and still hear your voice in my mind. My only regret is I wish you were here to see the outcome of your endeavour.

"Thank You" feels inadequate for all that each of you has done for me. So, for the time being, I am still thinking of a better way to say, "Thank You."

My Editor, Carolyn Wilker

Honestly, you deserve an accolade. I came to you as a 'writing toddler' and now I am feeling like the adult version. You taught me so much. Although some pockets of my stories were nothing more than soul wrenching, I still felt safe to share them because of your wise, calm and compassionate disposition.

As I pen these last words, I cannot begin to express the inner peace and joy I am experiencing because you have shown me how to put those venomous feelings where they rightly belong.

My Publisher, Glynis Belec – Angel Hope Publishing

Thank you for honouring my stories. You did not stifle my voice in telling it, nor did you dismiss the emotions they generated in me. When I completed writing my manuscript, my baby, it felt like I was sending it into the world all alone. I was sure that printing would be the next step after the editing process. I was in for a big surprise.

When I began this work, I knew almost nothing about publishing and what it takes to present a polished manuscript to readers, but I gained confidence in you, knowing you intended only the best for my book.

Amanda Belec Newton, graphic designer for Angel Hope Publishing, and also my photographer.

Amanda, thank you for your patience in not only snapping those photos but also in introducing this seventy-one-year-old to the world of Facebook. Technology always seems to baffle and frighten me. This is just another hurdle to clear towards promoting my book. I am happy to say I feel more comfortable using this tool now.

Foreword

Thank you so much for supporting my mother in her book writing journey! When she first mentioned she wanted to do some writing about her life, I was very excited for her, and a bit worried for both of us as I knew I'd have to provide technical support for this endeavour.

While she had some familiarity with computers, writing a book using one would pose a challenge as she had not been exposed to computers until later on in life. The use of a kindly donated computer and dictation software greatly assisted her, however, there was still a substantial learning curve. As you know or will find out, Grace is no stranger to difficulty. She quickly learned and wisely took notes of important concepts, resulting in an ever-diminishing number of support related calls and emails.

As a curious individual, she did some experimentation in the word processor, which sometimes led to gentle reminders by me in order to maintain our relationship (which is still fully intact) and all of her hard work. Apart from a near disaster of 250 pages, she had very few issues and I can say without bias she was a great "student."

Over the course of many phone calls, it became apparent that it was powerful enough to evoke a range of emotions in both her and others, in addition to great amounts of support from a wide range of individuals and organizations.

Had I the chance to reflect on Grace's two great accomplishments, I would say the first is pushing herself to detail her life, some of which is heartbreaking and emotionally difficult to write. The second is overcoming her fear of technology to dictate, type, and edit over 370 pages.

Mom, you are extraordinary in your ability to persevere, better yourself, and above all else, to inspire those you interact with, and those you don't, the world over. There is no way, literally or figuratively, for me to be more proud of your work and thrilled to have been there to support you, as you have done for me.

Love always,

Isif "Baggin" Ibrahima

I'm so proud of my Mother and in retrospect her path to becoming an author was fundamentally driven by two key attributes:

Courage. Over the years, Grace has never been afraid to share her deepest and darkest secrets with anyone who could potentially benefit from her experiences. This typically occurred at the individual or small-group level. But opening yourself up to a much larger audience and revealing almost every aspect of your life is a completely different level of vulnerability.

My Mom had some hesitancy and reluctance prior to embarking on this literary process.

However, she took a very unselfish approach to resolving her own personal fears. Grace decided the potential discomfort would be irrelevant if even one person gains perspective, inspiration or receives comfort from reading about her life.

Growth. My Mom is never stagnant. My brother and I are continually amazed by her thirst to acquire additional skills and undertake new adventures. Consider this: My Mom didn't finish high school as a teenager and yet ended up writing a biography. That's a pretty sharp academic ascent. Grace would be the first to tell you that she didn't do this by herself. Throughout her life, Grace has been fortunate to always find enthusiastic and supportive individuals to help her push further.

My Mom's accomplishments would not have been possible without a host of people, including my late Father.

The most recent addition to this incredible support system is this book's editor— Carolyn Wilker. Carolyn, I can't even begin to describe the effect this entire literary process had on Grace. This book has been more akin to a journey leading to an awakening. Thank you for your help!

Halim Ibrahima

Grace Ibrahima is truly an amazing woman. All the adversity she's faced with strength, courage and determination to achieve her triumphant life is inspiring. She's a very loving, caring, helpful and fun-loving lady.

So thankful to know her the way I do. Thank you, Grace.

Sherry Sheldon

In the Beginning

Procrastination and more procrastination! That was how I felt for a long, long time. It was like I was trying to face a fearful and anxious situation. What or why, I simply didn't know. I wanted to write about my life many years ago but was almost in a state of paralysis.

So I vowed with all my heart and willpower that on my 68th birthday, there would be absolutely no excuse. A few days later, I took out a folder with a stack of blank lined paper and placed it on the kitchen table. I just left it sitting there. For me it was a start, a little one, but nevertheless a good start. The next evening that same folder was in my wicker basket that holds the things I take outdoors when I am relaxing. It always contains things such as reading material, pencils, dictionary, telephone and a healthy snack.

But today, the fear and anxiety barriers have been cracked; I have started my lifelong dream.

There are many things in my life that I want to tell my children, about the good and bad times, the sadness, and the abuse (physically, mentally, and sexually). To tell them, too, of my childhood dreams and hopes, and how they never materialized and died even before they had time to germinate.

As a determined child, I knew it was just a matter of time that I would be able to work towards realizing my dreams. I also knew that to achieve those things, I needed to improve my life, though it would be difficult. The roads would be bumpy with many potholes. There were many times in my life I had absolutely no idea how I should go about carving out a better one for myself, but I kept hoping.

Yes! Hope kept me going when everything seemed hopeless.

Part 1 ~ Trinidad

"We must accept finite disappointment, but we must never lose infinite hope." **Martin Luther King**

Chapter 1: Early years

As a young child I saw firsthand how adult members of my family and community behaved. My understanding about human behaviours was still in its infancy. Somehow I knew what I observed and experienced was simply wrong. At that time, I had no word to name their ill behaviour. But feelings of anxiety, fear, and doom were almost constant companions. I was born on May 8, 1945, with no choice of the family that was my bloodline. When others talked about their childhood and those formative years full of nurturing, love, hugs and kisses, and encouragement, I could not relate. I had no achievements, small or otherwise. My life was the fields. In my family, school and education were regarded as a waste of time, time that could be better spent working as a child labourer. I worked on many crops, but more regularly on those that produced quick yields, such as peas, beans and cucumbers. Yes, child labour operates even in family circles, and whenever mistakes were made, major or minor, the discipline was predictable. Leather belts, twigs, the full strength of the hands were used to correct the child. Sometimes twigs were bigger and thicker depending on the deed and the present mood. While other children were developing life-long friendships with classmates, organized sports or other early childhood gatherings, I did not have those same opportunities. The order of the day was distant, cold and full of name-calling.

As a child, I often wished to relieve myself of the cursed family I was born into and, at times, wished that I had not been born alive. One of the worst things, there were absolutely no government agencies I could have turned to for help. Our society was so tightly knit that if my parents knew I had complained to another person about being mistreated, there would be consequences in the form of more abuse. So, what was I to do? The best and simplest way was to cope quietly with the beatings.

There were many times when the punishment for something as simple as making child-type noises resulted in me going to bed hungry. Somehow I simply could not understand that type of adult behaviour. Could there have been any other way to correct a child?

Often, I wondered if being in a large family of 12 siblings contributed to the dysfunction. I do not believe the size of my family had much to do with this conduct. My best guess for my parents' heavy-handed approach was that they simply did not know any better, nor did they understand children's developmental stages.

Other parents, adults and the school system were of the same mind, as far as discipline was concerned. That was the fashion at the time. In fact, this type of behaviour could have been handed down from generation to generation, as though it was in the DNA and difficult or impossible to avoid. Sometimes I planned to run away to avoid such a sad, miserable and unpleasant life, but there did not seem to be a safe place or person to turn to. Let me say, this was not a pleasant place to be for an adult, but worse for a vulnerable child. I clearly remembered when my father thought the previous punishment was not severe enough, so he would increase his power.

Whipping Sticks
A mosque separated our property and our neighbour's. On the far side of that building grew a mixture of trees, including guava. Guava was a variety of fruit tree. Their branches were stronger and straighter than the other plants. My father must

have decided that they were ideal for whipping, and my siblings and I would be sure of what was to follow when father returned from his search. He would bring back an arm full of sticks of different thickness for different ages. Somehow I felt as though the girls in the family suffered the worse fate; maybe it was because there were more females than males at that time. Our eldest brother did not suffer the same fate as the rest of us. This brother was regarded as the brainchild in my father's farm business. If he chose to withdraw his expertise, then the business would surely collapse, and that would have been a real disaster for all concerned, especially the workers whose livelihood depended on the weekly pay.

The most baffling thing for me was thinking about how a person could go to church, so frequently, pray, call out God this, God that, and God the other, and yet be so cruel. I clearly remember the wild glares in my father's eyes when he flew into uncontrolled angry spells. They would change into what I thought was a clear message: "get out of my sight or else."

Abusers in My Family
I have experienced first-hand the methods used by my abusers. They did it secretly and by degrees. Frequently the meanness might start with body language, including eye contact. Those quiet unspoken, yet powerful, messages that could stop anyone, especially me, in my tracks. Then the raised voices, yelling and threatening, would be followed by physical abuse.

As a little girl, I clearly remember how my late mother suffered at the hands of my father and grandmother. My mother was the more educated of the three. She could think for herself, her ideas were usually sensible, and if followed through, she could have moved the family forward. This was a very difficult concept for my father to grasp.

His thinking power was not fully functional. Consequently, Mom's bright ideas were viewed as threatening. I believe at that time, the poor man was doing his best, but for me, it was not good enough. We learn from our experiences. I struggle to understand why I saw no behavioural changes. Surely, the anguish on the children's faces would be enough to tug at most peoples' heartstrings. Well, changes never materialized, and the abuse continued. And those behaviours continued with different faces and the same negative effect.

Mealtime Carry-ons
My father did not have to say much for his mealtime demands to be met. His body language spoke louder than his words. The almost steely and determined look in his eyes, furrowed brow and shifting from one foot to the other, said it all. The saying 'actions speak louder than words' applied in this occasion. After his performance, whatever food was available, you could guess who got the lion's share.

For several reasons, we did not enjoy the luxury of having a complete dinner set. First, we did not know about those things and did not have the money to buy a set. Second, we lived in tight quarters, so storage space was an issue. Third, having food, and not fancy dishes, was becoming a matter of survival and not a luxury. Our odd assortments of patterned dinner plates were collected from here, there, and everywhere. I knew they were not from fancy china shops.

They were decorated with more chips than their original designs, and would be piled high with rice, beans and meat. Meat, from whatever the source, was as scarce as finding water in the Sahara.

My father did not appear to care whether his children resembled undernourished war victims, with vacant, pitiful looking eyes, height and weight under par and sporting distended bellies. That was irrelevant. How sad! Was it lack of knowledge? I wonder. I sat at home like a bird in a cage, with an extremely strong longing to fly to freedom and to be at peace.

That was another valuable lesson for me once I became a parent: Never eat before my children were fed. Some days when my belly felt like a bottomless barrel, I wished they would leave me some leftovers. I felt good in a weird way because my boys had enough to eat.

Time with Mom

I felt the happiest being alone with my mother. Mammy was the more educated and forward thinking parent, but my mother was no angel. She had her faults. And yes, she also made several foolish choices. In spite of her faults and blunders, I loved how she spoke about sensible things—the importance of children's education and how their time should be spent primarily in the classroom, rather than in the fields.

She was a strong advocate for open communication, especially between married couples. Her other hot issue was limiting the number of offspring. This last topic—fewer kids—was considered the most unpardonable sin of all and only added fuel to an already uncontrollable blaze. I never knew about my parents' love life or marriage vows because their lips remained tightly sealed.

In those days, birth control was non-existent. Women in that era used a few tried and failed contraceptive tools: the kindness of their lucky stars, the mercy of a higher being, or hoping for the best. And at the end of the day, or the night, the result of these best practices resulted in one thing, yet another mouth to feed.

When my mother presented her admirable ideas to Dad, they died a sudden death. These strange visions must have sat in my father's stomach like intolerable undigested meals. I often wondered whether these bright attitudes might have been the last thing that tipped the scale. Mom never talked much about topics of schooling and having fewer children. I know that because I sneaked in and eavesdropped when my parents were quarrelling. At the end of a particularly heated argument, she would say, "I wish I never married your good-for-nothing father."

My mother's swear words were 'blooming and good-for-nothing,' that's it. I felt like saying "He's your good-for-nothing husband," too. I did not have the gumption to voice my opinion because I would have certainly been on dangerous ground.

Had I been as inquisitive then as I am today, I would have loved to look straight into my parents' eyes and ask them three important questions. The first, how did they initially meet? Second, what was their love life and relationship like early in their marriage? And third, what were their marriage vows? If I had answers to those queries, maybe I would have seen their lives differently.

Chapter 2: Family

W hen I was very young, about six or seven years old, my father insisted that I leave school. My breast buds were not even developed properly. I was, oh, so young! There was not time to notice the changes to my body. There was no time to discuss what this all meant for a young girl. As for bras, what's that? If I knew nothing about a young woman's developmental stages, then how was I to even talk about it? How was I supposed to talk about brassieres and breasts?

The jobs I had to do took priority over me getting advice that would mold me into a sensible young lady.

Grandma

My paternal grandmother lived with us. Because of rheumatoid arthritis, Grandma's movement was compromised. There was no special medical treatment for the crippling disease, however, she managed some of her personal hygiene, walked short distances but was unable to climb stairs. I groomed and dressed her most days. As the years rolled by, Grandmother shuffled, faltered, limped and moved much slower. Eventually her legs grew weaker and weaker. I had the feeling that Grandma knew and did not like the next step.

My Grandma's passion was singing. If she had equal opportunity, she could have shared the stage with Aretha Franklin and other famous gospel singers. When she started bellowing out both those high and low notes with ease, neighbours were forced to take notice. Boy, when she sang, her melody could be heard high on the mountain tops and down in the valleys. We had a bad-tempered, delinquent bull that bolted once, but my grandma's voice could have easily stopped that fella in his tracks, with only two of its hooves touching the ground.

She loved quietly humming a tune or broadcasting her song for the world to hear. I, too, enjoyed that activity. Whether I learned from mimicking her or it is stitched in my DNA patchwork, I will never know.

What I do know was, many times I have chased the blues away, just by singing. I did not often hear her singing after her mobility was reduced, and that saddened me. And this was when my grandma started showing her true colours.

She presented as easily irritated, angry and increasingly discontent towards everything and everyone. She threw things at us or hit any unfortunate soul within her reach.

As her list of complaints grew longer, my patience and compassion towards her grew shorter. This lady became extremely demanding, in spite of my best efforts. Nothing seemed to please her. She even threatened to put an evil curse on whoever refused to bow to her unreasonable demands.

Some of her grandchildren and my mother were on her hit list. Luckily, my name was excluded. I was spared from I do not know what. Some family members teased me frequently. They say I was spared from that list for two reasons. The first, she loved me, and the other, our close resemblance. Whether her curses were real or imagined, I do not know.

Her nonsensical moaning and groaning to her son—my father—became a regular pattern. Her son took these grievances as gospel truth. My hunch was that both mother and son's thought processes were wacky, with a sprinkle of paranoia. It's like the blind leading the blind. Surely, both minds could not be thinking clearly. If Dad's thoughts were unclouded, he, at least, would have realized the inconsistency and foolishness of those complaints. He did not pause to analyze the validity of his mother's concerns, and what followed was a whole lot more physical and emotional abuse.

I witnessed some things Grandma complained about. But I dare not disgrace with her version. It would only 'add insult to injury.' I tried to separate the person from the behaviour, but it was so hard. I did not dislike my father and his mother. What I disagreed with was their hostile ways. My dear cousins and aunt suffered similar fate at the hands of my uncle, my father's brother. The only way these two brothers knew how to settle a conflict was by the use of physical force.

Reflection

All humans, and especially children, need care, love, protection and positive reinforcement to fulfill their destiny. It is impossible for a person to offer these qualities if they do not have them in their emotional skill box. As I turn back the script of my childhood, I felt a tremendous sense of grief for my parents, especially Dad. Their nurturing and relationship skills must have presented a significant challenge. I wished I could rouse them from their everlasting slumber and teach them the little I have learned.

As troublesome as my life was, at the end of the day, I hope to walk away with some positive qualities. I have had to exercise great caution to avoid history repeating itself, not so much for myself, but for my children and others.

Petrol Saga

My mother said that when I was a very young child I drank petrol[1] that had been kept in a sweet drink bottle. Sweet drink was like our modern day sodas. I don't think the bottle had a lid on it, but it looked good to me. I must have created quite a bit of excitement, because I drank some and was taken to the local San Fernando Hospital. Unless you are critically ill or dying, medical care was uncommon for anyone in our circle. Money was too scarce to waste on such a thing.

Vaguely, I remembered the really nice nurse who treated me with the kindness I had never experienced. At home, I got sweeties (candies) only occasionally. And it was infrequent indeed.

In the hospital, those treats were dished out after each medication round. The bed was made with clean white sheets,

---

[1] Gasoline

almost too good for my scrawny little body. My childish eyes near bulged right out of their hollow homes. I was not accustomed to this type of good life, food in abundance, free flowing unconditional love, topped up with a real bed with real sheets. I sincerely believed, for that short time, my life could not have been any better.

I wished the nurse had kidnapped me and taken me to some far-away place. After my stay in the hospital, I did not want to return home. Even as a small child, my appreciation for kindness was by no means dimmed. This same nice nurse had her mind on other ideas—me! At the end of my hospitalization, my nurse asked Mom if she could adopt me.

My mother had many offspring, so one less would have been a blessing for her, but no sir. I was discharged into Mom's care and back into the life I knew.

After my petrol-guzzling episode, my family did not trust me with anything resembling a bottle. They took care to keep bottles, full or empty, away from me. I wondered why don't they trust me? I should have learned from that accident not to do things that would hurt me. The next worrying thing I did was put peas up my nose. That was not too bad. It did not cause me any great distress. Apart from a few leather belt wallops across my behind, I went about my business.

Something was happening with those beltings. Either the giver was getting feebler or I was getting less sensitive to them. Still, I kept looking for more things to amuse myself, as the saying goes 'an idle hand is the devil's workshop.'

Boredom might be called something else, but even for adults who have no purpose, goal or focus, their lives could be meaningless. This worthless life could feel so intolerable that mischief could be mistaken for fun. The key to breaking that useless feeling was to be useful, no matter what. I felt a craving for something bigger. Instead, it almost felt as though my fate was sealed as in a time capsule, and I was to live a dead-end life.

Despite this dread, there was a very small voice in my head whispering, No, your life will not be a dead end. Could there be a better life out there for me? But how would this change happen? After all, I had no available resources to escape, where would I go?

My First School

I cannot remember just when I was out of school, but I do remember that I was more often out of school than I was in. Penal Rock Presbyterian Elementary School in Trinidad was perched on a slight incline. This entire structure was of two levels and built of wood, probably cedar, because that was the word I often heard. The roof was made of sheets of well-worn galvanized metal, similar to other buildings in the area.

The sound of doors and windows opening irritated me, because they screeched as though a ghost was fighting to enter the room. I often wondered if that was the reason for keeping them open almost all day, except during the rainy season.

The juniors were taught on ground floor, while seniors were on the first level. The authorities did their best to maintain this small wood-frame building. Anyone expecting padded or plastic seats would be sorely disappointed. The long, unpolished benches were built of fairly smooth planks.

There were no ceramic tiles, carpet, or linoleum under our feet, just a plain coarsely cut wooden floor, because, in those days, wood was the material of choice, common and readily available. What I enjoyed the most was the well-groomed surroundings dotted with beautiful flowering plants. My favourites were the white, red, pink and yellow hibiscus and breathtaking red and purple anthurium.

Being much older and less sensible than the other children in my class was no fun. Most of my classmates had been to nursery school or were in some other type of educational environment to prepare them for school. They were able to read, write, do simple sums and copy pretty good images of familiar things—pictures, leaves, animals, fish and houses.

Some students' drawings of family members were excellent. They were comfortable with paper, pen and pencils. They were light years ahead of me. I felt insecure and out of my depth, because those children were much younger than me, and yet so educationally advanced. I heard words I never knew. Those words were not long or complicated. Just simple words as I am, he is, it is, which most children used in day-to-day vocabulary. Both youngsters and their teachers seemed to speak the same language. I only muttered under my breath flowery words a girl should not have used.

My school days continued for a while longer, whether it was years or months, I do not remember precisely. The teachers did their best to teach and discipline their students. Reading, arithmetic, spelling, and singing were included in our curriculum. Singing was my favourite subject. I loved that period and, God, I was good at it. Perhaps I boast, but during that brief time, I felt 'as happy as a pig in mud.' Some of the class 'big mouths' were too shy to sing, but not me. I still remember one of the songs:

"All the world in trouble, that is true.
It worried you, I am worried too.
But dear old mummy says it wouldn't do…"[2]

I found school troubling because I could not grasp what was going on in the classroom. Hearing those word lists whizzed me to some bizarre faraway land. My world felt as though my five senses were hibernating. I looked and saw nothing, listened but heard nothing, felt numb, unable to concentrate with a mind that felt as blank as a grey slate.

At some point in this experience, I returned to reality. I gave my muddled head a good shaking and questioned, where on this God forsaken earth am I? Regaining my wits, steading

---

[2] Author and date, unknown

those two shaky stick-like fittings that were my legs, I realized I was still on the schoolroom floor. At about the same time, I grappled with my own group of humiliating words: stupid, unworthy and less than. Around and around in my head they went like a dog chasing its tail.

While I was still trying to figure out the simple sums and which side of the pencil was up, my peers had finished their work. They stared, putting their hands over their mouth and giggling so hard over my slowness to catch on. I hated school! I hated school! This place was unfriendly. I tried hard to focus on schoolwork, but each time the result was the same—a blank. My brain felt as empty as a hollow shell.

Instead of completing school projects at the end of a school day, I had to help care for the cattle, harvesting vegetables, especially cucumbers, peas and beans at certain times of year. Delaying harvest meant the cucumbers got fat and overripe, full of hard seeds, and beans could be used as dental floss, and lettuce turned to mush on the vines.

My other chore was delivering lunch to the workers on roads that were long, isolated, unpaved and uneven. My ultimate balancing act was keeping a large heavy lunch basket on my head, and at the same time treading gingerly to get the lunch safely to the workers. All this time I was falling behind on my homework.

I missed too many days to catch up and fell further and further behind in my schoolwork. My irregular attendance made bad matters worse, so I felt like an outcast. My classmates were new and those students who I started with were promoted to a higher class. And there I was in another year, almost at the same place as when I first started school.

Contemplation
As I write about my thoughts as a young child, I clearly understand how easy it was to look elsewhere for support to ease the pain. I would have taken anything—anything to make me feel better. On second thought, it was just as well I had no

quick fix. How much worse could it get? I felt that I was on an icy slope. I had no self-confidence, felt worthless and had no worthwhile support. Fear and anxiety were constant companions. I was unable to keep up with the junior class lessons. My confused brain worked much harder with no real result.

That challenged me. It was not enough to fall behind on my schoolwork, but being bullied added to the pain.

My irregular school presence plus fatigue might have kicked off my misery, consequently, I felt like some creature from outer space.

As I look back on that time and know something of the early Mennonite way of life, that was similar to what my life was like. For my family, modern gadgets were not within our reach. There was no electrical power connected to our house, so gas lamps were used sparingly to save on the consumption of fuel. Using the lamps to read was frowned upon as a waste of fuel. Besides, returning home to start schoolwork was nearly impossible as I was too weary. If I had walked any faster than the snail's speed I was going, I felt that I would fall apart, one bone after another, piece by piece.

Uniform

Our school was about half a mile walk from our house. This distance was comfortable, especially with other siblings and acquaintances. Even so, it was a struggle to be punctual, because my father felt that school was of little importance, so little or no effort was invested in it. School presented yet another sore spot—the purchase of school uniforms, for not one child but for a whole army of us.

Most people could tell to which school a particular student belonged because each school had a different type of uniform. The girls in our school wore white short-sleeved blouses and navy blue V- necked pinafore dresses with a white belt.

According to the Presbyterian School rules, the dress length had to be no shorter than below the knee. I guess that was to avoid temptation. The boys wore royal blue short-sleeved shirts and khaki-coloured trousers. I think that both boys and girls wore black shoes, most likely running shoes, because they were cheaper than leather shoes. The easiest ways to solve this quandary was to buy one pair and pass the shoes down from the oldest to the last one in the family, but my parents still had to buy the first one and likely more as there were a good number of children to outfit.

Canadian Red Cross
The Penal Rock Presbyterian School (the only school I attended) was under the sponsorship of the Canadian Red Cross. I really liked that school, not only for the singing, but also for the treats. At the end of the term, we were sure to get a 'doggie bag' of candies, pencils and a little toy. Something told me these goodies were not expensive, but whatever the price, we loved them. To add to the end of term gifts, someone supplied milk and cookies every Friday for the poor and malnourished children. This was the time when my gratitude was at its highest level. In fact, this was one of the happiest times in my school life.

Good does come out of bad situations. You know, I can still remember the delicious cookies and milk. As an adult I've tried different types of food, and I think we were given skim milk and cheap bulk cookies or biscuits, but in my mind, they felt like a banquet fit for a queen.

Milk and cookies were not very common in our household, save for rare occasions, yet my memory seems to fail me when I try to recall any particular occasion. I do remember that milk was added to a cup of tea, but only enough to change the colour to a paler shade of brown.

Seats
My short school life continued, but it got worse. The wood-frame school was too small to accommodate all the students. We took great care not to slide from one side to the other on

the unpolished benches, because there might be an odd sharp splinter ready to attack a soft fleshy innocent posterior.

The seating arrangement was allocated on a first-come, first-serve basis. Latecomers, like me, were easily identified and given special places. We ended up either standing in the corner or sitting on the cold, bare uncomfortable floor for the duration of the lessons.

Playground Tittle-Tattle

The school playground sat on a huge piece of land close to the school. Some local residents' theory stated that landowners donated pieces of their property to the school to bribe the teachers to give their children better grades. I wonder if the idiom 'you scratch my back and I will scratch yours' applies here. Although unproven, this 'bribery rumour' appeared like the truth to me, because the children of wealthy parents got better grades.

On the other hand, being rich meant the availability of better resources, more time to focus and complete schoolwork and practically no pressure to do non-educational chores. Whatever the reason, the poorer students' grades, including mine, were simply shameful.

At recess we talked with our friends, ran aimlessly around the grounds or playing with a ball or privileged students' toys, when they allowed it. It was like a mini social club. Membership to that society was exclusively by invitation from the toys' owners. Offers were usually given to equally rich personal friends, and family members. Unfortunately, I failed to qualify for those offers.

The school days seemed long, perhaps from 8 am to 4:15 pm, and were uninteresting, even despicable after a while. I just wanted to escape from this world and hunt for my identity. At times I wondered, Who I am I? Why I am here? But most importantly, where am I going, and what is my purpose on this planet?

Reflection

Sixty-eight years ago, the only form of contraceptive was abstinence. I think having too many children carried enormous financial, physical and mental hardships for parents. Everyone 'flies by the seat of his or her thin pants.'

And yet, in a large family, there were always more hands to help. Whatever the reasons, I tucked this concept securely in the recess of my impressionable mind. Too many to feed, too many to clothe, too many to bathe, and certainly too many to educate, nurture, love and keep safe.

Even though I cannot remember everything that happened, I am stunned that my emotional response to the past is still so sensitive and strong, but perhaps not as raw as some years ago. My memory is still good and it helps me to see things more clearly, at least those things I remember well.

Water

My parent's slogan was: "If you are old enough to go to school, then you are certainly capable of helping with daily chores." I was fully aware of these unwritten rules. So in order to save my hide, I did not engage in any extracurricular school activities or socializing with friends. It was my responsibility to hurry home to complete my chores.

It was also my job to fetch water. Sometimes it was not so lonely, because I walked with siblings and other water carriers. We walked a long ways and sometimes had to go deep into the bushes to find a pond or lake. Roads were unheard of. We attentively picked our way through the well-trodden, overgrown, uneven dirt trails. Trekking was problematic because we spent most of our time in the 'Hunchback of Notre Dame' position. We shoved our way through the thick brushes, pushing and breaking branches with bare hands and mostly unprotected feet, avoiding the branches from whipping at our faces.

When luck graced us, the city portable water trucks rumbled up the road hauling a large tank that resembled a tortoise carrying its shell. The truck delivered our water quota to barrels placed strategically along the roads for easy access. We scooped the water into buckets, small drums, or other handy containers and poured it into other barrels. The container we kept indoors was used strictly for cooking and drinking while water kept in the outdoor drum was used for laundry, washing up and watering both indoor and outdoor plants.

Weather

Trinidad, located in the tropical Caribbean, lies close to the equator. As opposed to the four seasons we have in Canada, this island has only two weather variations. The rainy season, from June to December, is a time of frequent and heavy showers when water is usually in abundance. And the dry season (January to May), when the weather is mostly sunny with light showers. We regarded water as a precious commodity, so it was rationed at this especially earth-thirsty time.

As the saying goes 'water, water everywhere' was a prime example of the rainy season. At this time, we learned about the poorly built and maintained buildings too, because water is a good assessor of how a building is maintained.

Sometimes the owner knew it was raining even before looking outside or into the sky. It was not only their arthritic or migraine aches and pains but also the sound and uninvited appearance of water indoors. Pails, buckets, rags, even cooking pots were used to collect water that poured through rusty leaky roofs.

Our House

Our house was a large single story structure with two high sets of stairs, one at the back and the other at the front. The only other way out was to jump through a window, which is quite a drop, with the danger of being injured. These stairs were our 'fire escape.' Our house could be compared to modern day bungalows, except that it was built on strong high poles to protect the living space from critters and to avoid floods during the torrential rainy seasons. Considering the number of occupants, we desperately needed more space.

All living spaces, except the laundry, were on the same floor. There were two steep stairs to climb before reaching the front entrance of our family sitting room.

This room was almost as sacred as an altar, because only on exceptionally rare occasions were the children allowed to sit in the easy chairs. The chairs were made of special wood crafted by expert carpenters and the cushions were sewn of gorgeous gold and satin material.

My mom loved her chairs and treated then like priceless porcelain dolls. She banned us from putting any part of our body—bottoms, legs, feet, or any other bits—on the cushions.

We dared not entertain thoughts of turning Mom's pillows into mini trampolines. It baffles me why these unresponsive pillows were put out in the sun. I know they did not need any colour enhancement. The Caribbean sun is usually 27 C. I am positive if those cushions had a voice, they would be begging for mercy or would dive under the shade of a tree.

Straight ahead of the sitting room was my grandmother's bedroom. This room seemed a fairly good size for one person, and it was out of bounds to anyone, especially us pesky children. Entry was only by invitation and without exceptions.

From a very early age, our parents said that we must stay out of her room. Now that I am more versed in mental health disorders, I believe that there might have been some link to paranoid behaviour.

To the right of the sitting room was my parents' bedroom, spacious and furnished with a large bed, a medium-sized chest of drawers and a chair. There were books, Bibles and religious books stacked for safekeeping, only to be used at frequent prayer times. The two other rooms were one for the girls, and the other for the boys.

Shortcut

I was affected with 'the laziness' and refused to walk around the veranda. So I created a shortcut. Like a thief in the night, I would sometimes creep cautiously through the window separating these two rooms and then jump to the floor as quietly as a cat preparing to snag its prey. At that moment, my limbs would feel too shaky to support myself. Fear raced through me and my throat constricted as I watched, listened and looked around, making sure all was clear before sprinting either to the kitchen or down the back stairs. I would not want my siblings to snitch on me, because I didn't fancy any more beatings.

The dining room, adjoining the kitchen, was the largest room in the house to accommodate our large numbers and any last-minute invited and uninvited Sunday visitors. A large light brown wooden table with chairs of different kinds competed for the space. Sometimes when more seats were needed, we got creative and placed pieces of broad planks across rusty metal cans.

No one complained about the seating arrangements, because the main focus at the time was the food. There were years when meal times celebrated the highlight of the day.

Food from our garden was plentiful and what had to be purchased from the grocery shops was affordable. Although life was difficult, it was bearable.

Kitchen Appliances

Our kitchen was very different in its humble arrangement. The very basic things needed to cook were present; after all, there was no electrical supply in our home until I turned 21 years old.

The cooker[3] was made of a mixture of sand, dry grass and mud. These materials were mixed with water until the texture

---

[3] stove

was pliable. With the builder's skillful hands, this mass was worked to form a common 'M' shape to accommodate an assortment of pots. The builder then trimmed, smoothed, cleaned the piece and then started up the cooker.

We gathered firewood from dry trees and carefully cut the pieces to sizes that would fit the length and inside of the 'M'–shaped space. If the wood stuck out and fell on the floor while it was still burning, our house would have been reduced to a pile of cinders. If all went well after the first trial, then it was cooking time! This homemade invention was called a Mud Cooker. It is amazing how delicious meals could be prepared using this rudimentary appliance.

Sitting next to our brand-new mud cooker was a coal pot, a modern version of its sister, the mud cooker. The coal pot is a metal cooking device shaped like a raised bowl, with a central grid that uses coal as its fuel. It is still used by some people. The coal is lit, burned to ember, and then the cooking begins. One has to be careful and pay attention to the food being cooked because this cooker is very rudimentary and has no heat regulating system.

In addition to the above-named appliances in our kitchen, there were a few homemade wooden shelves where clean dishes and bits and pieces were stacked. A well-used and stained plastic washbowl perched in a suitable corner served as our kitchen sink. Our dishwashing system was similar to a production line. There was no time to lose. As soon as one meal was finished, the dishes were washed ready for the next sitting.

I had to share a plate of food, due to a shortage of dishes. The amount of food received would be based on two main things: the health of your teeth and how cooperative the stomach was to accepting the partly-chewed food being dumped into it. Picky eaters, food allergies and special diets were unheard of back then. The mealtime rule was simple and very straightforward—either eat what food is available or go without.

Laundry Appliances

We knew nothing about that wonderful, labour-saving apparatus, the washing machine, but we did own a twin set of 'state of the art laundry technology.' The first piece was a wooden washboard for hand washing clothes. The second was the good old-fashioned, dented grey metal well-used laundry tub. Before we started our laundry, we half-filled the metal container and securely positioned the washboard in it.

These dependable vessels knew about multitasking. The beaten-up tub functioned as the family weekly bathtub, too. Many times, that weary looking washboard was converted to a seat to rest weary bodies or as a place to store extra items.

Rice Field

In my day, our food was mainly gathered from natural sources (our farm) and was grown and harvested throughout the year. We grew rice in the equivalent of paddy fields, in almost knee-deep muddy water.

First, we sowed the rice seeds thickly in a suitable place and kept them moist until they reached a certain height. Then the sprouted rice had to be planted. The objective was to plant as many bundles as possible by the end of the day.

The workers were assigned different jobs. One such task was pulling the shoots from the germinating area, washing the soil from their roots and binding them into bundles, with a few longer rice shoots. These bunched sprouts resembled miniature soldiers, waiting for their marching orders.

Staple Foods

Besides rice, we grew peas, beans, lady's fingers[4] and sweet potatoes as staple foods. We also grew most of our fruits such as oranges, tangerines, grapefruits and mangoes in our back yards in abundance. We sold some of our excess produce to

---

[4] Okra

the local market vendors or we put up a sign, "Produce for Sale," along the byways or on our property and sold it to a continuous stream of buyers.

All of the food we ate was made from scratch and from natural sources, with no fillers or additives. We raised animals and poultry on the farm. They had free range privileges. We raised domesticated birds in small cages, but only until they were old and wise enough to find their way into the wilds. When these animals and birds matured, we either kept some for family consumption, for a tasty Sunday dinner, sold some in the market, or frequently to other farmers.

Bakes
Bakes are made either with plain or brown flour, corn flour, or with other ingredients such as cassava, which is grated and dries to a grainy consistency. Cassava[5] is similar to our regular potatoes.

The chosen ingredients for bakes are mixed with grated coconut and baking powder, and a small amount of baking soda, sugar and salt. Add water to make the dough firm to the touch but not sticky. Then after leaving the dough to rest and rise, it is portioned and placed either on a baking tray, or on a flat surface, before being baked. They can be deep fried or baked as large as the size of a dinner plate. There are many different types of bakes, but this is how I did it.

You can pair these hot and tasty breads with anything that tickles your taste buds. Left- over stew, salted fish, curried pumpkin, peas, beans or almost any type of vegetables could be used. Yummy!

---

[5] A tropical plant with thick roots that are used to make small white grains (called tapioca) that are used in cooking - http://www.merriam-webster.com/dictionary/cassava

Roti

In Trinidad, any mealtime is a good time to enjoy this flat bread. Roti shared the same status as our Canadian burger, meat or veggie wrap, and could be eaten 'on the run.' There might be as many as seven varieties. This mouth-watering treat is mainly made of flour, split peas, salt, ghee and other spices and baked on a tawa, which is a round, flat metal griddle used in Indian cooking.

Rotis are similar to pita bread and are eaten with curry stews. Hot peppers (chilies) are commonly added to the stew, or they could be used as a side dish. We had no need for nasal or sinus decongestants when eating this, because this spicy casserole works miracles.

Vegetables such as lettuces, chives, watercress and cucumber were usually made as salads. We were not very fond of cold foods in spite of the hot weather. Maybe because of tradition, and also salads were not as satisfying as a hot hearty healthy meal. Working long hours on difficult and energy-sapping jobs required foods like peas, beans and rice that boost the body fuel reserves.

Pack Rat Mentality

The Second World War was still being fought with 'the fury of hell,' as my parents would say. Our family motto at that time was 'economize and save as much as possible' because supplies were frequently unavailable. The government regulated the supply of basic food items, such as sugar, flour and salt, and also household materials such as nails, screws and timber.

My parents said it was necessary to save bits and pieces of old objects, such as pieces of lumber, farming equipment, old cart wheels and frames, just in case. I never knew the meaning of 'just in case.' Was it for days, weeks, months, or even years?

My children sometimes referred to me as being a 'pack rat.' When they suggested or attempted to pitch out my collections, I protested, "I need them, just in case." My youngsters looked confused and puzzled and shook their heads in utter disbelief, just as I did when my parents uttered those words. Most times I debated between having absolutely no valid use for keeping things, and my reluctance to toss them.

My habit might have some relationship to being brought up in the post WWII era. So, I have a good reason for my economy pursuit.

Cleanliness at Home

One thing that was extremely important, regardless of our financial status was the cleanliness of our home. My mother expected the house to be clean inside and out. On Saturdays, each family member was given chores, which had to be completed before day's end. We dusted the walls and surfaces, washed and hung out the laundry, swept and scrubbed the floors and gave tender loving care to the beautiful plants. My older sister was assigned as the 'interim mother' in Mom's absence. She tried bossing me around and I made her life miserable for the duration of her internship.

My sister and I were only eighteen months apart, and I felt she was not old enough to order me around. A touch of sibling rivalry! I love my sister dearly, but not in a temporary mother's role.

Generational Conflict

Our house sat on a low hill facing the main road and other neighbours' homes. Commonly two, three, or even four generations occupied the same house. Everyone lived in this area for generations. Babysitting was free and easy, having a choice of several available family members.

Regardless, the wife was not always happy and agreeable with living in such a large family. The problems started rearing their nasty heads during and after the marriage of an adult child.

In some cultures, the eldest member of the family started to dictate to the young bride or groom, and this was where the relationship turns sour and even bitter. The younger the couple, especially the bride, the less accepting she was of these old-fashioned practices. Squabbles, shouting matches and even fistfights happened between the new bride and her mother-in-law.

Other family members took sides, and before long there was a full-blown family feud, resulting in separation and ending with divorce. I have witnessed many such instances of family violence. These were accepted behaviours. Soon new brides refused to accept abuse of any type and started hitting back as a way of defending themselves. Sometimes it worked and other times the results were less favourable, even tragic.

If the walls of our house were to talk, they would relate much more than I could ever remember during those hard times. I experienced that same abusive treatment as a child. I am convinced they were old and seasoned behaviours that must have started much before my mother's time. To be truthful, my siblings may have viewed that was how life was supposed to be, but I was not satisfied. So I vowed that I would not stay in that deep dark hellhole for the rest of my life. I made that promise at the tender age of 6 years old. This planted seed would eventually help me to change my life.

Chapter 3: School

School continued. I had very little interest in what was going on in the classroom. The year slowly and painfully dragged on, and I continued to wish that this mental torture would soon come to an end. Having quite an overdose of consequences, as a child, I prayed not to God, but to myself.

But it was perfectly sane as far as I was concerned. Even though I did not believe in God, yet I was forced to attend church, yet I wondered if God protected fools and children. As far as I was concerned, I fulfilled both requirements. I was a child and I was a fool, or at least I was repeatedly led to believe that.

After what seemed to be an eternity, my prayers, hopes, and wishes were heard. Somewhere out in this big neighbourhood, this large island of Trinidad, this huge world, and this vast universe, something heard me and answered my humble plea.

Spending More Time in the Fields

One morning, news came fast and furious by way of the local 'busy-body' residents that our local school had burnt to the ground, leaving only ashes. Oh! The joy and relief I felt was beyond explanation. No more school, no more sadness, no more battle with homework and, even more importantly, no more feeling dumb.

Some parents would have viewed this disaster as a loss, but not mine. No school meant more time to help on the farm. It meant hard manual labour in the rice, sugar cane, and vegetable fields. Mechanical equipment such as plows, tractors, reapers or diggers were unheard of. All work had to be done by hand, so you see why my parents were happy to have additional manpower.

Some problems ended and others, even larger, started. Now almost all my time was spent in the fields. The golden sun was still sleeping when the trek to the fields began.

Tropical sun is very hot and shows its strength in quite a relentless way. Most people awake early and try to complete their chores to avoid the sweltering sun. We rose before the rooster. Sometimes we need to rise as early as 3 a.m. depending on the task at hand.

I did not need a doctor or medication to have a sound night's sleep. The heat and weariness of the backbreaking work acted like a natural sedative. Other times, sleep seemed as though it had grown wings and flown to the other side of the world. My mind would go back to what I lived through. I could not help thinking whether my life, even a short part, would ever get better. If I were to use colours to show parts of my life, I'd choose black or brown. Black, symbolizing the ongoing sadness, and brown, signifying shards of light sneaking into a crack in a dark room.

Work in the fields started as soon as there was daylight and continued until nightfall. I thank the universe for the blessed nights when the field workers were forced to lay down their tools and then their tired bodies.

Discontented Bull

To get to the field, we rode in a bumpy buggy drawn by one of our bulls. This creature desperately needed anger management therapy. He was bad tempered and pulled his loads grudgingly. It was as if to say that he was doing this job because he had no choice. This particular beast of burden reminded me of my feelings, because I felt the same way.

The bitterness that was festering in me had to be kept under a tight lid; I dared not show it.

My dad and other farm employees exercised caution at all times when working with this strong brute. The bull was dressed in neck halter and adorned with a huge three- to five-inch diameter metal nose ring. I believed that a bull with a nose ring is easier to handle than one without.

One day this angry creature decided that enough was enough. During the night he broke his rope, pulled the wooden stake free and bolted with his tail in the air. Freedom.

The birds were singing, the trees nodding in greetings, the sun smiling down from the heavens and all seemed well, but not for our family. Our family dealt very poorly with any wrench in the wheel. In the morning when my father discovered that Mr. Bull was missing, he called in the untrained 'standby search team.' The response was encouraging. The helpers came out in droves. The local labourers dropped their tools, farmers secured their gates to prevent other cattle from following the delinquent beast, and then the search started.

In those days, farmers were protective of their cows to prevent undesirable breeding. How many cows could one bull impregnate in a day? I do not know. Mr. Bull was found and he seemed happier after his brief taste of freedom. And back to the fields we went.

Humiliation
Field trips were dreadful but not as much as the heart-gripping fear of my schoolmates seeing me riding a buggy packed with bags of vegetables, bundles of cut grass for the cattle, piles of dry branches of firewood, and me perched way at the top of this precarious contraption.

I called it a contraption because everything on the cart was tied with old rope of different types. To add insult to injury, buckets (some dirty, others rusty) hung at the sides, swinging like ancient pendulums. If Mother Earth could have opened and swallowed me at that time, it would have been blessed relief.

Shame and embarrassment were indescribable; it was like a circus coming to town and children were pointing fingers, whispering and laughing to one another and running a short distance behind the cart, which helped to increase the feeling of embarrassment and worthlessness. Oh, Maker of the

Universe, how was I going to face these horrible taunting kids again? I had absolutely no idea! My best hope was that no replacement school be found for the school that was gutted a few weeks before.

The choice between going to the fields and going to school was 'six of one and half a dozen of the other.' Real difficult choices!

Chapter 4: New School

Several weeks passed and news circulated that a new school was found, four miles from our house. This structure was similar to its now charred predecessor. It took hours to reach the new school. The roads were mostly uninhabited, with only a few shacks along the way. Although the journey to the school started early, I was still late for classes, which only deepened the sadness. Children in rich families were driven to class by car. So, the lateness to classes, poor attendance, inability to keep up with lessons and homework added to my intense useless feelings.

In those days, the teachers spoke to my parents and they decided on my future. My opinion, even at the age of about eleven or twelve years old, was unimportant. I was not a party to this decision. That was the end of school and the start of another life.

New Status

As time went by, I became a village female labourer. I spent my time doing menial jobs, going into the fields almost every day, walking long distances in the burning sun to carry lunch to the people who worked for our family. Other times my tasks would be to work in the vegetable garden where many seeds had to be planted for tomatoes, peas, cucumbers and others.

Depending on the season, the young sugar cane shoots needed to be fertilized to ensure stronger mature plants. When I started to go to the sugarcane field with my eldest brother, I was so small. The most efficient way of keeping track of me was to call my name at frequent intervals. I worked mostly with my eldest brother who always looked out for me.

When I was totally exhausted from the combination of intense heat and gruelling work, sleep came easily. My bed was anywhere in the tall grass or being propped up under a shaded tree. Any place was good enough to rest my weary body.

For whatever reasons, the regular fields were not yielding crops as expected. My guess was because Mother Earth was as exhausted as what I felt in my body. New avenues needed to be explored. My father received word from other land seekers about available forestry land to rent at a reasonable price. That was just what was needed to boost production. The land required clearing before any crop could be planted.

Clearing New Land
The lumberjacks strolled into the wooded area. The men sported a reassuring smile. Their heavy well-worn uniforms showed patches upon patches. Over their shoulders, they carried the tools of the trade—axes. They sized the huge trees from crown to bottom. With each stroke, the axes' blades flickered like a shooting star in the midafternoon sun. The tree started leaning as if pushed to one side by an invisible force, as the pair—men and axe—worked together. Soon, the tree fell to the ground with a dull thud, grabbing leaves and weaker shrubs with it.

The tree trunks were sold to the local sawmills. Specially equipped lorries (trucks) hauled these logs away to be cut into lumber.

Without fail, my parents always found jobs for us children. We were responsible to drag, wrestle and deposit those smaller uncooperative branches, and other pieces of clearing onto the bonfire.

I cannot recall hearing about any governmental or environmental hazard bylaws. If any regulations were mandated, I wondered how many citizens would take notice. Survival was of paramount importance and rules next.

Accommodation and Inadequate Sleeping Arrangements
Daily travel to this newly acquired land was too time-consuming. We needed temporary lodgings, and quickly.

Raw materials such as thick tree branches, large banana leaves and rough woods were the material of choice.

During good weather, this shack worked well, but in strong winds or in the rainy season, it left a lot to be desired.

The makeshift bed was made of similar material as the shack.

Only one bed was available for my mother, father and me. I was frightened for my life because of the earlier abuse that I had suffered at the hands of my parents, especially my father.

Morbid thoughts of 'what ifs' circulated in my mind. What if that out-of-my-control anger started to show its ugly face? Such unpredictable adult behaviour frightened me. I really hated the sleeping arrangement. Here was a girl in her early teens, sleeping in the same so-called bed with her parents. Although I strongly despised and hated this idea, I had zero choice.

When the land was no longer profitable, and the rent was too high, this interest was soon abandoned. My small humble heart was so excited, and I felt as though I was bubbling with delight.

Hardship
The writing was on the walls, so to speak. Signs of hardship lurked around the next corner. Shortly after enjoying my wonderful moments, our lifestyle slowly started worsening.

First, our money was insufficient, so we had fewer names on the payroll. Next, our food supply shrank dramatically. Then our precious land started to vanish. Signs of poverty were as clear as daylight, for all to see.

First Mentor
I did not realize it at the time that my grandfather was my first mentor. Later I added my brother and my husband to this cherished list. The most vivid and memorable of them all was the memory of my maternal grandpa. My grandpa was the best of the best men who ever walked on the face of the earth. Well, one of the best. There were more such good persons, my eldest brother and my late husband.

To me, my Pa was a real earthly angel, if there was one. He grew a lot of fruits and vegetables and I clearly remembered him saving the best of his produce for his grandchildren. If I had known that he was a man I could trust, maybe, just maybe, my life would have been less traumatic.

Or, perhaps if he had acted as my house of refuge, he would have been the receiver of threats or violence. In the end, I am glad that my grandfather's safety was not jeopardized on my behalf.

Seasons came and seasons went, and so did some members of our family. There were more births and then deaths. My recollection of all the souls that have gone over the Jordan River to their celestial home was rather vague, but there is one person I still remembered with fondness, and that was my maternal grandfather, who we called Pa.

Grandpa's Personality

My grandpa was a special person. He was neither famous nor rich. He was a man of humble beginnings and very modest means. On the contrary, financially, he was as poor as a church mouse. He did not own a big rambling expensive house or drive a luxurious flashy car. Nor did he enjoy the pleasure of modern day house gadgets, such as fridges or freezers. Probably if this man had a fridge or freezer, they would have sat empty or almost empty.

My grandpa lived off the land and used the produce he cultivated. Fruits and vegetables, such as tomatoes, beans and peas were common commodities he enjoyed. Also, he had a gift for raising a variety of feathered friends—hens, ducks and turkeys. He understood the birdies' language, and they showed their love for him by laying hundreds of eggs. My grandpa made tasty meals from the flesh and eggs of his fowl. My Pa had a generous nature that benefitted not only his family, but also friends and neighbours too. He kept only enough food for his consumption, sold some yield to the local market, and gave the rest to friends, neighbours and family, and especially the disadvantaged.

Rules are made, rules are broken, and there are also exceptions to some. Grandpa's exception was to keep some of the best he had for his dearest loved ones, his grandchildren. And he had quite a few of them.

In my short period of going to school, the best part about that time was our school holidays. School vacation meant two things. The first was helping on the farm. The other, and by far the best, was spending some time with my grandfather. If I had to choose, I would have voted, hands down, for the latter.

Even after more than sixty years, I can still see him standing, waiting patiently, in the door of his very basic home that he had built himself. His clothing was of earth colour, shades of brown. It was like his uniform, with patches upon patches, and at times it was difficult to distinguish the colour of the original garment. As for his boots, they were riddled with holes and the soles peeling off. The holes were stuffed with whatever; I do not quite know what. Paper, even newspaper, was in short supply and at times unavailable. So, my most educated guess would be that my grandfather used natural products such as leaves to plug the holes, coupled with vines or strings to reinforce the tired worn-out shoe soles.

Whether the day was gloomy or sunny, the smile on this man's wrinkled, weather-beaten face was almost enough to brighten up a whole village. What was it, as a very young child, that attracted me to this wise ancient-looking man?

Was it because he saved all those goodies for us? I thought it had to be those biggest, fattest and ripest yellow bananas. Or could it be his best sticks of juicy sugar cane? His traditional Trinidadian Palau dish of rice and black-eyed beans with coconut milk was a real taste-bud teaser. I appreciated and enjoyed all those delightful treats. The thing I valued more that anything was my grandpa's love and kindness.

Coming of Age

The age of majority snuck up on me, unnoticed. I did not know exactly what that phase meant. Still, everyone was expecting me to not only to think, but also behave like an adult. I felt strange and equally confused. For me, it was having a child's brain in my grown-up body.

Adults are usually wiser than children. The useful skills that adults acquired served to guide themselves and others to safety, like a lighthouse leading to safer shores. I had not found that safe shore. Certainly, I felt unskilled, unwise, unsafe, with no self-awareness, and incapable emotionally and mentally to cope with life.

Body Changes

I started to menstruate and this added to my already muddled state. "What do I do?" Mumbling to myself, I didn't have the faintest clue how to proceed. It seemed really crazy when a confused person (me) is asking another muddled one (me) for help. I heard the village's untrained midwife once say that your insides could come out, so that was exactly what I thought. My end was near. I felt an overwhelming sensation of fear and was afraid of almost everything in my life—the past, the present and the future. I learned much later in my early adult life that menses, periods, monthly, and woman troubles are just that, words. The same way there are names for parts of a tree, so too names are given to bodily functions.

When I think back to what it was like when I was growing up, two things come to mind: a sense of sadness because I realized that these experiences, whatever they were, would forever change the course of my life, and that I must have been a strong and determined character.

Female personal products were unavailable in my level of social culture; improvisation was the order of the day. Tampons and sanitary pads were considered frivolous and too expensive, so the other and only choice was to go local and make your own from old rags. My first lesson in health education occurred when I turned 21 years old. I felt a dash of control by this new and exciting education. Control, because of the learning opportunity and glimpsing a sliver of light, although small, that was at the end of the tunnel.

Nursing School Application—England

Wheels of change slowly started to turn in my favour. My elder sister had immigrated to England (UK) to pursue her nursing career. In those days, immigration rules and regulations were easier to manage than they are today. Good health and having a sponsor, whether family, friend or any organization, were important contributory points to gain entry to England. Plans were put into action to help me apply to an English nursing school, but self-study proved to be more difficult and confusing than expected.

Because my school life had been so short, I could have been classified as illiterate. I had absolutely no credentials showing I had attended or completed any formal schooling, and this would cause a huge stumbling block when I applied to any nursing organization.

Still with strong determination, I made plans to continue with my studies and forward my application to England. Any reasonable thinking person might have considered me insane, but I called it persistent, which gave me the feeling of a little more hope.

One or two days after posting the application to England, I was expecting a reply because I was totally consumed by excitement. Postage wheels in those days were much slower than today, so patience was essential. Personal mail was not delivered to our home. I trekked up the roads, and back down the roads. The waiting seemed unbearable as days turned into months.

My visits became more and more frequent and my legs began protesting. My questions, "Any letters?" remained unchanged and so were the postal worker's answers. "None."

I was beginning to have a low mood sensing that my applications would be rejected.

Replies

Then one day my repeated visits paid off handsomely. I received a letter, all dressed up in red, white and blue stickers. The joy I experienced was unexplainable. I held my letter with increased heartbeat and shaking hands. I received very few letters, so this particular one was especially exciting, because it was from England.

As I hurried home, my mind started to ramble on and on, like a broken record. I could not shut it off. Two thoughts, as dissimilar as opposing parties' policies popped into my mind. These were my first thoughts: I said all these things in one sentence, and one short breath. "My letter was from a big foreign country, with a Queen who was head of almost the whole world, where hospital workers were all white people, and they wore white aprons and their snow-white caps had different colour bands signifying how many years in training, and the staff wore black lace-up spotless shiny shoes." I thought dirty shoes could cause more sickness. Believe me, I needed a good dose of life's sustaining air after this long exposition. I bounced out of my daydreaming-like state, realizing my views were right over the top.

Second thoughts brought the flaws of my unrealistic reasoning to the forefront. It pointed out that the Queen was indeed the head of some countries, but definitely not the whole world, and that the country's workforce was a mixed bunch of people, and it was questionable if dirty shoes caused hospital-related infection.

I had very little knowledge about England, so this was where my imagination led me.

I ripped the envelope open because I had no letter opener, and in my eagerness, the enclosed letter was in two pieces.

Disappointment literally wrapped its arms around me, like a vicious octopus, when I read the response. This was the first reply to many applications, but still I felt a feeling of failure. I had no sense that there could be a "yes" among the replies.

More letters came from different hospitals with a similar answer—no. The reason stated that I was not adequately educated. This statement, "not adequately educated," brought back more shame and worthlessness.

Somewhere in the recess of my mind came the thought, do not give up, all is not lost, and so I waited with a heavy heart and low mood for more replies. There were two more schools that I had not heard from and I pinned my hopes on having at least one favourable reply. My belief then, and even now, is that having a positive spin on life pays off. I am not saying that I was 'Miss all positive,' but at least it helped to give me hope in almost hopeless situations. After all, I had dreams for a better life.

More Replies
Another day, another trek to the postal office, and other mail had arrived. This time my excitement was too overpowering. I was too impatient to wait until I reached home to open the letter. This letter was not a clear rejection. I had to fulfill some educational requirements before the hospital could send me an acceptance letter. Later I learned that this same hospital was among the best in England. It was in the upper echelon and 'riffraff,' such as me, were simply unwelcome. As a child, school had always been problematic; now as an adult it would be equally difficult, but time was my ally and so I waited, hoping and wishing for a favourable last reply.

Faith
Asking for help did not include me praying. I was not too happy with some members who ran through the church doors twenty-four hours and seven days of the week. I did not see the thread of kindness that connected their behaviour to what was preached. In other words, deeds and actions were

incongruent. They repeated God's name so much, yet they were as mean spirited as a serpent.

All of this confused me just thinking about where godliness stood in all this hypocrisy. It would be unfair to paint everyone with the same black brush. I met few genuinely compassionate members who reminded me of my late grandpa.

As my memory turns back through these pages, I clearly remembered when I vowed not be affiliated with any type of organized faith, regardless of its name. I was done and finished with it.

A Package

I waited for what seemed like eternity for my final reply from England. One fateful day, I received a package. This parcel was unlike all the others, the envelope was larger, thicker, carefully sealed and plastered with stamps. It looked very impressive. Adrenaline was pumping through my veins. This surge of hormones started to do funny things to me, increasing my heartbeat and blood pressure, and my legs felt too weak to support my body. My hands were shaking like someone withdrawing from some sort of addiction and I felt deliriously happy. My body was simply vibrating with excitement. For the first time in my life, I felt a sense that all would be okay.

These emotions feel as strong now as when I experienced them many years ago. As I held this mysterious package, I passed it back and forth, from my right hand to my left.

At about this same time, my emotions sat at opposite poles, overjoyed and totally terrified. I felt happy to possibly receive a favourable reply, and nervous because of what lay ahead for me. Maybe, just maybe, luck had eventually come to my rescue. If that were the case, then there would be a lot of rejoicing and dancing on earth and in the heavens.

Overnight Star

Rarely did I receive any letters, especially one from Britain. So the residents' curiosity was at an 'all time high.'

Inquisitive parents, brothers, sisters, and spouses were asking whom, what, when, why, and how, even though the envelope was still sealed. I was the big fish in a small village pond and considered to be knowledgeable about international communication. Imagine, Grace, with almost no education, being asked her opinion! I knew the meaning of overnight, but not sensation, and I did not care to know. I was in the spotlight and basking in this brief newfound fame! A pig in mud could not have been happier. Truly, I felt like an overnight sensation.

As far as I could remember, it might have been the very first time that my opinion mattered. From that day forward, I held my head higher and walked taller and even pushed my chest out like a proud peacock. The tide of change might have been ready to visit me to improve my gloomy, dead-end life.

News reached far and wide about my big fat thick envelope from England. As far as the villagers were concerned, this was 'breaking news.' It said, 'I was going to study to be a medical doctor, a dentist and whatever else people chose to add.'

What I found rather interesting was how this news took on its own personality when it passed from one person to the next. I was certain of two things: the facts were completely distorted and I had become the International Star.

Chapter 5: New Horizons

What a truly memorable day! My last reply proved to be the best of all; the letter said that I had been accepted into the nursing school in Harrogate. All I knew of this place was that Harrogate was somewhere in England. We had no proper map, no access to Google, and no other access to the school, so this place, which might soon be my temporary home for many years, remained a mystery.

The feeling of being on 'cloud nine' lasted for a long time, and I enjoyed it. But reality started to creep in, and I started to wonder how I was going to prepare for my journey. Money was extremely short; the produce from the farm was at an all-time low and money from my labourer's job extremely small. Frequently, instead of money I got a cooked meal for the completed job. And sometimes I received neither money nor food.

The employers fabricated excuse upon excuse for not paying me. Some of these made-up tall tales seemed so dumb, and when I could see through them, you know they were really pathetic.

Mom's Wisdom

Thankfully, my mother was an intelligent and shrewd woman. Her motto was 'save for the rainy days.' It took me many years to understand and appreciate what she meant. The logic in this wise saying was to spend some money, but also save some in case of emergency. My mom's motto proved true based on the amount of dollars that she had saved in spite of our financial crisis.

Preparation

My acceptance offer was not indefinite. The hospital had given me a deadline in which the agreement letter, employment forms, and medical clearance certificates should reach them. Also, travel bookings had to be made, and clothing and luggage had to be purchased in preparation for my departure. I would also require a passport. I never had the opportunity to plan anything in my life. I was told what to do, and I followed the instructions.

So, I almost passed out when I had to take on this project.

Help

Can you imagine what the situation was like for my family? I bought a few new things because I owned no suitable clothing or personal items. And that caused even more strain on our already strained pennies. But even with limited resources, my mother was determined that I would not miss this great opportunity. And for the first time, family members joined in to make my opportunity a success, and I was very thankful for their help. Family members offered their help in whatever way they could. Some bought material for dresses and nightgowns, others bought shoes, and still others gave whatever money they could afford.

I believe the deadline was two years. Within this time, I had to complete some educational remedial work. I felt that the time was still too short to get everything ready for my departure. Mentally, I could have used this time to clear my mind.

The biggest and the most expensive item on my list was my mode of transportation. Would it be by air or by sea? Travelling by air was much easier and quicker as compared to sailing.

Making Travel Plans

Some say that poverty contributes to poor health and increases the risk of danger. In truth, being underprivileged forced me to tolerate intolerable behaviour beyond my control, because I felt I had no voice, no input in what happened in my life, no strong support system or the ability to hold others accountable for their dreadful actions.

Almost all the travel plans were made for me. Occasionally, I would travel to town accompanied by another family member to sign the necessary papers. I must have been an introverted young woman with little confidence if I could not travel to town to attend to my own business. This was my biggest concern. If I could not find my way around my tiny island, then how was I going to survive in a huge county such as England? I was such a naive and gullible person, an easy target for those human birds of prey.

I would classify my childhood as sheltered and restrictive, with strong focus on religion and its related activities. To put it simply, I believed that my parents gave me an overdose of religious teaching. Other important aspects of life such as nurturing and safety to navigate life's dangerous waters seemed to take a backseat. This type of thinking stirred up in me an angry and rebellious attitude.

Passport Office, Trinidad
I was in my late teens to early twenties, as I was preparing to go to England. I had never even been to any of the nearest cities. What a culture shock. I was a real hard-core village girl. I asked myself, was I in another world? I believed that my eldest brother accompanied me.

Seeing so many different types of vehicles almost put me in a state of trance. How about those females all dressed up in high heeled shoes, tight, tight skirts, short and skimpy hot-pants? According to my simple, narrow, limited, and so-called religious upbringing, these fashions were a definite a no-no! It was a good thing I was not alone.

I paid little attention on the roads but looked around on the way having a real 'Aha' moment. What did I think about these city people's outfits and their way of life? I loved them all, but I kept those thoughts and feelings to myself. Some seeds were already planted in my mind. One of those seeds was that life is much more than being a labourer or worse still, an unpaid labourer.

I needed to get my first passport, but I had no idea what a passport was. I had never heard nor seen one. Even though one of my sisters was already in England, I had no idea about how to get one. I had only been told that I needed one. Acquiring a passport was considered to be exclusively adult business. And since I was under 21 years old, I was not considered an adult.

Eventually we found the passport office and went in. The room was big, clean, well-kept and brightly lit. What was even more wondrous to me was the use of electricity. We didn't have it at home at the time, though we would have it later and use it sparingly.

Completing Forms
The official handed me a form that seemed never ending. I had never seen or filled out anything like this before. The clerk must have been a very good reader of body language, including facial expressions, and so she offered her help to get through it.

I felt extremely tired from the trip there and all the stimulation, but I was also overwhelmed. My already fragile brain had reached its saturation level and I couldn't think. Still, my quest to keep my plans going, getting out of Trinidad, kept me focused for the moment. To me, few things could be as painful as my present life. It was much better to have even a glimmer of hope, than none at all.

Something deep within me kept reminding me that my situation would get better. And whatever happened, my life was in that safe and secure place. The saying that God or a Higher Power helps those who help themselves seemed to ring true for me. Things seemed to work out well even though I was almost clueless. What was the trick? What was the magic? What's the secret formula? I had no idea. But what I did know was that I'd keep trudging the road to wherever it led.

Thanks to the sympathetic and helpful clerk at the passport office, who assisted me to complete those complicated forms;

at least that is how I felt. Was she a guardian angel or someone put in my path to help me?

My Brand New Passport

When my passport arrived in the mail, I realized this was not just an ordinary run-of-the-mill document. Oh, no! It represented a long, long-awaited independence and freedom from the long toils of being a female village labourer. I saw a little streak of light at the end of that dark tunnel and called it hope. When I held my new passport I felt the shackles that had held me so tightly for so long had been loosened, not completely, but simply a link or two.

Although I hadn't the opportunity to read about human slavery, I had heard stories about what it was like. It was not only being made to do hard work in inhumane conditions, but it was working for little or no monetary gain. It deprived people of social benefits such as health care and no days off from work or vacation leave, to rest and rejuvenate the weary system.

These things reminded me of my younger days and much more. I was once more bathed in unwelcome emotions. I felt an anxious sickly sensation in the bottom of my stomach and felt uncertain about making simple decisions. My self-confidence was at its lowest point.

At the time, I literally prayed not be asked to express myself on paper. I would have either peed myself, fainted, or died because of fear and lack of self-confidence. But I would be studying and starting out on a new learning process. That meant I would have to work at it.

Could you imagine an adult starting out from a junior school grade level? It was truly embarrassing and humiliating. I felt stupid asking simple, but important, questions. I knew those questions were necessary to help me understand what came next. Like building a house. Unless the foundation is firm, the structure will be shaky. I needed to understand process number one to move to the next.

I coped with the embarrassing moments, waves of anxiety and humiliation. Yet I still asked questions and still more questions. I was prepared to be vulnerable to have a new life elsewhere. I realized there was plenty to learn and so little time to do it.

Chapter 6: Seat Booked

My seat was booked and the final payment made. Plans were well on the way and I felt excited as I remembered the beautiful photos that my sister, Ruth, posted from England.

She was well groomed and smartly dressed in her white crisp uniform. And she was looking as intelligent as any well-educated scholar. She wrote about the delicious food, beautiful flowers and a variety of plants. She commented on how life was in England and so much more.

The photographs and letter turned me into a true believer that life in England was exactly what I needed to turn my life in a different direction. There was no doubt in the vision she shared of England through her photos and what she had written. After all, I had no access to magazines, books, radio, television or computers to advance my knowledge of what to expect.

I made both voluntary and involuntary visits before I left the island. Voluntary visits were to immediate family and close acquaintances, and involuntary ones to people whom my parents thought I should visit. I hated some of these visits, especially to people whom I had absolutely no idea who they were. I had never met them before and, more importantly, where were they when I needed someone to comfort me, or a shoulder to cry on? Yet, in reality, I lived in a tightly knit, unhealthy village. It was likely that the things that happened in our household were also happening in others' homes.

Families tried to turn a blind eye to those problems, feigning ignorance and sweeping their issues 'under the carpet.' These denials did not solve the dysfunction issues.

It's impossible to use tools that you are naive to or that are not available or used in your segregated society. A person will only use what they know in their learned behaviour, including how to give and receive love, but love was mostly unheard of in my home, and I never heard it used in reference to a human being.

I'd always wondered at this thing called love. It must be a good thing to say to another, and I swore to myself that I would try to use it someday. And I did.

Departure
The day of my departure finally arrived; I would be travelling by sea. I stood before this massive vessel with the stature of a Queen, and sadly I said my last goodbyes. Truthfully, I forced myself to remember if I had received any farewell hugs or kisses and I only drew a blank. Nothing came up.

Her Highness was my pet name for the ship. She stood, quietly waiting and assessing her potential passengers. I felt frightened and isolated. As I mounted the intimidating gangplank, I felt as though I was walking toward the unknown, to my demise.

The crews scrambled to prepare to set sail, and after everyone boarded, final checks were done until the crew was satisfied that it was safe to sail. The all-clear whistle sounded. My thoughts started to race. Most of them were natural while many were unfounded, bordering on panic. Fear of the unknown was causing the greatest uneasiness. But then my thoughts started to drift to the ship sinking, and whom I could ask for help if I needed it. Endless concerns and worries plagued my thoughts.

The accommodation and meals onboard were excellent compared to what I was used to. There were clean bed linens and regular meals with generous portions daily. The days dragged on at a painfully slow pace, and blue skies and open water were all we saw for many days. This was one of the times I wished I knew how to play board games, Scrabble or just plain regular cards. Cards were forbidden in our family, because they were related to gambling, heavy alcohol consumption, and low lifestyle.

I often smiled to myself when I thought about the people who took it upon themselves to pass such drastic judgment on others. How easy it must be to accuse others and point out character defects rather than deal with our own. For me, I believe that the defects of characters were rampant and flourishing right there, under our noses. What's worse? Playing cards or abusing the family? Almost all of my life I was baffled by this type of nonsensical reasoning. I felt inspired when seeing my life through a different, independent emotional lens.

My journey was long and seemed to take forever. The water was calm. It shimmered as if dusted with fine crystals. A few dark objects, which looked like birds, were hovering about, unhurried. When the captain announced we were nearing land, I was elated! We spotted landmass within days of the skipper's announcement.

Shattered World

To this point of the journey, I felt safe, but this feeling would be short-lived. My world totally fell apart one night when my cabin companion was out and a strange man unlocked the door and entered my room. He approached me quickly, leaving no time to ask questions about who he was or what he wanted. What he wanted, he took forcefully—all I had as a woman that I called my own. I was in shock. And who would I tell, even if I knew how to express it?

Part 2 ~ England

Yesterday is gone. Tomorrow has not yet come. We have only today. Let us begin. - **Mother Teresa**

Chapter 7: Southampton

In the summer of 1966, a giant, magnificent vessel slowly cruised like a well-dressed confident woman into the Southampton Harbour, England. I did not notice the water or the skyline shape until the signal was given for the passengers to disembark. These monstrosities sat patiently, waiting their turn when the hooter would signal them to advance.

The same way that the ships were unique by their sizes, design, insignia and status, so too were people of different ethnicity. At that time, I only knew people of African, Asian or Caucasian descent. Arriving in Britain, I felt like a wayfaring stranger. Mass confusion and pandemonium confronted me.

The whole situation reminded me of the nursery rhyme, "The Farmer in The Dell." The farmer takes a wife, wife takes the child, child takes a nurse, and on and on. In this case, the crew members were barking orders at already perplexed passengers to follow a specific route. Puzzled and anxious parents were hollering at their unmanageable kids, trying to comply with the authorities' commands. Then adults were hustling others to pick up the pace.

The expression carved on travellers' faces said it all—lost. Probably that countenance and more was also etched on mine too—lost, lost, lost—and completed baffled and totally crushed by this apparently complicated process. I was in a right fix. A question came to me during a moment of clarity, Girl, how the hell do you end up in these quandaries? Are these calamitous happenings just coincidences, or are you the unfortunate victim of evil gods? The present position was "six of one and half a dozen of the other."

After saying adieu to my old life, I did not want to experience this confusing gathering. Honestly, I felt there was only one thing to do. Drop my one-piece small ancient-looking luggage, take a long deep breath and bawl in the highest soprano's shriek, splitting my seams wide open. My mood could not have been any lower. My defenselessness must have been like a beacon flashing on full beam, for all to see. Insecurity was my temporary name.

Many, many years later, I observed my pathetic, unconfident self in the presence of others. I did not like what I saw. It was like being afraid of the silhouette of the entire world, even my own. This unlikable realization ignited something within me. Someday, someway, I vowed to change my demeanor. I would cultivate the confidence I had never possessed. Then I would stand upright and hold my head high.

At the completion of the ship's usual formalities, the crowd headed for the exit sign. I felt as though I was one of a herd of cattle rounded up to a particular pen for either feeding or milking.

After going through customs, I was in for still another surprise, maybe the last, and that was seeing the hair colours of the people who lived there. My poor eyes must have almost bulged out of their sockets in amazement. There was black hair. There was brown. There was also yellow hair too, but I loved those heads of hair with bits of brown, red, pinkish and sprinkles, and rainbow colour tinge. Hairstyles were distinctive. My vote would have been for the Mohican style that a young man wore, with the hair shaven off on both sides, leaving a straight colourful line of hair only about two inches wide from the front of the head to the nape of his neck. He looked as colourful and as proud as a peacock in full display. Later I realized that not all light-skinned or, for that matter, dark-skinned people were sporting their natural hair colour.

Fashion, for me at that time, was nothing like I had seen prior to standing on English soil. My outfit was fashionable while in Trinidad. In Britain, it was nothing near to what was shown in magazines. If they looked at me sporting old-fashioned wardrobe, a vulnerable appearance, matched by defenseless demeanour, it must have been quite a feast to the public's eyes. [Later I often enjoyed a hearty belly laugh thinking how I was dressed up when I landed that day in Southampton, England.]

Absolutely no one could have convinced me that I was not a top-notch model. After all, I had something in common with our Royal Highness, the Queen. It was my snow-white gloves. Not all passengers followed my flair. Royalist or not, I wore my fine new white gloves and hat. My matching handbag contained my worldly wealth of 120 English pounds. I used this money frugally, because I would have to wait a month before receiving my first pay cheque.

I was a member of the British Empire, and that, my friends, was rewarding. Was I not in my Queen's country? And was I not dressed like our reigning monarch? Well, a bit. My outfit might have been a tad cheaper than Her Majesty's, nevertheless, I had that complete new suit of clothing! I could honestly say that I could not remember getting a full wardrobe ever in my life. I was 21 years old at that time. Amazing, and more than amazing. This was more than one hundred percent progress from only a few months earlier.

Walking out of the ship's waiting area, I began scanning one face to the next of the people to find out who was waiting for me. I knew I had to look for a male Caucasian representative, but I had no photograph to compare with him, so I could not recognize him. I supposed a man is a man. My little problem was this. There were a multitude of males standing in the lobby. Was I to walk up to them, close my eyes and pick one, anyone? I passed on that idea.

As I continued skimming hundreds of faces, I hesitated on a particular person. Yes, a man, a Caucasian man. In his right hand, he held a placard higher than the rest. It displayed my name. Ours eyes met and he gave me a shy type of smile as if to say, "I have found you." That must be the representative of what would soon be my new home—Harrogate Royal Bath Hospital. Who else would know my name?

Mumbling to myself, I saw that the letters on his poster were clear, large and bright. And I knew that someone would be coming to meet me, but at first, I thought it was for another passenger, and not for me. That insignificant feeling stuck to me like glue. Who would care to waste his valuable time to come to the seaport to meet me? This happening was unexpected, puzzling and joyful. Petrified and fearful, because of what had happened on board the boat, and because I knew no one else, I cautiously approached the gentleman and introduced myself and told him my name. I have never met anyone happier to see me. Looking at him, one would be sure that he had won a major battle and was finally presented with a medal of honour. His mission was, no doubt, to gather, welcome and safely deliver these new people to their destination.

There were other prospects for the nurses' training who had travelled on the same ship, "The Montserrat." But I did not know them. It was only when their names, country of origin and destination were announced, that we knew who was who. Some of these prospects seemed to be, what would be termed, wise to our world. I felt as shy as a schoolgirl and did not have anything meaningful to contribute to any conversation. I felt as though I were sinking into a bottomless pit.

A few of the travellers had previously been to England and other countries. They said they even travelled in those magnificent flying machines. I had never been near one or even saw a real plane.

News networks like CNN in America, BBC in England, and our own local CTV frequently broadcasted the breaking news. Well, my breaking news was meeting people my age or younger, having flown in real airplanes travelling to places farther than Trinidad. What bigger news could there be? News of the so-called Cold War, war in the Middle East or in Eastern Europe, had almost no impression on me.

Harrogate Town

Royal Bath Hospital would be my home for about two years, and here was the place that I was bowled over by devastating news. It hit me like a china cup slamming against a concrete footpath, never to return to its unique form.

I do not remember much of the middle of my journey to my first hospital, Royal Bath. The wings of doubts were frantically flying everywhere in my mind like bats in the night. My subconscious mind was at the helm. For a short time, it felt as though my memories were blotted out or even buried somewhere deep, deep, in the back of my mind. I did not want to think because I felt too disturbed. Sometimes it is beneficial for the health of the brain to know little or nothing at all. It was impossible to keep some frightening, unwelcome thoughts securely under lock and key, yet still some squeezed through. My questionable reasoning powers sowed seeds of doubt, and how little effort would be needed to open a window or door and fling myself in front of a speeding locomotive, committing my final act. I felt so inadequate to face a challenging world.

I had to survive even though I felt frightened and alone. I energized myself, saying, "You are standing in the darkness, but you know you are going to get back in the light, the one at the end of the tunnel." One specific pleasing thing brought sunshine to me and that was the memory of the Canadian Red Cross people who visited my local junior school, in Trinidad, for their end-of-term treats, the skim milk, cookies, and a little paper bag of assorted goodies. Cheap or not, I still enjoyed not only the treats, but also the givers. As a young, vulnerable, desperately hungry child, even the smallest act of compassion to partially relieve the situation was appreciated greatly. I felt confident I would enjoy similar empathy in my new place.

I felt mistrustful of almost everything and that even my own shadow was out to get me. There was one main thought which felt strong or even stronger than the destructive reaction and that was tenacity. It had me moving forward before I took this trip and it would give me the drive I needed to clutch this once-in-a-lifetime opportunity. Again, inner reassurance would not let me be. I did not give up and hung on for survival with all my might. Regardless of being trampled emotionally, physically, spiritually and sexually, I refused to stay down. My life's journey had thus far been merciless, bumpy and pitted with potholes, except for this new opportunity that lay ahead. That tiny voice inside me whispered, this time, ever so gently, "You will be ok." Along I trudged. I did not give up and I hung on for my survival with all my might.

Train Journey
And so we were finally on our way, ready to board the train that would take us to our destination. Once again our instructions were read out clearly and loudly, one last time. We responded and took our seats in the railway coaches.

The snacks looked strange. A variety of tasty foods were served in paper or plastic packets. I had never seen food served in this way, and so I called it ready-made food. I thought, for a fleeting moment, that I was on the train for glory, not the Harrogate-bound Pullman.

I wished those foods were available for my family, but everything has a price. Our treats were for eating, but they were wholesome foods. The foods that my family ate were cheap, freshly harvested, wholesome and readily available. During that time, I knew nothing about nutritious meals. All I cared to know was where my next meal came from. We had absolutely no idea that we ate good foods, in line with healthy diets.

The train started moving. Its noisy engine puffed out smoke as it travelled along the steel tracks. As it picked up more speed, the noise was almost deafening and frightening to my unaccustomed ears. It was as if the whole world was moving as the train whisked past people, buildings, places and other things in its path. Everything seemed like sheer magic.

The speeding train rattled along, giving the impression of the mammoth creature pushing its way along the tracks, but after a while this fiend began slowing down. I was curious to know if it was short on fuel, or was something much bigger blocking its path? Neither! We had reached our destination—the Harrogate station. This ride took 5 to 6 hours and 17 minutes.

The other candidates and I grabbed our scanty luggage, and again performed another game of "follow the leader" and hurried towards a fleet of shining, spotless, black automobiles. Our fearless leader directed us to one of those shining taxis. Off we headed, riding for what seemed like an eternity on wide, straight, well maintained, but very busy roads the driver called 'a motorway.' Soon, we exited into narrower winding streets that snaked their way up moderately steep hills, then down valleys, and eventually the driver stopped. We had arrived at our destination—Harrogate—that would be my home for possibly two years.

We repeated the process as we did at the wharf, following our organizer's instructions. Our leader stepped out of the car and onto the sidewalk. Aching from sitting so long, we understood how older people must feel who have arthritis. We followed, stepping out like ducks in a straight line. Our chaperone led us into the huge brown brick house to a cozy room. It felt good to move around and know the journey was over.

This spectacular looking dwelling was adorned with breathtaking colours, blushing pink roses, blood red zinnias and sun yellow buttercups. I had never seen such a well-manicured flower garden. It looked like artificial pieces of tapestry spread on the ground. These patches were so meticulously cultivated with beautiful vibrant flowers that I felt in a pleasant daze. Some shrubs were shaped like birds while others were in the shape of squares and balls. There was not even one yellow, one brown or a dry leaf on the lawn. The landscape and structures were all in pristine condition. I felt like singing that jingle, "How many types of sweet flowers grow in the English country gardens?" There were many.

I seriously thought I had spent all my emotions. I was mistaken. Some surfaced in degrees, others too robust to keep under tight lids. I stood looking in admiration at the large greyish-brown building. It seemed so powerful and glaring that it made me feel truly insignificant. There were windows and more windows, and not as many doors. I tried to compare which was bigger, that massive ship or this majestic structure.

In the tale of Gulliver's Travel by Jonathan Swift (1667-1745), the Irish writer described his thoughts about travelling into several remote nations of that world. How a particular mountain, which resembled a sleeping giant, would safeguard the city. Now, I was the modern-day female equivalent of Gulliver.

Nurses' Home
The heavy well-built door opened, and a prim and proper looking female walked out. She held a paper folder in her hands. She smiled, held out her hand, and with robust handshakes, she greeted the others and me in the group.

"I am the Home Sister," she said.

From her head to her feet, she was a picture of sophistication. There was not one strand of disorderly hair. Her face looked as if she just walked out of a high-end beauty salon. As for the attire, I had never seen anything like it in my life. The best I could tell you is that her navy blue suit, which fitted her extremely well, could not have come from a second-hand shop. In spite of her upper class appearance, I felt reassured about one thing—her gentle and considerate attitude—as she escorted us into the building.

She placed the paper folder on a desk, and we had a brief conversation. The necessary new-recruit paperwork and procedure completed, the Home Sister escorted me to my chamber. This space, in this strange land, with its unfamiliar citizens, would become my family and home away from home. That building and its occupants would be my residence and my protection. Being inside this comfy mammoth structure was one thing, but how was I to navigate my way through this apparently strange maze? Hopefully I might be assigned a mentor to help me find my way around the community. Luckily I was assigned one.

I needed to learn how to use modern gadgets, stoves, washing machine and clothes dryer.

Although I knew I was standing on English soil, it was not until I was actually shown to my room that reality clouted me in the face. There was no time to change my mind or turn back. Having no other place to live, or extra money, I stayed.

The best way to describe my emotions at this particular point was perplexed, with disorderly thoughts and anything in between. On one side of the coin, I was glad for this once-in-a-lifetime-opportunity, but on the other side, well, I was near panic.

Flowers
The Home Sister had turned to leave my room. It excited me having my own room with a beautiful flowering plant as a welcoming gesture, especially since I'd never had a room to myself. I was delighted by the thoughtfulness until I looked at the plant's label. I knew virtually nothing about any plant's ordinary or botanical name, but when I read the label that said it was a begonia, that name was enough to unnerve me, and I felt rooted to the floor, unable to move.

No one knew the relationship between this plant's family name and me. My older sister, Ruth, had travelled to England on the "Begonia" in 1964. It nearly caused me to throw up because it reminded me of my journey and what had happened on the ship. I gasped loud enough to cause the Sister to turn, giving me a peculiar look. She might have had doubts about me, wondering what a strange creature this girl is. What she couldn't have known, besides the fact that I sailed on the "Montserrat" from Trinidad to England, was that the "Begonia" was her sister.

At that moment I had absolutely no notion of what was happening to me. Much later in my life, I learned those feelings were called triggers or recollections. It felt like that past hideous scene was being played over so vividly and so painfully. Having no skills to cope with these emotions, I somehow managed to pull through. Whether my so-called coping strategy was right or wrong, I dragged myself through those unpleasant days and equally God-awful nights.

Often I questioned if this plant had unknown meaning. There might have been a deeper reason, apart from brightening my room and intending to warmly receive me to my new home. Whatever the reason, I would never know.

In late evening, on the day of arrival at the student home, the Home Sister briefed us and gave us a written plan for the next few days, including medical appointments with the infirmary's physician. We learned that the Home Sister was a qualified nurse employed by our hospital; she looked after the smooth running of the resident nurses' program.

The day for my medical appointment arrived and the same women who welcomed us the evening before greeted me. The medical examiner was more thorough in comparison to some of her colleagues. She started with the routine examinations of ears, nose and throat and the conclusion was 'good.' The doctor was methodical; she was good and she was not going to miss a darn thing. I cannot remember the time but it seemed to me too long. My physical examination continued to my upper chest area. She examined my breasts, but this was followed by a grunt and a change of facial expression. The physician's final check was the dreaded internal—a vaginal examination.

Chapter 8: Unplanned Pregnancy

At the conclusion of my physical checks, we had an emergency meeting. It was then that I heard the worst news ever. The doctor explained her concern of a "possible pregnancy." These words shocked me, but I had to tell what happened on the ship. And that's when I received my first lesson in sex education. The doctor explained that, because I was a virgin, the rape had caused the pregnancy, and I related that to the blood I'd seen on the sheets.

To add insult to injury, I was informed that I would not be allowed to start my nursing training if the pregnancy continued. At the precise time, if the staff could have had a sneak peek into my mind, they would have seen only a blank field. I felt empty. An emotionless wave swept over me, and I did not care about anything anymore.

Tough Choices

A few days later I was summoned to the doctor's office, and the laboratory's report confirmed my fear, that I was pregnant.

My sympathetic organization offered me two options. The first was to terminate my pregnancy.

"What's terminating?" I mumbled.

"To get rid of the pregnancy," the doctor said.

"Rid of it? Kill it?" I said in an inaudible voice.

The second option they said was to discontinue my career. That one was just as hard. It was the reason I had come this far. It was an extremely difficult decision. This crisis was too much for me. I felt as though my brain was going to explode at any minute. These two issues were equally important to me. I would have to face consequences regardless of what I decided.

I felt like sticking my fingers tightly into my ears, screaming at the top of my lungs, bolting with long strides, and jumping over the chairs, tables, medical couch, and right out the main door like a racehorse. But how could one run away from one's shadow?

No Common Cold
Early signs of pregnancy started to make their presence felt. Generally, I felt as if I was having a touch of the common cold, my body ached, my energy was low, and I was too tired to do anything. My belly was uncooperative, rebellious, even violent, and as ferocious as a wild animal. I was neither consulted nor had a say when this system decided to try turning itself inside out.

So this was it. Anxiety, worries and hateful moods frequently disturbed me. I had thoughts of doing something dreadful to the man who did this to me, but there was one drawback, I could not think of anything that was more dreadful than what he did to me.

Final Decision
This final decision was one of the most challenging ones I've ever had to make. I asked myself one question, Am I ready to receive this child? I carefully considered numerous things, such as my support system, the understanding of raising a child alone, and the time and financial resources at my disposal. Considering my limited experience and hopeless situation, I was convinced that I was making the very best choice. And that decision was made and executed in a place away from the hospital or health clinic.

My Greatest Loss
That chapter of my life was over. Over, but definitely unresolved. I was told that I had a male fetus. As I glimpsed briefly at him, I broke down and wept as if my heart was breaking, and it was. I could not stop the hot tears from flowing. It was as if I were crying for not one, but two souls. Probably both my child and I were crying at the same time for our loss. His life started and ended in violence. And for me, it

was the loss of my son. Much later in my life, I learned that I could have asked to spend some time with him. I would have cherished hugging him close to my heart and talking to him. No, I think I would have whispered, instead, and asked for his forgiveness.

That enormous loss, grief and sadness followed me—even now—like an unwelcomed pelt. I had millions of unanswered questions. I did not know what to do, or where I could find a sympathetic listening ear. Who would listen? Who would understand? Was I the only woman in England to terminate her pregnancy? Maybe there were other women, in similar unfortunate situations, who wanted to tell their stories but were too terrified of societal reaction.

Chapter 9: Collecting the Shards

Very soon after the abortion, I went back to address my nursing career and to focus on the task at hand. The Home Sister, who was present when my pregnancy was confirmed, greeted me with nothing but warmth and kindness, which I appreciated greatly. I was sure that she had a good idea what happened to me over that weekend, though no questions were asked and no explanations were given. With the offer of support, only love and extra care were showered on me.

This Home Sister was the most senior staff and she operated with a military-style attitude, living by the rules, and there were thousands of them. Some were fully obeyed by the resident nurses while others only partly obeyed, and still others were blatantly disregarded. Rules such as changing bedding, or placing soiled uniforms outside doors made perfect sense and were followed. After all, the consequences for not acting meant there was no fresh laundry. Another rule was cleaning the kitchen after we used it. Well, this cleaning was done, depending on who was there. We used to say, "Some people are probably allergic to cleaning up after themselves," meaning they detested housework so that chore was not done. But the most disregarded rule was curfew.

Most of the nurses who were in my particular building related how they went to parties and dances that did not end until the early hours of the morning. This was certainly breaking news to me. In my simple ill-experienced, unworldly life, I never knew that girls were allowed to go, not only to parties, but also allowed to stay until the wee hours of the morning. Partying and dancing were unheard of when I was a young person. Parties were seen as a sin and abomination in the eyes of those who lived as though they were holier than God. Though there were a lot of other things far worse than parties, I was very confused with what was right or wrong, and so my state of confusion continued until I was able to use my own common sense to reason and come to a conclusion.

Despite my ignorance, I searched and searched for the answer, trying different churches for guidance but still unable to find one whose doctrine appealed to me. In the end, comfort came when I simply started using what I truly believed was right and what was wrong, what felt comfortable, and how easily could I live with my actions. In other words, was I willing and able to stand up to the consequences of my behaviour? This simple mantra became the beacon in my life and still proved useful after many years.

Knowing my educational limits, I devoted my time to focusing on my career. I knew the program would be challenging because rigor mortis almost set in upon receiving a copy of the course outline. I had absolutely no idea what some of the words, terminologies and sentences meant. My new English and nursing dictionary were my Bibles for a long time. I jotted down any new words I heard on a piece of scrap paper, and when I returned to my small, but comfortable, room, I learned the pronunciation, their meaning and how they were correctly applied in the job.

The first few months of my training, my listening and observation skills were as sharp as a razor. My new vocabulary was not to impress anyone; it was crucial to my nursing job. Using new words such as diaphragm, diarrhea or dehydration came slowly and felt weird initially, but by applying these words more frequently, my comfort level increased and I was able to expand my knowledge. Learning these big new complicated words was not easy. I almost bit my tongue in the process. I repeated after other health professionals, such as nurses, doctors, physiotherapists and anyone else who sounded educated. One day I was even brave enough to give the daily report to a group of senior staff members, and they actually understood what I was saying! That was when my confidence started to blossom, and I developed a strong hunger to learn new words and how to use them properly.

All of my classmates were graduates from either high school or college, but I was starting at a very basic level. Biology and science were foreign to me—I had never heard of these things. Because of that, my workload was twice or three times more than that of the other students. I had one main goal, to study and study hard, and be successful. I simply could not afford to fail. To fail would mean going back to a life of misery, so the only way to free myself from such a burden was to educate myself. That was my goal.

Chapter 10: Keep Focusing

My studies were my parties. I did socialize with a few students, but only after I was satisfied with the amount of studying I had done. It was never far from my thoughts that I needed to do extra work to accomplish my goal. I knew why I was in England, and it was definitely not to waste my time.

During frequent library visits, I requested the help of a senior staff member and I asked numerous questions, which was very helpful.

Exam #1: Success

After a few months, it was time for our first non-state examination. This particular exam was set by our local Harrogate Royal Bath Hospital. It was almost like a dry run to the bigger Final State Examination. Naturally, I experienced fear, but this was different. I felt in control and hopeful as opposed to a sense of helplessness and impending doom. It was as though I was peeking through a tiny window and saw for the first time what my life could be like with some education, and this realization was exactly the encouragement I needed to carry on.

News travelled fast when the exams results were delivered to our rooms and pushed under the door. That particular day, my excitement affected my appetite so I skipped my meal and continued to my bedroom. There was a letter waiting for me. With weak, nervous trembling hands, I ripped open the envelope. I read only the first few lines and that was enough news for me:

'Dear Miss Cooper, we the Nursing School are pleased to inform you that you have been successfully...'

The rest I cared little about. Crying, I ran to my friend's room and learned that she, too, was successful, so she started to bawl. I had a companion in the weeping arena, so we howled with all our might. When we finished using up our quota of tears, we looked at each other and started to laugh like two foolish girls. This was the first time, I think, in my life that I shed happy tears. Oh, it felt so good. Now this was a perfect reason to celebrate and we did it in our quiet way.

The students who had the biggest room hosted the celebration. Nurses from different countries such as Hong Kong, China, India, and the Caribbean prepared delicious meals. We played music, danced, laughed, and told stories about being nervous before the exams. On returning to my room, I was sure that there was no happier person on this earth than me. My world was not where it was supposed to be, but it was not as upside down as a few months before. Success felt good. I wanted more, much more.

The next day I was back in the world of reality, doing my job, my studies, and chores of daily life. My life felt easier mainly because I had a better understanding about what nursing entailed and the successful completion of my first exam. A fairly firm foundation was taking shape that I used to improve my life, not only in the nursing field, but also in other areas such as changing my thought processes.

Even though I was in my early twenties, I had never heard of positive thinking before. I believe I first heard the words on a radio show, or perhaps spoken by a learned person, or I read it in a book. Correction, it could not have been from a book especially those 'make you feel-good types.' The only books I was interested in at that time were those related to my work. In fact, periodically I was almost brain-dead after only a couple of hours of studies. I worked on my studies either before or after work, depending on my schedule. Besides, I was fearful of those feel-good books. How would I cope with myself if I started to feel positive or believed I was a worthy person and using better words? This would be like going through the different stages of metamorphosis. Surely, I would be changed into the person I was created to be. In spite of travelling those tumultuous and bumpy roads, I had never accepted my lot, but instead looked ahead to a happier life.

About one year after starting my nursing career, my life started to change in so many ways. Mentally, all those negative feelings of anxiety, fear, and low-grade depression subsided. Contempt and loathing towards Grace was no longer a constant companion. The powerful self-defeating statements, such as, You were not bright enough to read a book or pass a test, were replaced with a resolve to do all those things I previously did not think I could achieve. Freedom was slowly replacing my gloomy and despondent existence. I could see that bright light at the end of a pitch-dark tunnel.

Chapter 11: Promotion

In those days being promoted to a second-year nurse came with its own types of accolade—a unit celebration with cake and juice, and also a new clean stiff uniform with an emblem marking you as a 2nd year nurse. This was a grand occasion, at least for me, because it was the very first time in my life that my achievements were truly celebrated. What a glorious feeling it was!

As my career continued, others began to have more trust in not only my everyday life, but more importantly, in my professional life too. With support, if needed, just the right kind and amount of responsibilities were offered to me. Negative thoughts about my ability to undertake responsibility drifted back from time to time, but they did not prevent me from completing the task at hand.

I held my head higher as if I had graduated from a young women's finishing school. I felt worthy of my accomplishments and my vocabulary was improving. I was confident, although not cocky or arrogant; humility propelled me to be the best I could be under the circumstances.

Although I was eager to complete this basic nursing course, I was equally nervous about the next step to further my training. As I mentally flicked through the pages of my life, I realized that I always got help from somewhere. My guardian angel or my Higher Power, whoever or whatever that was had always protected me and would continue to do so in the second phase of my career. But first, I needed to continue to focus on the immediate studies, and then I would think of the next step.

Final State Exam

The months flew by, and it was time for last-minute preparations for the Final State Nursing Examination. The residence took on a business-like attitude of its own. The television sitting room grew less occupied and much quieter; the common kitchen area became almost deserted; the telephone rang, but there was no hurry to answer it. Hanging out and chin-wagging was almost a thing of the past, and visitors—even the regular ones—came by less often. It was as though a sign was posted that read, Examination Revision in Progress: Please Keep Away.

It was pretty easy, because I was not one of the regular partygoers. My studies were pushed up a few notches and so was my determination to succeed. Nights turned into days and vice versa. I always used my time wisely, but now it was even more valuable. An interesting thing occurred to me during this time of intense revision. Terminology that used to confuse me was clearer and easier to pronounce, test situations were a breeze, and I was able to think about solutions to problems and list important points before consulting my textbook. I was feeling fantastic and confident to challenge the test. On the day of the exam, I believed I had challenged the test instead of being challenged by it. I felt good.

A celebration was planned to mark the end of two years of hard work. Stresses were fewer; sleep came more easily, and relationships with friends and colleagues resumed while we anxiously and impatiently awaited results. Patience was definitely not my strongest virtue.

Our regular English postal workers were familiar with what was going on and knew that the students were anxiously awaiting their exam results. They delivered our mail as quickly as possible, even if it meant back tracking to the other side of the street so they could deliver our letters first. The wait became almost unbearable.

Some former candidates said a thin envelope from the nurses' examining office meant failure. They knew firsthand what they were talking about, because they had passed through the doors of disappointment, some of them more than once, experiencing the distress of opening that 'slim packet.' These so-called 'advice-givers' continued their prediction with the confidence of an expert. On the other hand, they said a thick envelope was a favourable sign. It meant various forms were enclosed in order for us to start the registration process. We all knew our fate was sealed the second we handed in our test papers. Still, we all hoped and prayed, crossing our fingers, and probably toes too, wishing these uncomfortable positions would bring us good luck.

Reflecting
Before I left Trinidad, I had been disappointed with what was done to me in the name of religion, so I decided to cast aside any and all things that reminded me of God, religion, or church. In England, I was free! Free from being forced to go to church. Yet I still needed help so that I could pass my state exam, so I asked for God's help, and he reached out and helped me.

In time my understanding of an organized religion or church and being near to a Higher Power was not the same. When I understood this difference, I was at peace with myself. For a long time, I had blamed God for all the mean things people, who went to church regularly, had done to me. My reasoning was simply this, if those people go to the house of God, worship him and call his name so often, even to the point of uttering threats in the name of God, then God must be aware and have a part in it.

My sincerest apologies to my Creator for putting a heavy load of blame on you, I know better now.

Chapter 12: Awaiting Results

For the next while I looked in the mailbox literally from morning to night, before the postman commenced his shift and long after it ended. Even on weekends when no letters were delivered, I thought, by some miraculous means, an envelope would magically appear. Still I waited, and nothing came. By this time my patience was at its all-time low and so was my reasoning power. I continued to go to my job but hurried home on my meal breaks just in case the examination results were there.

Success #2

Then one bright and sunny morning, my long wait was over. I received another official stamped envelope addressed to E. Grace H. Cooper. Although my anxiety and fears were at the forefront of my thoughts, it was completely different from one of doom and gloom. Sweating and trembling, I quickly ripped open the letter to find out that I had been successful in my examination. I did care about the rest of the letter, but at least not at that moment. I had to sit down because the intense emotions felt as though my heart was about to fly out of my chest with joy.

No one ever told me joy could be as nerve shattering as in time of sorrow. Fortunately, there were many nurses who had received similar news. Expectedly, there were tears and laughter, hugs, jumping up and down, waving of letters in the air and generally happy silliness. I am unsure what time we returned to work, or maybe we took an unofficial afternoon off. We simply did not care about punctuality. Timekeeping flew out the window, like a bird just set free from captivity, but only for a brief period.

Congratulations, good wishes, kind thoughts and the jubilation were over and the next step in our career had to be addressed. We completed and posted registration forms for both our employer and the college. My 2-year contract with my present employer was near its end, and so I applied to another hospital in Liverpool, England, and was accepted as an Enrolled Nurse[6]. What a day that was! The new title was not only accepted in Britain but was internationally recognized, another positive milestone. I felt like a Super Star for the second time! I tell you, I was doing the equivalent of the happy dance.

Fear of Success
These successes started giving me cause for concern. I felt like sabotaging it, because, although I appreciated my progress, I was also frightened by how to cope with it.

For the greater part of my life, I truly felt as though I was in a deep dark cocoon and now that shell had begun to crack. I was reminded of the stages of the butterfly. Mine was not silky by any means, but I was determined to go through all those stages and eventually show the person who Grace was born to be, in spite of life's roadblocks. I kept reminding myself that, yes, I'd been beaten down, but I would not stay down regardless of what happened to me.

Determination, having a positive attitude, and help from what I call a super human being has brought me safely thus far, and I was convinced that these qualities would see me through, whatever my lot.

Small but significant changes were happening in my life; the tide of positive change was replacing the old negative ones. I could not stop wondering why so much help was suddenly coming my way. Who or what was the driving force behind this? What was the reason for so many pleasant changes in the space of only a few short years? When would this help end? Where would this collective aid lead? No reasons or answers were available because I could not see my life's road map, but I wanted answers.

---

[6] Registered Practical Nurse in Canada - RPN

The Unknown

As I recalled the barricades in my life, many question surfaced. One in particular was "why was I still alive?" I was sure there had to be some important unfinished work to be completed by no one else but me. I nearly went out of my mind trying to figure out about the incomplete job business. The more I tried to question the 'unknown,' the more the answers drifted further and further away and then a part of me 'threw in the towel,' but only a part. Then I approached my question from a new angle. I still wanted answers.

I wrestled to keep control. My only obstacle was I really did not know the name of what I needed. I recalled the time when I desperately needed help but did not know what to ask for, because it was like a 'no name brand.' Imagine me going into a shop to buy a certain article not knowing the name. I took some action, settled myself and accepted those things I couldn't change.

Chapter 13: New Employment

For a second time I had to pack up my belongings. This time was different from when I was leaving Trinidad, and I was excited with a positive outlook. There was no dreadful fear, instead I was quite happy. During my interview I had been introduced to the Head Nurse on the cardiac unit where I applied and would be working. She was a pleasant woman and reassured me that she would support me in my new job. I was ready to get started.

The first things I packed were my nursing textbooks and my dictionaries; everything else took second place. I was prepared to face this new challenge, accept any help and be successful on this cardiac ward. At the time, I did not know what happened in the cardiac ward, but I knew I would learn. I was so hungry and appreciative for the additional knowledge and the encouragement that were given so easily and freely.

The manager gave me the necessary textbooks, dictionaries, special magazines, relevant printed articles, opportunities to attend special cardiac procedures and operations. I learned many complex words such as tachycardia (fast heart beats), bradycardia (slow heart beats), heart valves, and heart rhythms and was able to use them in the course of giving and receiving reports to my colleagues. It felt so rewarding when I used the terminology appropriately. I felt as though I had won an honours degree in medicine by just using the right words in the right context.

I was ready to go to my new hospital in the Beatles' town of Liverpool. The train seemed to be travelling almost as fast as the speed of light and with clanging, rattling noise and a strong side-to-side motion. Soon I was standing on Liverpool's soil, and after a short ride in the taxi, I was standing outside Sefton General Hospital that would be my new home for at least five years. Another pleasant and kind woman, the Home Sister in charge of the nurses' residence, welcomed me. I was shown to my room, given a light lunch, time to unpack my belongings and settle in my room. The room was small, clean and comfortable. Later I was given a tour of the surroundings including my new unit. My new manager welcomed me with a whopping bouquet of flowers. One problem, I had no vase to keep the flowers fresh. That problem was quickly solved when someone loaned me a vase from the unit, and I returned it when the flowers 'gave up the ghost.' This experience was so wonderful; it was nothing like I had ever known or felt in more than twenty years on Mother Earth.

Earlier I referred to that feeling of being in a concrete cocoon. Now, it felt more like silk than the hard unyielding concrete. Yes, there were changes. I could feel them.

For an instant I paused as I approached the sign that pointed in the direction of my new unit. Cardiac Ward. It was at this time that my own heart started to skip a beat, and it felt as though a few birds were doing small quick flutters in my chest. I felt weak in my knees and as though I was going to faint, but in a few short minutes I was sitting in my head nurse's office and being introduced to other members of her team. The Head Nurse literally took me 'under her wings' and introduced me to the ward's routine and the different areas where specialized cardiac assessments were performed.

This was one of the few times when I was strongly encouraged to ask questions, however simple. I must have asked many child-like questions, such as what are those scissor things? I learned they were forceps. I had so many questions before the end of my shift. Before I left the ward, my mentor asked me to make a list of anything I wanted to know, and we would discuss them the next day. My brain was working overtime, because I did not want to miss a single point. Well into the night, I was jotting down question upon question. Even when I was in my bed, I would jump up and add another point to my already long list.

Back to the ward I went the next day, armed with a long list of queries. My mentor was pretty impressed. After spending a long time answering all the questions, she told me that once I got familiar with this area, I should consider studying to become a Registered Nurse (RN), a step higher than a RPN. I was totally freaked out by this suggestion, and I had to pinch myself to make sure that it was real and that I was also real. Me, Grace Cooper, who had not even one academic qualification prior to this training, was advised by an experienced senior nurse to consider doing advanced studies!

The very thought almost made my poor already weakened heart want to give up completely. I said already weakened heart, because of the many happy unexpected positive things that kept coming my way. The most awesome thing was the help that came spontaneously. Growing up, being abused and treated cruelly came easily too, very easily. It was the same with this kindness and support that I was presently enjoying. Most of the time that help and support just flowed smoothly.

It was as though I was at the right place at the right time. How wonderful!

Chapter 14: Cardiac Ward

After a few months in this new and exciting field, I had acquired additional knowledge of the heart's anatomy and physiology. Then it was time to move to a different area. Now that I was comfortable with the structure and the function of the heart, it was time to move to the assessment area to observe this small, but mighty, organ. In action, it worked 24 hours and seven days a week throughout a person's lifetime. Watching this machine actually beating rhythmically was simply breathtaking and jaw dropping; it was awesome and incredible. Seeing the action of the heart made me want to learn as much as possible. I found cardiac catheterization very interesting.

Pronouncing the word 'cardiac' was easy, but catheterization was a mouthful. Only if I was more articulate or knew about phonetics, learning this medical terminology would be less problematic. However, articulate or not, phonetic or not, I was determined to succeed in learning these words. Personally, knowledge and education gave me more confidence and added self-worth. It was like laying a foundation, adding knowledge, and building on it with each new learning experience.

One day when I was in the cardiac assessment room, a doctor performed a cardiac catheterization. He fed a small tube through the blood vessel in the groin, and did some tests to diagnose or treat diseases of the heart. I was fascinated by how easily a tube was fed into the heart with little or no pain to the patient.

There were many new and interesting procedures that I initially observed. Later I would come to prepare, accompany and stay with the patient throughout the procedures. Having observed numerous tests, I started to identify the odd cardiac abnormalities that were pleasantly surprising, not only to me, but also to some of the medical and nursing staff.

Being in a positive environment with equally positive professional people forced me to change my thought processes. My focus was to see the good in the world and in my personal life as the glass being half full and no longer half empty. I suddenly began to appreciate some of the simplest things around me. The dawning of a new day, regardless of whether it was cloudy or bright. I appreciated the beautiful flowers and the green leaves. The path I was now walking was a far cry from a few years before. Even though I continued to try and understand all the miraculous changes, the answers still evaded me. Maybe I needed to graciously enjoy my blessings and stop expecting answers.

I did not realize guardian angels, in the form of human beings, were placed in strategic paths, corners, and crossroads in my life's journey. Perhaps due to past behaviours of those I had earlier encountered, my trust in mankind was almost nil. I painted everyone with the same dirty brush instead of seeing people as individuals. In the back of my mind were always distrustful questions, such as: What's the payback? What was their ulterior motive? What did these people want from me? No one will do good without expecting repayment. The answers to these questions were nothing! My colleagues seemed to simply recognize me as a capable woman who would benefit from a helping hand. It was that simple. My brain might have been programmed to see all of my fellow human beings as foes whose main goals were primarily to use and abuse others. It was a hard thing to overcome.

Ever so slowly, my brain was being reprogrammed to avoid viewing everyone in the same light. I knew that there were wicked people just waiting to attack the weak and vulnerable. On the other side of this equation, there were many genuinely caring and real individuals who scatter joy, love, and kindness in our troubled world and aim to leave it a better place.

On many occasions, when someone was sincerely trying to help me with my work, I could feel the monster of fear and mistrust creeping back into my brain. At times, many times, my reactions were almost as clear as daylight. People told me, "Grace, you've got to trust a bit more" and "Everyone is not here to harm you." There were days when I was too scared to ask for help, and it was even worse to accept it, such as if a person smiled or presented with a pleasant expression. That was enough to trigger a negative reaction. There were still restless and troubled nights. A particular small noise like clanging of metal chains or even words of special music as "Amazing Grace" would send fearful shivers up my spine.

One unforgettable day, while at work, one of my colleagues was sharing about a miscarriage she recently experienced. This was the first time since the termination of my pregnancy that I heard of another woman's view of abortion. I had a flood of negative emotions. Shame, guilt, and remorse were only a few of many self-blaming thoughts. I knew that I had a lot of work to do to reach a stage of closure, but I was not anywhere near that stage yet. Those wounds were still too raw and far too deep to tackle by myself. I needed long-term professional therapy, and I promised myself that when I had reached a more comfortable level in my life that it would be addressed. Now was not the time; it was too painful and I was too weak.

Triggers were positive or negative. Listening to that woman's story reminded me that I had unfinished business that still needed my attention. This was the first item I placed in my emotional memory box. Undoubtedly, there would be many more to add to that list. Oh, how I wished I had only one concern that needed my attention, but as fate would have it, I was not so lucky.

There were things in my life that made me feel truly blessed and fortunate, even though life was not always easy. Some days it could be compared to a raging sea, other times it could be unbelievable calm. How delightful it was to enjoy a calm and meaningful life.

Chapter 15: Scared of Knowledge

The days, months and year flew by quickly. My knowledge started to scare me. Those big long words I alluded to earlier, I was now incorporating them into my reports and using them in correct context. I had a very simple way of testing whether or not I was using them properly. I paid attention to the facial expression of the person to whom I was speaking, to see if he or she responded appropriately to my statements. These methods worked well, and I called it my 'compass.' The experience, love and incredible support I received on that ward were almost too much for me. This unexpected treatment was the opposite from what I knew when I was growing up. I felt so undeserving, but I soon got used to accepting kind words from people who really mattered. It was simply wonderful. It felt as though each time I had received a kind word, that cement-like cocoon grew yet another crack and would finally crumble, setting me free.

One morning as I arrived on my ward, my senior nurse said she would be going to a staff meeting that afternoon and I would be in charge. I don't remember if I asked her if she was sure about leaving me in charge of a cardiac ward. Could she really be talking to me? Grace? What would I do if a patient's ticker started to misbehave? Whatever questions or doubts, spoken or unspoken, I am convinced they all registered on my face. This nurse had her plans, I am sure, but I was still left in charge. My knees felt weak, and I felt my energy ebb, my forehead was moist, yet my biggest fear was my heart. I wondered if I should be the patient instead.

The meeting seemed as long as eternity. I was unsure if there was really a staff meeting, but I gladly handed my report back to the senior nurse. There was no catastrophe, and all residents were alive and well. Although I made ward rounds much more than was required, I kept my eyes on those patients whose cardiac conditions were being closely monitored. Being in charge was one of many new experiences. After that day, I was regularly asked to be in charge. Initially, I felt uneasy and nervous, but with time my comfort level increased and I began to enjoy the journey and felt more and more confident with both my work and my private life.

That evening when I went to my room, I looked in the mirror. I did not merely glance, but for the first time I had a good hard look at myself, and what I saw almost knocked me off my feet. I did not see a weak, useless, stupid and uneducated young woman. On the contrary, I saw a strong resourceful, smart and intelligent young woman, and I reminded myself that I was going forward, no matter what. This was my little pep talk then and still is after more than forty years.

Years later, I learned that those in-charge experiences were a testing ground for bigger things. The recommendations from both the nursing and medical staff would be valuable if I decided to pursue further studies, which meant applying to the nursing school to study to be a registered nurse or in other specialized fields. My senior nurse was convinced that I was capable of going further in nursing.

Chapter 16: Now I Understand

Sometimes it was impossible to see myself. I knew that I was not a stupid person and the only reason I did not have any school certificate was that I simply did not get the chance to complete any worthwhile education. When children were going to school and progressing to higher grades, I was subjected to backbreaking work that served no useful purpose. For me, this lack of education presented me with great problems because the thought of writing even a simple shopping list generated anxiety and negative feelings. So I found a solution.

Unless it was absolutely important and there was no alternative, I avoided pencil, pen and paper. To be truthful, it was like being in a foreign country with no idea of the local language. When I initially applied to the nursing school, I got someone else to write my letters and then I recopied it in my own handwriting. My English grammar was so poor that I doubted whether anyone in Britain would be able to decipher what was written. I believed that the reply would have a quick 'sorry to have to inform you...'

My memories sometimes take me way back to my childhood days, and it felt as if I was in constant state of grief for those wasted years. I learned that the first six years of a child's life are called the Formative Years, when the brain is impressionable and learning new things.

Lack of education seemed almost like an incurable disease. It seemed to show its unwelcome head at frequent intervals in my life. Some consolation for this deficit was that something could be done to improve the situation, such as enrolling in an organized educational institution and starting at a comfortable grade. That was one of my goals, to pull myself from the fear of putting a pen or pencil to paper. How would I educate myself? I had absolutely no idea, but it would be done. Whatever helped me thus far would surely help me in the near future. I had faith in this something, whatever it was. I still did not know. As a steadfast employee, I continued to perform my assignments as efficiently as possible.

Challenges presented themselves almost daily, but I was able to overcome and rise above them with a feeling of great triumph and satisfaction. Some people may have thought that this was such an easy thing to do, but for me overcoming any obstacle was a huge deal. Even something as simple as problem solving could present challenges for me, such as how to defuse a volatile situation, how to be a good listener, or how to prevent any situation from becoming uncontrollable. All of it was a learning process.

Secrets

As I continued to adapt to my new world and gain knowledge, I also learned how to articulate my own feelings, especially in response to an action and interaction with others. For instance, I could say that when someone shouted or used inappropriate language towards me, my newfound awareness allowed me to recognize that I felt put down and devalued.

For many, this ability to articulate and understand their feelings may be natural, but not for me. It felt, whether I wanted to or not, as though I was gradually stepping into a new world not only in my career but also in major changes in my life. How I yearned to return home to tell my family about my new life. I was not barred from returning home, but I still felt traumatized by the long-term abuse I had endured. I felt that someday I would return.

My colleagues and Senior Nurse (who felt like my away-from-home family) only knew superficial snippets about me. I felt cloaked in disgrace and dread, unable to even bring myself to explain what happened. I feared being scorned or ostracized by them, and that if my senior nurse were made aware of my past, she would be tempted to involve the police. Could I see myself as a fairly new landed immigrant in England, scarcely able to cope with the everyday language and appearing in the justice system to answer for myself, and to answer technical questions? No, I would certainly be struck temporarily dumb! Had I more command of the English language, going to court might have been an option. So for a while longer, I bore my heavy burden alone, the memories never far behind me.

I wished my memory could be intact at all times. On the other hand, lapse of memory might be a safety device to protect my brain from overloading and malfunctioning with anxiety or unhappiness. I often pondered what could happen if every single hurt, every single pain, or every single unpleasant incident were registered and constantly remembered! I believe that there would be a lot of people who would find coping very disturbing. So I would say thank goodness for fleeting forgetfulness.

Preconceptions

I yearned to share my memories with an understanding person, but I was scared. Often I found that when situations were vague, disparaging attitudes tended to fill that gap. The worst part in indulging in this type of behaviour is the ignorance that accompanies it, like judging a book by its cover. I am guilty of this behaviour.

It's time consuming getting to know a person, but I have also learned that by taking even a little time to listen and understand, although we are unique creatures, our stories are similar. Others' stories have helped me to unlock doors to parts of my life that desperately needed unlocking, such as not being who I am, avoiding uncomfortable circumstances, and confronting facts and facing personal challenges.

Frequently, I am amazed how easy it to discard judgment and just see the person without any preconceived ideas. I had to learn and I had to learn quickly.

Chapter 17: Self-Acceptance

Having a better understanding of human behaviour, especially my own, I was beginning to find new peace of mind and acceptance of my blunders.

Cardiac Unit

My daily chores, socializing and work were more balanced, yet I had to keep the main focus on my studies. I frequented our unit library and flicked through a few cardiac periodicals. I was more overwhelmed and not much wiser. I did not like those long complicated words. I thought that my nursing textbooks had been difficult to comprehend, but now they seemed like ABCs in comparison to these new materials. Initially, I easily understood some of the words, while others came with difficulty. I had absolutely no idea what the authors were talking about. Somehow I had to get the gist of what I was reading. And then I remembered!

The senior nurses in England are addressed as Sister, plus her last name. Sister Gill told me that I could ask her anything that I did not understand, and I asked a lot of questions.

Initially, while working in Sefton General Hospital, I felt shy and embarrassed to ask for help, because I never thought anyone would truly help me and that I only been paid lip service, but I swallowed my pride and asked Sister for help, so that I could start to comprehend the difficult literature. What surprised me the most was her eagerness to offer guidance. Sister Gill provided me with a dictionary suitable for the literature I was reading. In all honesty, I did not realize there were different types of dictionaries! I was encouraged to use it often and make a list of the baffling words, and that's exactly what I did.

At first, I only managed to read a few pages, and so at the end of the week I presented my list of words. We discussed and applied them in sentences and later in work-related reports. Though these were the most difficult things my poor brain had to learn and apply, I learned so fast that at times I shook my head in awe. I went from being unable to write a simple letter to being able to study and successfully pass the Nursing Council State examination, and then being comfortable in the cardiac ward, and eventually reading medical expert reports and understanding most of them. I was definitely grateful for the changes, yet at times I felt they were coming way too quickly.

Gratitude was my new word. I do not know where I first heard or became familiar with this word, but it kept me from having a sense of entitlement and reminded me that the universe owed me nothing and was not all about me. It never dawned on me that, in spite of the bumpy roads that I had travelled, I should consider myself to be blessed and also appreciative.

Looking for new Opportunities

After working in the specialized heart unit, my confidence level began to increase and I started to socialize with some of the nurses. My ears were tuned into their experiences on different areas of our hospital. What they talked about in their day-to-day jobs interested me greatly. Some worked on the kidney unit and described how magnificent these two little bean-shaped organs keep the body clean by filtering the waste products from the blood, and how this strainer thing with tiny parts worked so well to prevent stuff like salt and protein from literally poisoning the body.

They described a certain machine that when it was hooked up to the patient's veins could pump out the person's bad blood, clean it, and then return the clean blood back to the body. It would take all day to do this procedure, and all of this was done without even spilling one drop of that dark red fluid. My jaw dropped in amazement.

Superstitions or Lack of Knowledge

Certain people back home, who knew absolutely nothing about medical technologies, would say this machine must be magic that it could do such a thing. Because this equipment was comparatively modern to some communities, they might even suggest that it was sprinkled with a satanic spell.

I recalled a similar situation when I received that decorated letter from England. A group of neighbours had their own interpretation of what I was or was not going to study in England. Had I not been introduced to this amazing nursing and medical field, I might surely have added my doubts and said it could never happen, because I knew absolutely nothing about modern day medicine at the time.

I clearly remember growing up as a child listening to those illiterate adults sitting on the veranda or some other place in their houses talking with an attitude of authority about how the human body worked. How this part is joined to that part, how the blood is the body's lifeline, how the veins worked, and if one starts to bleed, that person could die in the blink of an eye. If these explanations were to be followed, as directed by these so-called specialists, our bodies would be in a tangled mess.

The prime example is that no knowledge is bad, but a little of the wrong knowledge can be extremely misleading and, at times, even dangerous.

Chapter 18: Not Knowing

Sadly, I have heard one too many horror stories on the topic especially 'woman's curse.' I have also heard many a heated conversation and many self-taught theories about this topic, so much so that I was afraid to become a woman. It seemed to me that a terrible thing would befall anyone approaching womanhood.

These made-up unproved village theories were passed down from generation to generation, adding more fuel to the already stupid theories. The danger here was that no one knew the truth about the how the female body functioned or developed. The energy and enthusiasm with which these talks were delivered were truly convincing. Sometimes I thought that few, or no one, knew when a girl should expect her first menstruation cycle. As a result of this basic information, young girls were frequently faced with frightening and embarrassing situations when they experienced it for the first time.

I remembered how fearful I felt, thinking my insides were falling out, and no one could convince me otherwise. There was so much blood, I thought it was a sure sign it was time to leave this earth, as I knew it. Occasionally I did not sleep, because what if I did not wake up? It was not until a big red spot seeped through the back of a garment I wore, and drew the attention of my mother, that my limited education of womanhood started.

"Grace, now you are a woman and you must stay away from the boys," she said.

What exactly did that mean? Was I not to even say hello to boys, even in my neighbourhood? Was I supposed to cross to the other side of the street when I saw them? Now I was more frightened for fear of the boys and even more confused.

My parents always spoke in parables, using them to answer and respond to life as if it was the only way to relate to life's occurrences. Devoted to the Good Book, they often used them to apply to their daily lives, but as a child, all it offered was confusion. They had a saying that "anything you did in the dark will soon come to light." In my child's mind, I thought it made reference to a flashlight or an electric light, perhaps candlelight. It was not until much later in my adult life that I found out through my elder sister what the statement meant. Hearing those kinds of sayings day after day made me feel like I was caught in a sticky spider's web, unable to find my way out. Something as simple as explaining my woman's cycle only left me with uncertainty and made my body feel foreign.

As a young adult, I knew nothing about menstruation. When I started my nursing career, we were required to learn the different parts of the body and where they were situated; this presented me with a problem. I felt rather ashamed that as an adult in my mid-twenties, I did not know the proper names for some basic body parts.

One of our nursing tests was to name them. Our class was given a sheet of paper naming the canal in the female leading inwards to the uterus that is called the vagina. For all my life that part of the body was called all sorts of funny names, even The-Girl-Part, but never the vagina. Equally, the male anatomy had even more weird names, but never penis. Back home, either these proper names were unknown or they might have been considered the equivalent of cuss words.

Taking a leisurely stroll on a sunny evening and enjoying nature and her patchwork of creation was a good way to recharge and renew my brain. There was the danger of overfilling it with all those interesting and new things that were so foreign, yet so inspiring, to me. I just could not get enough information to satisfy my hunger for knowledge.

Chapter 19: More Education

One morning I arrived on my job bright and early, wearing my snow-white stiff beautifully pressed nurse's hat with a bluest of blue narrow band on it. The whole world would know I was in my third year as a Registered Practical Nurse. My blue dresses had long sleeves, which could be rolled up and kept in place by white elastic cuffs.

Some say only senior nurses were given uniforms with long sleeves because they were assigned to more clerical and managerial jobs. They were exempted from the unpleasant tasks such as attending to the basic care of patients. They had already done their duty with basic care, and now it was my turn. Faithfully, I had fulfilled my role and honoured my commitment with pride as a short-sleeved cadet. Dedication and hard work helped me to join the status of the 'long-sleeves.' I must admit, I felt a cut or two above those nurses who had to wear short sleeves.

About midmorning, one day early in 1970, my senior nurse (manager) approached me and asked if I could come to her office at a certain time. She had already arranged for someone to monitor my patients. Knowing this, I was petrified and beside myself with worry. My mind started to race. At first in a fairly logical way, I went over the last few hours of my last assignments on the ward, but I could not pinpoint any concerns or mishaps. Then suddenly, in the space of no more than a few minutes, my mind started an irrational scramble of the worst kind. Hundreds of questions bombarded me with scarcely time to process an answer. Had I given the correct type and dose of medication? Were all my patients alive and well? Had I ever failed to show up or inform the ward if I was absent for a shift? These were only a few questions that plagued me, but I would learn I had absolutely no reason to worry. I later realized that those feelings were referred to as 'fear of the unknown.'

I arrived earlier than the appointed time and was given a warm welcome and "thank you for coming." After a quick glance around the room, the people I saw there almost caused me to faint. My heart was fluttering in my throat, like a bird frantically trying to free itself. Palms clammy, I wondered, Would I be fired from my job? If so, what would I do?

There was a panel of senior members in the room. Senior members of the nursing profession were rarely seen outside of their offices, and only on special occasions, such as when an executive from the nursing head office or some special high-ranking public figure was visiting the hospital. Then the matron would be busy doing her pre-visit rounds, making sure the nursing staff was dressed neat and tidy, shoes clean, and hair either pinned up, or if not, at shoulder length or shorter as per protocol, and that beds were properly made. That wasn't the case for this day, for they were all sitting in the office waiting for me, and I was scared of what they might say.

I saw the head of many of the different areas in the hospital, from education, payroll office, the cardiac ward and others. I felt a wave of nausea wash over me. As the meeting was called to order, the manager finally provided a reason for the meeting. I was grateful. After all, passing out and falling off my seat would not make a good impression.

The opening of this meeting reminded me of the novel, Lord of the Flies, when everyone sat around and presented their case about what should be done to keep them safe. The members present spoke of what they had seen and observed of my work. One said that I was a clever young woman and a dedicated nurse.

I was in disbelief and in a partial state of shock and surprised. It was gratifying to hear complete strangers, who had no ulterior motive to publicly say what they observed in my work ethic. The last person to address the group was my Senior Nurse. What she said was even more powerful than all the other recommendations. She spoke about me coming to England with no formal education and how I had been more successful in all my tests and examinations and made much better grades than most of my more educated colleagues. They offered me a chance to enroll in the Registered Nurse's program.

Perhaps I looked shell shocked, too, for that was the way I felt at that moment. I was given a few days to consider the offer. I had not expected to hear all these kind words. My unfounded fear was put to rest. On reflection, did that group of professionals see attributes in me that I could not see in myself? Or perhaps I did not believe I was worthy.

A few days later I mentioned to my manager that I did not have and 'O' or 'A' level certificate of education. In the English educational system, 'O' or 'A' level is equivalent to Canada's Grade 12 and 13. She reassured me that she had an appointment with our Matron (her manager) the next morning, and she would talk with her about my concerns. I was anxious until the manager finished her meeting with the Matron. I saw her enter the ward, and she asked me to meet her in her office. I felt as though I could not cope with even one more bit of excitement. I entered with much more emotion than I realized.

Their decision meant I would have to write an educational test and get a passing grade of 75 percent. Thankfully, my manager was very good at reading facial expressions and body language. She quickly realized I was clueless, and she soon put me at ease and explained the statement in simpler terms. "If you were to write the test and score 75 marks or more, then you will be accepted to the Registered Nursing program."

Seventy-five seemed so high. Couldn't they knock it down to accommodate my educational deficiency?

Later I learned I was very lucky to be accepted to the program by such an unconventional route. What a sobering bit of knowledge that was. I was one of the few fortunate nursing candidates. The tutors loaned me textbooks, provided me with samples of previous test papers. I found that encouraging. My determination was at its apex, and I was trying my hardest to be successful and do more than scraping by with a pass mark, but to do much better than expected. My goal was not only to make everyone proud of my achievement, but most of all prove it to myself.

The day of the test came. I said a quick prayer. Calm came over me and I was able to think and comprehend the questions in front of me.

My results came through; I learned I had been successful. My tutor, my manager and many others congratulated me. I was not only successful, but also my mark was in the high 80s. There was a celebration with a special cake ordered from our hospital chef. What a happy day that was, especially for all the people who believed in me.

I would have liked to take a long break after all that work, but there was no time to waste. There was a deadline to get the registration in. Forms and letters were completed and admission fees sent to the Nursing Council main office by registered mail.

Soon a thick envelope arrived containing my acceptance letter, forms for completion, and a list of recommended stores where the textbooks were available. A twist of luck had unexpectedly come my way and I had faith things would work out.

Once the paperwork was done, there was time for a rest.

Chapter 20: Taking a Break

One evening, my friends from work invited me to go for a casual walk with them in an area in Liverpool, locally known as The Valley Gardens. This area was noted for its well-manicured gardens and beautiful flowering plants, such as impatiens, marigolds, zinnias, and lupines—my favourite.

We walked and walked, oohing and aahing at the various brilliant colors. We talked casually and laughed about funny things in our lives and enjoyed the delicious ice cream from the local vendors who'd be found there in the evenings. The weather was surprisingly sunny and warm as opposed to the usual chilly damp English weather. We continued our casual stroll and were soon honoured with the presence of a young man, a stranger. I was rather surprised and so were my friends. I thought they set it up and only acted astonished.

Something seemed out of place to me, because this man was not behaving like a total stranger. He seemed to know my friends but glanced frequently at me, and at times flashed a million-dollar smile. What could this smile mean? My plans were not focused on this sort of relationship. I simply wanted to have a nice walk in this peaceful and welcoming place and to enjoy life, focusing on nothing in particular, but it led me to thinking about relationships.

I sincerely believed that we are destined to meet someone we're born to love. Who would my special person be? I did not know, but I had to smile because I thought this man was a real cultured gentleman. For such an unusually hot and humid evening, this young man was dressed in formal attire. He wore a navy blue suit—I believe it was wool—and a white shirt with dark matching tie, cleaned and highly polished shoes that were so shiny they appeared like a looking glass. His face was radiant with a smile that would brighten any dark room. When I looked at him, I noticed a peaceful pleasantness about him. It was truly pleasing to be in his company.

I had never experienced any human being with this type of personality. Some of the people I have met reminded me of myself—unsure of who they were—while others seemed to drift aimlessly through life with no real purpose. I sadly remembered when my life felt like a dry leaf in the wind, and I was at the mercy of a strong gust with no goals, no purpose. What a dangerous place that was! I wondered what life held for me in the way of relationships. Might he be a part of it?

I was so wrapped up in my studies that I could barely consider a relationship. We said a special goodbye and he went home. I knew that was certainly not the final goodbye. Spellbound but pleasantly confused, I could not get him out of my mind however hard I tried.

I thought as he walked away, Is he real? What I saw in his face, I felt that this would not be my last visit with him.

One evening while I was in my room at the nurses' residence, there was a decisive rap on my bedroom door and the messenger—a nurse—said, "Grace, there's a visitor for you." She was excited delivering that news as though it was her visitor, but I was not expecting anyone. With a broad smile she added, "It's a young man, a nice young man."

Could it be that person my friends and I met on our evening walk? Surely he did not know me that well to come and visit. Being naïve and new to the world of dating, I was confused at how this person knew my name and where I lived and worked. He must have done much research because he found me. I casually walked downstairs, and there he was, standing erect and well composed in his gentleman's suit and wearing his radiant smile. What a feast for the eyes. He even stood up to greet me.

I felt first uncomfortable and at the same time special by his treatment. This type of attention was so new to me and I did not know how to accept it. Should I have bowed? Or should I have curtsied? Looking back, I could not help but giggle about that particular moment. I am sure I looked as awkward as a cow on ice. We sat in the sitting room and talked, but the thing that almost knocked me off my feet was his keen interest in my job. I'd just enrolled in the Registered Nursing program, and my thoughts were on how I was going to get through this monstrous undertaking, with my lack of sleep and the fear I faced about getting through it. This situation seemed far greater than the others.

There were many attributes I admired about my gentleman. He was not boastful, but he used gentle and encouraging words and bore a presence of humility. Was this man even real? It was unbelievable to be presented with such incredible luck. At the end of our visit, I felt twice as excited as when I received the congratulatory letter from the Nursing Council. I was almost on the verge of falling off my seat (again) when he asked me about my upcoming program.

I told him of my concerns about learning it all. He seemed to know in great detail the different parts and functions of these organs, the brain, the heart, the lungs, the kidneys and a lot more. The next day when I went to work, I thought about the words he had used that evening; they were similar to those used by some of the doctors on our ward. I was even more convinced of his intelligence and education. Several times I have heard about a guardian angel. I was not sure he was my guardian angel, but I believed he was sent to help me get through my nursing program.

We agreed to meet and make a study plan. I soon learned that his idea of a plan did not look at all like my plan. His was more detailed and included a fairly precise timeline as to when I should complete studying a certain organ and write a test he would set similar to the real thing. I thought this approach was too tough. I also realized I was attempting a much higher level of studies that called for more discipline, if I was going to be successful. I chose to abide with the so-called tough plan that might help me succeed, instead of doing my own thing and failing miserably. Failure was not an option. Too many people had gone out of their way to support me—the latest addition being my gentleman.

All of our time together was not confined to pen, paper and books, or to him visiting me decked out in a suit and tie. There were times of fun and casual visits like going to picture shows, having picnics on the grass and strolling in the park. Money was in short supply, so we became creative how we spent our leisure time, and it was fun!

Curiosity got the better of me, and many questions about this earthly angel started to flood my thoughts.

Who was he? Issah Ibrahima. Where did he come from? Ghana, West Africa. How did he acquire that radiance that surrounded him? And his intelligence! Or that calm and clever way he presented himself? Much more than everything else was the sense of peace he seemed to have and gave to others, including me. Words were simply not enough for me when I described this gentleman.

Chapter 21: Training

As time went by, our glances at each other became more than just a glance. My focus was still very much on my studies, but the other part was on strengthening our working relationship. My studies progressed exceptionally well, and the mystery of the complicated body organs that used to baffle me was less frustrating. This earthly angel could not have been sent at better time.

My idea of angels was someone or something that comes from above with wings, completely different from a human being. I never thought an angel could be my grandpa, my Ward Sister, the medical staff, the Home Sister, or the Matron at my hospital, and my gentleman, Issah. Why were all these people dotted along my journey? There may never be answers to my questions, so I would continue to not only accept their support with gratitude, but also to work as hard as I could to help myself. I could not expect others to exert more effort on my behalf than what I was prepared to give.

Discipline in my Studies

My studies continued under the careful supervision of my gentleman, who was studying to be an engineer. I was frequently amazed about the depth of his knowledge. It was not only his knowledge about my entire nursing syllabus, but also about life in general. He was clever in how he associated learning to everyday things, so that I could easily remember them. He made learning fun instead of dry, boring and tedious sessions. He related how, as a child growing up in an extremely poor family, he kept his enthusiasm for learning alive by writing out words and solving mathematical problems in the sand in his yard. He said that he earned pocket money by doing other rich boys' homework for them, and how some were blessed with a brain and no money—not even to buy the basic necessities of life—while for others money was never a problem. The problem for these individuals was the discipline of settling down to their studies.

I never knew discipline was simply the ability to put one's life in some kind of order and sticking to it to achieve a certain goal. Be it the goal of arriving at work at a certain time every day, reading a book, studying for a precise period, or even exercising two or three times per week. Whatever the plan, it needed to be a regular undertaking and not haphazard.

With Issah's guidance, within a relatively short time, my thinking process started to change. I paid close attention to his words, deeds, and actions. His words were not used to impress but to help me improve my basic English language. This was Issah's natural way of speaking. He used nice words; I loved to hear them because they were precise and made perfect sense.

The Oxford English Dictionary supplemented my knowledge of English. I acquired two faithful and trusted friends—my fellow and my dictionary—and they stayed with me as constant friends for many years. I read various printed materials, including novels, but the dictionary I used almost daily. It held an abundance of knowledge, with words that always seemed to refresh and challenge my vocabulary. I was never bored, even when the pages were casually flicked. I was starving for knowledge. Learning, to me, was like an eternity of never-ending new things. It seemed to go on and on, without an end.

One day, my earthly angel was working on his university assignments in the library, furthering his education. That was the day I learned that he was already an electronic engineer.

I saw some funny letters that I had never seen before and was curious as to what they were and asked about them. Issah said they were the Greek alphabet, not like the A, B, Cs, but quite different. In the space of a few short minutes, I had a crash course on the Greek alphabet that consisted of 24 letters. He wrote them out in order: alpha, beta, gamma, delta, epsilon, zeta, eta, theta, iota, kappa, lambda, mu, nu, xi, omicron, pi, rho, sigma, tau, upsilon, phi, chi, psi, ending in omega. Originally I thought that the reason for writing, in particular these letters, were simply for me to see these weird shaped letters, but it was much more than that. He encouraged me to first learn the pronunciation, then to read them, and try to memorize them.

For a long time, I was convinced that my angel was of sound mind and body, but soon I started to doubt the sound mind and body business. After all, I was still struggling and trying to feel at ease with my basic everyday English.

Now, I had this foreign language sitting squarely on my lap too. I thought, really, this man has gone bonkers! It was ludicrous asking me to learn, not one, but twenty-four new foreign letters. But I continued because I really loved to learn things, anything that I didn't have the opportunity to learn as a child or a young adult. It was like having free education. In the end I was grateful, because I learned how many times, during the course of my nursing studies, some complicated words could be broken down into simple parts and their origin traced back to the Greek language.

Learning this language gave me a stronger understanding about the important connection between English and the Greek language. I was becoming clever and was able to not only identify but also to fluently pronounce these funny letters.

My nursing program went on as per the syllabus and soon it would be time to prepare for an important test and later a state examination. These were some rather stressful times again, but this time was different, because my support system was more concrete and we were actually working on what was important to me—my studies. I had a better feeling this time even though my program was far more challenging than the previous one. It was reassuring having a mentor who knew what my studies were all about and having actually studied most of these topics. I clearly remember, even before I was given the text for future courses, my coach had already drawn up a plan. That man was nothing short of brilliant. We still had periods of disagreements, which was mainly due to me wanting to do things my way, even though my way could have certainly put me at a disadvantage. Was it being stubborn or was it pride? Perhaps both!

At times I was reluctant to accept help because of too much false pride. After all this time, I still saw requesting or even accepting help as a failure.

One particular day, when my mentor corrected me on the better way to approach a particular test question, I decided to do it my way. On receiving the corrected paper, I noticed that my marks were the lowest since I had started the program. I learned an important lesson. That I should learn to listen and accept guidance from someone more knowledgeable than myself. If I had continued on that obstinate path, total failure would certainly have been the result.

My marks did improve as I continued to follow his directions and suggestions. I spent a few months in the classroom studying the theory of nursing, and as our tutor eagerly said, "Now it is time to get our feet wet." This water activity was not done in the sea, nor the swimming pool or in the bathtub. It was on a real ward, with real patients and real situations, which was scary.

On the Ward

My experiences on other wards were, for the most part, rewarding. My favourite areas during my registered nursing training were surgery—because of the fascination with seeing real body parts in a living person—and pediatrics—nurturing teeny tots back to health.

I almost fell to my knees one day during a surgery, the first time I saw the heart beating away to, what seemed to me, its own tune. I did not know how many beats it did in a minute. It could not have been too slow, but however many beats, the patient was alive at the end of the surgical procedure and probably many years later.

Pediatrics, the children's ward, was even more fascinating. Imagine the nurses or doctors trying to insert a tiny plastic tube in an equally tiny vein when the poor child is fighting with all its might to free itself from the human grip. Many times I felt sad and I cried simply because the body seemed so helpless, and because my memory took me back to the time I was sexually abused, held down mercilessly against my will. Unlike that situation, for this baby, we were trying to help. How amazing that those small everyday actions could be such powerful triggers. My consolation was this procedure would be beneficial to the baby's health, in spite of vigorous protest.

I was curious about the labour and delivery unit, too. How that big baby got inside the mother's belly was one thing, but how would the baby find his way out into this world? That was the biggest mystery. How comforting to learn there were tried and proven ways to bring babies into this world. So, I put this topic on my mental list and decided that would be my next specialized course after finishing my Registered Nurse's (RN) program.

Managing My Studies

My studies were progressing better than expected and I was becoming more confident. Confidence gave me a sense of positive self-assurance that my life would turn out alright.

The more I worked through and succeeded in both my short tests and major examinations, the more my level of confidence increased. Gone were the times I was almost scared of my own shadow, let alone even thinking about studying, no matter how basic.

Suddenly I realized it was in my best interest to fully cooperate with my mentor. I was greatly amazed that all the effort he invested in me was out of kindness. My guess was this man had so much to pass on to others that he found someone who he thought not only worth his while, but who was also appreciative.

I clearly remember the time when I brought copies of past examination papers to him to give him an idea of what my final state exam would be like. To my surprise, he glanced, or casually flicked, through the papers and said,

"Ok, that is easy."

All I could think was easy for you mister, but not easy for me! The speed at which he completed reading all the questions, including the rules of the exam, baffled me. I sincerely thought he was just trying to impress me with his know-how. This person was certainly not someone to show off, but it was not until a few days later when I finished working through those papers that I realized the brilliant person I had met. My knowledge about the strategy of major exams was minimal. It was true that I was successful in exams, but I had no idea how to divide the allotted time, depending on how many marks were given to a particular question. In other words, the higher the marks given to a question, the more time should be spent on it. I learned time management as related to studies too. I do believe that this new terminology—time management—almost knocked me off my feet.

Really, I have to confess how I continued to practise all the new words in front of my mentor. It felt so unnatural at first, but it became less of an issue to practise because I humbled myself, swallowed my pride, and asked for help as needed, which was quite often. My tutor and I made a plan for me to write mock tests frequently so that I would become familiar when it was time for the real thing. Initially, I did miserably scoring 40 out of 100. I felt disappointed and discouraged, but I had travelled too far to turn back. Before the next test we sat down and went through the questions and answers one by one. From that single discussion and his suggestions, I learned so much.

My grades both on my tests, and also in our hospital classroom, continued to improve. I became more enthusiastic and eager to tackle other exams and was better equipped to read and interpret the questions. Previous to these mock tests,

I secretly wished the date for our final examination would be delayed for whatever reason possible— maybe weather, an unsuitable venue, or the Asian flu. Any cause for delay would have been okay with me. Now, I was simply eager to write the final examination. I studied more, wrote more tests, and made more last minute revisions. It was more going over the most important parts of the questions and how to identify, and if needed, underline key words. I learned how to allocate time and was ready and feeling more assured of myself because of the progress I was making.

The day of the final exam arrived. The long-awaited day, the moment many of us were dreading or, on the other hand, looking forward to, was here. Some wore anxious faces, others worried and a few relaxed and looked forward to the challenge. I approached the allotted meeting room feeling hopeful but still a little nervous. I did not know what my facial expression showed, but I had a feeling that I would do my best because of my intense preparation. The other students and I listened to the rules and formalities relating to the examination, including both the starting and concluding time. The time allocated for the finals seemed almost too long. A bell was rung and we got started.

Those exams were mostly presented in essay format with a few requiring short sentence answers. For the Enrolled Nurse exams, I had used mostly memory of the things I learned on the ward to get me through. The RN exams required much more; I used a combination of what I was learning from Issah's sessions with me plus my practical knowledge.

Before long the time was up. At last the final bell rang to announce the end of the exam and the closing of this chapter in my studies. Results would be published and posted individually to us within six weeks, giving us plenty of time to perform a post-mortem and most likely worry about our answers.

Since it was also the end of the term and time for holidays, we celebrated in a small way, saving our time for a bigger one later when we knew the results. It was like a holiday; we could tuck books away and literally forget about them. It was a good time.

Issah was working for the University of Liverpool and money was in short supply. After paying his rent and the regular bills such as food, heating and transportation, spending money most of the month was simply unavailable.

Small Gifts

My relationship with my friend started to change. He visited more frequently and brought me beautiful flowers and books. He was interested in books, inspirational poetry, Shakespeare and other well-written literature. I did wonder many times how he could buy these books. My best guess was that he borrowed the money from his friends. My boy was infatuated and might have done whatever it took to charm his girl. Needless to say, I found it difficult to get through these books while keeping up with others that I received. We certainly had to cut back on the pace of purchasing books because I was an avid but slow reader, and also on account of the cost of books.

My live-in accommodation was in the same place as the hospital where I worked and within a short walking distance. One evening as I walked to my room, I noticed some bright pink roses on mature rose bushes next to the men's outdoor washroom. It was summer time and the flowers were in full bloom. That evening, my caller arrived with his usual bright smile, holding a beautiful bouquet of pink roses. I was sure they were not from the local florist, but I wasn't one to judge where they came from. Yet, they had a very close resemblance to the ones I that I saw outside, just a short walk from my building. The pink roses continued to be our private joke for many years after. Life could be difficult when a man wants to buy his potential sweetheart some roses when he has no money for such a thing.

Weeks crawled by, and soon the sixth week arrived. Tension was running high, similar to the emotions at the time of our final examination. Tempers were short, emotional fuses quickly ignited, agitation increased and tolerance level was at an all-time low. We were much like prickly cacti, and at last, that long-awaited moment had arrived.

The mail arrived, and with it a strange new professional envelope with Council of Nurses boldly stamped on it. I felt queasy. I wanted to run and hide, cover my head, because at that moment I felt like a coward and could barely open the letter, but I swallowed my pride and asked one of my colleagues to open it for me. As she looked at the most important document, she began screaming, jumping up and down. Unaware, I also started to do the same, uncertain as to why. Eventually I came to my senses and asked her what the letter said.

"Cor blimey," she said, "Grace, you are almost a State Registered Nurse!"

All I needed to do was pay my registration fees and I would be a Registered Nurse, or RN. That's when we both started screaming and jumping up and down, and quickly we were joined by others sharing in our happiness. I was in a happy fog with poor concentration for the rest of the day. I kept repeating, "I am almost an RN." It was all I could think about. My patients, their families and my colleagues added kind words and congratulations. That was another time that my efforts were truly acknowledged and I felt proud. I needed to share this breaking news.

Chapter 22: Coming Alive

That evening, I decided to go and see Issah. I showered and dressed in my finest attire, and with a spring in my step, I walked happily out of my room. When I reached the ground floor, someone called my name. I looked into the nurses' sitting room and there, as usual dressed in his fine attire, was my friend Issah. He had come because he wanted to hear my results. When he learned of my success, he was equally overjoyed for me and the next thing I knew I was in his embrace. I thought he was going to crush me with the strength of his arms. I loved his embraces because they felt different; they felt right and comfortable.

Something definitely came alive in me when he held me. I was unsure what this something was. Some may call it affection, others may call it delight, and a few might say it was Cupid. Whatever it was, I would call it passion. It was the kind of feeling that if we were at the right place at the right time, I could have found myself in a whole lot of hot passionate trouble. So I was thankful that we were in a public place.

My friend did not strike me as the passionate type. But there again, we had not focused on that side of our relationship while I was studying. I had far too many educational needs to attend to, to think about romance. We, or at least I, was so consumed with my studies, that for most of the time, I worked, studied and socialized just a bit. No more studies for the time being, and so my thoughts turned to another part of life— relationship. We made plans to go out the next evening to where we initially met—in that beautiful garden.

Issah loved most types of sports. We watched different sporting events, such as track and field and cricket, stopping to enjoy some ice cream along our way, and from the same vendor as on our first date. I believe that the vendor may have remembered us as a couple; his smile said it all.

Our relationship suddenly took on a momentum that surprised us both. Visits became more frequent, conversations turned to a much deeper level, both personal and including family of origin. I felt ashamed to talk about my family simply because, to me, my family was unique, in what I later learned was totally dysfunctional. The abuse I had endured, the feeling of abandonment and the overwhelming anger then was too much to share with this man whom I was just getting to know.

I remembered what I had heard and been told since I was a young child. They said, "Do not tell strangers your troubles because if you do, then you would surely pay for it." Meaning, you would be whipped beyond pity, so why would I tell this man about my deep dark secrets?

He'd studied psychology and knew how to apply it to his daily life. He cracked this thick wall of emotional ice and started to tell me first about his family background and eventually about himself. My astonishment, in his sharing, made me feel as though we were truly on the same life's journey, because there were many similarities, both in our personal life and our family of origin. The poverty, the humble beginnings, the intense hunger for education, the different types of abuse we'd both suffered, and the indefatigable character that, no matter what, we would not stay down. Had we made a list of all the unfortunate experiences in our individual lives, it would surely be an extremely long one.

The Question

One lovely day as we were visiting our special garden, again, I closely observed my friend. I saw a much broader smile on his face with eyes as bright as any of the brightest stars in the heavens. He wore a new shirt and an extra flashy tie, as though he was going to a special function. Concerned, I asked why. Whether my special friend went down on one knee or both knees, I do not remember, but what I remember is the lovely way he asked me to marry him. At first, I was flabbergasted, because I did not realize the depth of our friendship, and second, I was still feeling somewhat unworthy of such a clever, educated, kind and generous person. I could not give a definite answer one way or the other but agreed to give him my answer the next day.

Restlessness led to a sleepless night. Many thoughts of doubt about our relationship occupied my mind. What if this is just a show and not a sincere request? Marriage, to me, seemed a sad and painful situation, because I could only judge on what I had seen and observed in my younger days, where young women were disrespected and treated pretty badly.

I tried to replay his visits. A strong sensation went through my body. I pictured those bright kind and gentle eyes, wide smiles and peaceful demeanor. I felt unexpected butterflies in my stomach. My mind was tugging this way and that. Then the doubt and dread washed over me. The thought of happiness I had never known scared me in the same way as possible success in the nursing field.

The next day I decided that before I made any firm commitment, I had talk to Issah about the promises that I had made to myself as a child. He was keen to hear them. I shared that I would not tolerate abuse of any kind, I would not wish to have more than two children, and I would very much love to educate myself so that I would better understand how society worked and help my family. My friend seemed overjoyed with these three very important wishes and vowed to honour them. I smiled and looked at him. Those few short seconds must have seemed like a lifetime to him. Eventually, I said, "Yes! Yes, I would very much love to marry you."

Now we were at liberty to give and receive hugs—real hugs—and kisses. We celebrated our relationship by preparing a meal at home. The engagement ring would have to wait until his next cheque. Despite our financial situation, those were happy days. Certainly it was uplifting to have met my dear friend, Mr. Issah Ibrahima. I wondered how many people of his integrity, intelligence and generosity existed in our world, but his kind seemed rare.

Imagine two young starry-eyed lovers, with intentions to marry soon, waiting for their next pay to purchase the engagement ring, and many, many paycheques to buy the wedding rings, and still trying to cover the wedding expense. In spite of that, we were quite happy with our lives. It felt as though we were truly starting from scratch; at least that was my feeling. Our relationship grew and blossomed, while we waited for those precious pounds.

We made plans for a simple, extremely low-cost wedding. By combining both salaries, we were now in a financially better position to buy not only the engagement ring but also to put a deposit on the wedding rings as well.

The engagement ring was yellow gold with one tiny diamond stone. At least it looked like a diamond to me because the stone sparkled. To be truthful, it could have been something completely different. I had never owned a single piece of jewelry in my life, so in my mind this item was amazingly worthwhile and was good enough for me. We chose a narrow band with delicate slash-like patterns. What was even more important to me was having our first names and the date of our marriage engraved on the inside. That was so neat, so unique and definitely so close to my heart. Some might call me sentimental, others may call me other names, but for me, it was truly a romantic feeling. I felt reassured and comforted.

Part 3 ~ With This Ring

All great changes are preceded by chaos. –**Deepak Chopra**

Chapter 23 - New Knowledge

Issah taught me many things. He was keen on a system called Time Management. I did not know what that was then, but he patiently explained it to me that it was how an individual uses a certain period to maximum benefit. In other words, do not waste valuable energy on useless things.

Issah taught me how to improve my English vocabulary, both in speaking and in writing. Some evenings we would engage in history or geography. I learned about the five continents—Africa, the Americas, Europe, Asia and that land down under called Australia. That was not the end of my lessons. That same evening, he brought out a map of the world, as large as he could find, and spread it out on the floor of his living room. The table surface was too small, only able to seat two people and the map was much bigger.

Initially I was astounded by the size of the map, with so many countries and so many blue colours. I learned that the blue represented bodies of water: rivers, lakes, seas and oceans. He explained that the scientific equation for water was H_2O. By the end of the evening, I was mentally exhausted. To make my learning even more meaningful, or should I say important, he was going to give me a quiz when I felt ready. Thankfully, the quiz would be a casual discussion with a question and answer session. I was glad this quiz would not be in written form, because the names of some of those countries seemed as complicated as learning to spell the name of the mighty river in the United States, the Mississippi.

The next big, or probably the biggest, topic on our mind was our wedding. Who should we invite? Where would the ceremony take place? Who should be in the bridal party? The questions were endless, and we soon realized that our wedding would have to be low-key with little to no fuss. The scarcity of money made our final decision quite easy. We visited the city's registry office and all the necessary plans were made with minimum hassle.

Our wedding was small, private and meaningful. The reception was a gift from our landlady. We simply could not afford a honeymoon. It would be too expensive for now, but maybe later. Later never came. Instead we went on a visit to our friends, John and Rachel Goodall, in Bexhill-on-Sea, on the southeast coast of England. John had lived in Ghana, West Africa, for many years. He had been my husband's godfather, teacher and housemaster since he was fifteen years old. Though this break was not the same as a real honeymoon, we were, nevertheless, very glad.

Maybe I am too old fashioned about a newly wedded couple going away on their honeymoon, or was it more about being unable to afford such luxuries. Okay, let me be truthful, we would have been ecstatic to have even a short time alone soon after our marriage, as other couples had. In spite of our living conditions, we were still rich in terms of love and support towards each other.

My education was improving by leaps and bounds. Even my husband was surprised with my progress. Soon I was beginning to identify the meaning of new, and the odd times, even complicated words. My memory took me back to the time when I had started to use proper English, and my husband joked that I was now using the Queen's English.

The expression on his face said it all—his effort was yielding results. Being in the company of Issah was such a happy, joyous and peaceful time. It was also a time to work on our relationship.

Relationship Building
The years went by too quickly, and during this time we had to put some effort into our relationship. Marriage, to me, was like

having two different pieces of material and working together with them to produce something unique. One of the most important things that prevented disagreements was proper communication skills. I had absolutely no idea what it meant at the time. I could not remember hearing such a word and certainly did not know what it entailed—another tool to add to my learning list.

There were misunderstandings in our relationship; I doubted that problem was unique to us. It could have ended with a brief marriage and a nasty divorce. One blessing was there were no children to add to this getting-to-know-you period.

Newlyweds Squabble
One particular day, we had a blazing fight, and I vowed never ever to touch or speak with my husband, and so I got ready and crawled into bed. My husband also crawled into bed and gently touched me, and I moved away from him. This touch-move away business went on until I had no more space in the bed to move. I did not realize that I was at the edge of the bed until I fell onto the floor. I was so angry, ashamed and humiliated with my behaviour and myself. I stared up at Issah and we both ended up laughing. This confrontation taught me a valuable lesson: instead of nursing a grudge, it is easier and less stressful to talk about it, especially before bed.

My thoughts went back to an incident I had witnessed some years before. One summer day, I was looking out of my sitting room window, admiring the beautiful scenery. I spotted a small object drop from a maple tree. Many times I had noticed birds busy building their nests, and after a while all was much calmer. A nestling had either accidently fallen out of its nest or misjudged the power of its virgin wings.

When I fell out of bed, that was exactly what I did; I had miscalculated the width of the bed. I was jolted by something much more important than falling out of the bed—my underlying anger. Was it rearing its ugly head for relatively small matters? Could it be past unaddressed emotions that I could no longer control, or was I starting to find my voice? I needed to pay attention and address whatever the reason for this outburst in more appropriate ways or the results could have been catastrophic. I had to work hard not to lose all the positive things I had gained.

My hope was to keep moving forward instead of going backwards, but how could this negative and destructive emotion be addressed? I had absolutely no idea, but if the problem was left to run its course, then it could be as corrosive as acid.

As time went by, our lives continued with much less friction and more meetings at what we called the 'table of communication.' My husband, bless his soul, explained to me, with practical examples. For the first time, as far as I could remember, I started to say how I felt without being judged. What a free and exciting feeling. This was only a minute part of a huge problem, because at times feelings just welled up like a raging ocean. Whatever these thoughts and feelings, they still generated sadness and fear in me, another issue to be added to my ever-growing list of concerns.

My husband was not what I would call a culinary expert, but credit still goes to him simply for his effort. I still remember how, when I worked all day and came home dog tired, hungry, and sad, because of unexpected news of the passing of a patient, Issah's love and support was always there. He had the aptitude to separate emotions from logic, and the ability to see an issue clearly. Another quality was his use of pen and paper to make notes of whatever needed to be addressed.

Sometimes I needed a quick solution to a problem. First, he would put on his eyeglasses and, at that moment, this man looked the part of a legal professional. Then, he would list the most troublesome points and number them. Next, we would discuss each one, and he made sub notes as we went. Eventually he would offer suggestions, and almost all the time the conclusion would be perfectly simple and usually worked very well. I have to tell you that it seemed like a never-ending process. I felt impatient for a quick solution and was about to grab pen and paper and say, "Forget it."

A few times in work-related issues, my colleagues would applaud me for my problem-solving skills. I could not accept these praises because it was Issah's skills and not entirely mine. Then my colleagues would refer to my husband as 'my problem-solving guy.' I felt envious. That guy was not only educated but also wise. I questioned whether such a God-given gift could not be acquired entirely from classrooms. My consolation was that everyone was born with a gift, so I would have to start searching for mine, whatever it might be. Could this gift be passed on to the next generation?

Chapter 24: Starting a Family

The time came when another important decision had to be made, about starting a family. So far I think that this might have been our biggest decision and discussion. We discussed when this process should start, how many children we would have, and what if there was an 'oops' pregnancy? Would it be welcomed? Would the child be loved?

Parenting was another worry. We had no model on how to rear a child. For almost seven years, I had taken birth control pills and luckily without any complications. When I conceived, we were extremely happy greenhorns as far as pregnancy, labour and delivery of babies were concerned.

There was an element of fear and apprehension sprinkled with the happiness. Even though everything was going well, doubts started to reign supreme. Were we making a wise decision? Even though I was equally a partner in the act, my husband should have known better than to agree with me to have a baby. After all he was wiser and more educated, so I felt that he should have been the one to make the final decision.

I was feeling pretty miserable with regular morning sickness and started feeling sorry for myself. I found someone to blame, and that was Issah. I knew few women who were fortunate enough to avoid early pregnancy discomfort, but I was not one of them. At least I did not require any hospitalization for medical concerns. At the end of the first trimester, I felt better—no more upset stomach, nausea and vomiting. Life was good again. My thoughts about the pregnancy were positive. I made my apology and Issah accepted it gracefully.

Whether requested or not, there was no shortage of positive comments and advice. It seemed to me that most people, if not at all I met in my daily life, felt compelled to let me know what was good or bad for me. There was some valid advice while others needed to be taken, as the saying goes, 'with a grain of salt.' And the others should just go in one ear and out the other!

I thought I had left old wives tales back in my homeland, but I was stunned that some of them were still alive and thriving in this foreign land. If I had been so naïve as to follow some of the advice, I am certain that the results would have been disastrous. Exercising simple common sense was key. It was unbelievable how those so-called experts, who have never been trained in certain fields such as medicine, were keen to counsel others.

Issah and I realize that the best way of knowing about pregnancy, labour and delivery of this precious child should be learned 'directly from the horse's mouth'—from someone who had the knowledge, so we enrolled in prenatal classes. This was a brand-new learning process for us. The sessions covered the process from contraception to the actual labour.

We learned briefly about the anatomy and physiology of the uterus, the trigger mechanism, and what possibly starts labour pains, especially the type that almost takes the mother's breath away. We also learned about Braxton Hicks contractions, pseudo-labour pains in which the uterus is getting ready or rehearsing for the real labour. And of course, we were told by the midwife when the delivery unit should be notified and a whole lot more. By the end of our educational sessions, we felt much more confident than before we attended. Another positive thing about these groups was that almost all the expectant parents in this group were rookies. We observed and asked basic, but important, questions; we were not alone. Couples asked numerous questions which ranged in complexity as the weeks went by.

The general consensus in the group was labour and delivery would be a piece of cake. This would be 'easy peasy,' and what is all the hype?

The instructor also said, "when a woman is in labour for the first time, the process takes about 8 to 12 hours, and for someone who has been through the labour process, the next time might be considerably shorter."

I hoped my name would be in the lucky group of women to have short and easy labour. From the vast amount of literature we read, our comfort level improved, knowing what lay ahead of us.

During the last week of our prenatal classes, we went on a tour of the labour and delivery unit and we were so happy and proud to show the world that we were soon-to-be parents. We felt on the edge of being cocky. It was as if absolutely no one in the world had ever been pregnant or had a baby. That over-confident attitude was almost shattered when we saw the delivery bed and given full details of how it worked. The birthing position brought back a flood of traumatic memories for me.

The labour coach took some time to answer questions in great detail, yet not too much as to scare us, but to help us understand better what to expect. We were young and didn't know what to expect and might still be getting used to relatively new partners, and now only to be told that our most private parts would literally be on show with the lights on as bright as daylight. I did not like this part, because I was still quite shy of being exposed.

Those eight months went unbelievably fast. There were some excited and happy periods during those months. We were still on a 'shoestring' budget, and felt so blessed receiving beautiful hand-me-down clothes, blankets and pram from friends, neighbours and colleagues. I have never been as thankful for secondhand items as I was then. Because so many baby items had been donated, we did not need to buy many things.

Prior to delivery, we made plans to reside at a relative's home in Nottingham. The home was located near the hospital where the birth of the baby would take place. The baby's things were washed and ready. We were anxious and ready, as the final countdown started. With only a couple of days from the delivery date, I wondered, would I make it to the hospital on time? After hearing stories about babies being born in their mom's bed, the back of dad's car, or in front of the neighbour's 4x4 pickup truck, and even by the wayside and having the police officers escort the ambulance crew to a safe place to deliver the baby. I hoped no one would find fault with me for wondering if I would I make it to the hospital on time.

I experienced Braxton Hicks contractions that our prenatal educator told us about many months before. It is one thing learning from books or in class tutorials, but it is something completely different physically experiencing it. If Braxton Hicks were as uncomfortable as labour pains got, then I figured my labour would be as easy as a summertime breeze. The discomfort felt more like dull menstrual cramps and was not hindering me from continuing my usual activities. I was unsure about all the fuss about having a baby. To me the whole process of labour and delivery seemed magnified out of proportion and grossly exaggerated.

Since early in my pregnancy I was under the care of a registered midwife and then under the combined care of the midwife and hospital medical obstetrical team nearer to my delivery date. This was the usual practice in England.

During my routine obstetrical assessment, the baby's head was found to be presenting by an abnormally large diameter. Following a long discussion with the treatment team, they came up with five possible modes of delivery that they would try. The baby might turn itself; or the doctor would attempt to turn the baby. Then there was vaginal delivery using forceps or vacuum extraction, and the last option was a caesarean section. These five options were very scary and generated even more fear and anxiety, despite any in-depth explanation and reassurance from the treatment team. I had a feeling of impending doom and, though minute, thoughts of having a child with permanent brain damage remained.

The discomfort continued. At times the discomfort was mild to bearable, and other times a dull ache. Infrequently there would be an odd, moderately strong pain that would make me stop in my tracks and take a few deep breaths in hopes of finding some relaxation. I did not like those stronger pains, and if they were a taste of the things to come, it would definitely be no fun when the strongest labour pains presented themselves. Ever so slowly, I was thinking that I might want to change my mind about the pending labour. Not about having my baby, just the labour process. Established labour had not started, yet those few twinges were enough.

My chores took on a slow pace, and simple activities such as bending to tie shoelaces or to dress in a pair of slacks were almost impossible. Thankfully, my husband was extra helpful. Being a first-time mother, labour was new to me and I was unsure what to expect, but one morning I woke up and felt different from the night before. There was more pressure and heaviness in my lower back and tail end. The baby had shifted, hopefully, into a more favourable position. After relieving myself, I walked out of the washroom and there came this huge gush of clear water-like fluid that ran down between my legs.

Fortunately, my bags were already packed and ready to go to the hospital. In a relatively short time, these weak to moderate discomforts changed from moderate to strong labour pains. By the time I arrived at the doors of the hospital, I could not get out of the car since I was doubled over in agony. As the contractions were now regularly every one to two minutes apart, it seemed as though there were no resting periods. Those spasms came with such strength. They were determined to bring me to my knees, and they did. Prior to going into labour, I had bravely decided that labour would be natural and I would not accept any pain medication. I figured that if some women could deliver their babies naturally, then so could I.

What I had forgotten was that all women are not born equal; that our anatomy and physiology might be similar, but our bodies might not function the same. Another point that slipped my mind was the size of the baby compared to the size of the pelvis through which the baby has to pass during vaginal delivery. Considering many more factors of having a natural birth, it became obvious that my initial decision was lunacy. In all fairness, I did not discard my idea willingly, but those excruciating and unbearable contractions forced me into total submission. Enough was enough. Never mind those women back in the ages who were heroines; I say "good for them!" I no longer wanted to be any brave woman enduring any more unnecessary anguish. Some might think I was a wimp.

Realizing my labour would take many hours; I made up my mind and accepted the pain medication. This was a whole new experience for me.

Chapter 25: Like a Kite

Whatever injection was administered made me feel weird, but good. In a few short minutes those awful pains were replaced by a nice warm calm and relaxed feeling. I clearly remember telling my nurse, "I feel like I could fly right through the window." Until this time, my comprehension about the relationship between substances, whether for medical or recreational purposes and behaviour, was vague. At the time I didn't understand how easily I could've injured myself under the sedative influence. Besides, windows were sealed, so even if I were determined to be a pregnant superwoman, the chances of jumping out would have been impossible. Thankfully, the vigilant nurse kept a close eye on me.

Labour continued for several hours more. I had arrived in the maternity hospital on Sunday morning and now it was early Monday morning. The nurses tending to me did their thing while I enjoyed the blessed reprieve from the dreadful contractions. Another assessment was done to check the labour progress and the position of the baby's head.

There was both good and bad news. The good news was that the cervix was dilated fully so the baby could be delivered vaginally, but the bad news was that the baby's head was presenting abnormally larger in diameter and could present a problem at delivery. The five possible modes of deliveries were again reiterated for my benefit, but as I was still under the influence of narcotics, Issah, who was present since our arrival at the hospital, did a pretty good job of giving me gentle reminders of my task at hand.

Delivery

The time came to deliver the baby. We went with the first choice to see if the baby would cooperate. I started to push but it took a lot effort, all my limited energy with no significant results. Next, a member of the team placed a small cup (ventouse) attached to the suction tube on the baby's head and applied a small amount of suction, but only enough to keep the cup in place to gently deliver the baby. This procedure was done under epidural block, which numbed me below the waist.

A few points needed to be taken into consideration in my situation. To start, I was exhausted; the epidural in my back had worked well, a little too well. I was numb, so even if I wanted to help, I couldn't. Besides, in my mind having been in labour for what seemed like an eternity, I felt that I had reasons to sit on my bed and do as little work as possible.

Then suddenly my eyes cleared and the tiredness lifted and the bone-tired exhaustion disappeared. I was in turbo boost and back to the world of reality. I was gently nudged to my main call so that I would be present to appreciate the moment. What a moment it was! There was celebration, not with food and drinks, but simply by the raised voices in the delivery room. In the split-second before my baby's delivery, there were more people in the room than I remembered.

I was later introduced to a pediatrician and his team. Thank God they were there to help, because my baby's heartbeat was fluctuating below the normal level and recovering slowly, which was causing some concerns and the need for the assistance of the pediatric medical team.

I saw my child a few minutes after birth, only after his airway was cleared of mucus and he was given a 'good luck' suck of oxygen, feet tickled and his body briskly dried off with a warm dry towel. All these actions helped to stimulate his initial breathing. It seemed to everyone that this baby was as tired as his mother and was in no hurry to announce his appearance in the big wide world. Finally, there was a whimper, to the joy of everyone in the room, and from this point on, this baby had no problems voicing his opinion. Whether he was hungry, uncomfortable or simply demanding attention, he let the world know, "Here I am!"

The baby placed in my arms simply did not look like mine, but how was he supposed to look? This was my first child, so

I had no point of reference. What I saw was a baby boy who looked pretty bashed up, as though he was part of a boxing team. His head was elongated (as if he had a cone glued to his head) instead of being round, and he looked shell-shocked and dazed. His eyes seemed glazed, crossed and unfocused, but in spite of his unusual appearance, I was still grateful for his safe delivery. I vowed at that moment to always love him no matter what, because he's part of me. I was filled with awe and wonder about the process from conception to the birth of my baby. Had I not observed all the necessary care and medical treatments administered to my son in the same room, I would have doubted if this truly was my son.

I named him Halim Ibrahima. And thank goodness for the persons who invented identification bracelets, because that was one of my focal points every single time I had contact with my boy, confirming the information that he belonged to me.

As time went by, his elongated head took on a less acute shape. He had relinquished his boxing team appearance and his eyes were more focused. It appeared as though he was looking here and not yonder. He looked more relaxed and less battered and bruised. One problem-free area in my son's life was feeding. He seemed to have graduated in feeding 101; he was a real pro and knew what to do.

Breast-feeding has positive and negative benefits. The good side was that this boy took his feeding seriously and fed well. The not so good part was Halim had strong sucking reflexes, like a vacuum cleaner. I was pretty sure if I were to lean forward while he was nursing, his powerful suction would keep him safe. I did not test my theory.

I experienced only one negative effect from the epidural. It worked well, in fact, too well, both during and after delivery.

The nurses encouraged me to get up and move around. I could not move my legs regardless of how hard I tried. My upper body felt normal, but lower parts felt lifeless as if they did not belong. My feet felt as heavy as two pieces of lead and it scared me. Irrational ideas seeped into my mind. Am I going to remain in this debilitating condition all my life? These crazy thoughts were unfounded. I started to feel tingling and was soon able to wriggle my toes.

Chapter 26: Watching You

The years flew by and my son grew fast and was happy. Halim became an alert, sensible and talkative child. His 'gift of the gab' continued throughout his life. Along with the usual developmental milestones came his awareness of being an only child. Everything, to him, became 'mine!' "This is mine" and "That is mine," refusing to share belongings with his little buddies. Bothered by this possessiveness, my husband and I agreed that a solution to this problem had to be found quickly.

My life, both as a wife and mother, went on at a fairly busy pace for a couple more years. When Halim was about 18-months old, my husband went away to the University of Essex, England, to study electrical engineering. Little did I realize that this little mite of a child would become such enjoyable company. He always wanted to know who, what, where, when, how and why.

Bedtime was another story. It seemed this child thought he was part of the royal family. In order to sleep, songs had to be sung, cradle had to be rocked and I couldn't leave his room until Prince Halim was asleep. There was no sneaking out. Oh no! This was not allowed and if His Highness was aware of such trickery, then he would deal with his subject—me—by making a sound like "ha-ha," and when he caught my attention, he would hold the side of his crib, vigorously shaking it, and give a big broad smile. What could a mother do but also smile?

Hunting for New Accommodations

Life for the three of us was mixed—sometimes happy, but mostly challenging. Prior to the birth of our first child, my sister, Ruth, had promised us secure accommodation. Ruth lived in Nottingham, England, which is a short distance from the hospital where I delivered our son. We understood that our accommodation was only for a relatively short time, so we had to find alternate housing. The living arrangements changed suddenly.

Her actions spoke volumes saying it was burdensome to have us there. Slowly and steadily, the atmosphere became so unbearable that we were forced to find emergency accommodations. I was fearful of developing postpartum depression and had heard how dangerous this could be for mother and newborn baby. Fear of being depressed haunted me to the point where I could not think clearly or keep the baby safe troubled me deeply. I knew I was the best person to care for my child, and wherever I go, he would go with me. Hence the quick decision to leave our former address.

We were faced with two huge problems; first, having a newborn baby while needing to look for new housing and second, no extra money to pay for any type of accommodation. What were we to do? We had no one to turn to for help. I had no other relatives in the country. Deep down in my heart, I knew that our lives would not be a 'bed of roses,' but I had a feeling we would be okay. I say okay because I was not expecting a life of luxury, only enough to survive.

On reflection, I still do not understand the reason for my sister's change of mind. She did not give me any concrete reason. I remembered my envy towards a casual girlfriend who lived in government-sponsored housing. I wished I had an apartment like hers. I often wondered, was there a little sprinkle of jealousy?

We left a nice clean, well-kept, cozy, but small room, with a sad and heavy heart. I shed many tears over that decision because our new living conditions were similar, if not worse, than those we had visited a few months before, while living in that dilapidated one-room apartment.

My husband was still a university student and would graduate very soon, and I was a relatively new qualified registered nurse. Although our combined salaries were small, we were still able to provide for a child and pay our bills, but we desperately needed outside help!

Social Services

After inquiring about possible government assistance, available to low-income families, we were introduced to the Social Services Office. Communicating with the government department was like having a full-time job, but without pay.

A good part of my life was concentrated on meeting the benefit office's numerous requirements: caseworker's inspection, receipts, from rent bills, baby expenses, family food bills, public transportation, gas bills and a lot more. The caseworker requested parents' birth certificates and most importantly, the baby's birth certificate. Nothing was overlooked.

As they say, "this lady was on the ball." I felt as though I was standing stark naked in front of the worker. In those days, immigration offices were not as strict with immigrants coming into the country, but it certainly was not an open door policy. We had to prove that my husband and I were legally allowed to stay in the country. It was comforting to be on the right side of the law. The worker dissected my entire life, leaving no stone unturned.

When I was out in public, I overheard remarks of wealthy citizens, that if parents could not support their children they should not have them. I felt sure they were talking about me.

Having presented all the requested documents, we waited a very long time. Lack of patience and a good deal of anxiety plagued me during this period of anticipation. Although all the necessary requirements were met, there were still some lingering feelings of uncertainty. It was only when we received a letter from the social services office that our application for family benefits had been successful that were we able to 'let our hair down' and relax. Oh, what a glorious feeling. My guess was that having a newborn in the family placed us on the priority list. Because the three of us were living in a small room, we carried our important papers with us, and after many more visits to the Social Security office, we were given a list of possible accommodations. We were now on another journey.

Armed with a long list of addresses, we began our search. We also had a pretty good list of the problematic areas that required frequent visits by the emergency services such as the police, fire, and ambulances. I am sure that such services were not called to have a picnic or be invited to 3 p.m. English high tea with the residents, so we crossed those from our list.

Another area to be considered was the transportation services. Luckily there was an abundance of regular public buses. Low-income citizens, like us, depended heavily on public transit to get us from point A to point B. Living on government benefits did not afford us the luxury of owning a car, so we relied on buses or went by foot.

I was grateful to spend some time visiting with my friends who lived in a government housing community, especially when I felt disheartened. I was 'green with envy' when I compared our situations. The thought of living in a high-rise and having my own place excited me, until I paid close attention to the surroundings. My jealousy became weaker the more I observed the lifestyle.

Around that time, I noticed subtle changes, joyous greetings became a mere hello, conversations were forced and not as spontaneous as before. We knew it was time to find our own apartment.

I started the dull and wearisome search for an apartment. Most of the addresses we visited were nothing more than slums. I did not realize there were different grades of slums, with some places clean on the outside and filthy on the inside. It seemed to me that the residents had an issue with soap and water, or maybe they had allergic reactions to cleanliness.

There were places where the residents all perched outside the door on the concrete steps, puffing away on their fags (cigarettes) and tossing the butts anywhere they chose, while others engaged in similar behaviours but with the added enjoyment of beer, whiskey or whatever tickled their fancy. It seemed as though most of these activities were around the day of, or shortly after, receiving their benefit cheques. This time was truly the time to celebrate. Not only were people settled on their doorstep like birds coming home to roost for the evening, but the children also ran here and there as they pleased. The dogs walked and barked their underfed lungs out, but at what? Perhaps they themselves did not know.

My friend commented that probably most, if not all, of the residents were either unemployed, taking odd jobs, had served prison terms or they were living on welfare. This was far from the end of this sad situation. When alcohol hit certain brain cells, a new type of behaviour started to rear its ugly head. The merriment ceased to exist and was replaced by irritation, anger, and loud voices. The tone of voice took a much higher level and the language was more flowery than an English garden. In other words, the air was almost smoking with the sound of obscene language.

The women certainly held their own in terms of drinking and responding to insults flung their way. This might be less than ladylike, but to those women I say, "Good for you!" Society would consider them 'rough around the edges,' but if that is the survival tool that kept them alive and maybe see them through life, well then who could blame them.

I became aware of a different type of living during my apartment search. I observed how the children stood like statues, their eyes staring with fright while the adults cursed.

Every show needs an audience, be it paying patrons or simply inquisitive neighbours enjoying a free show. After all, who did not like a free show? But as entertaining as the show may seem, a part of this sad situations made me think of my roots. Almost always, the next morning, that show would end with a gathering of neighbours for the final verdict of who was wrong and who was right. Even those who were absent at the time later added their own versions. My friend lived in one of these buildings and sometimes when I visited her, I accompanied her to the community post mortem shindig. This gathering was, and still is, commonly known as gossip.

We moved on with our apartment search and the next address was even more of an eye-opener. There were no dogs roaming the streets and howling to the moon, instead the garbage in the street proclaimed its presence on this crisp windy day. Papers, especially newspaper, were blowing to and fro. In the streets there were also all sorts of things, like garbage cans and anything that could be easily blown about by the wind. Where was the city's rubbish (garbage) truck?

The doors showed signs of mistreatment and the windows seemed to have suffered similar fate. Windows and door panels, or what was left of them, were either boarded up with plywood or patched up with plastic bags and duct tape. I could only imagine the condition inside these houses. Looking up at the roof, the tiles told their own story of neglect. The children, due to many years of living in these conditions, looked as pitiful as the surroundings. Their clothing was torn and mismatched.

Sadness washed over me. My heart felt heavy, as though a block of ice had been placed in my chest. The pleading eyes and sad faces tore me apart. What I saw in those innocent-looking faces pulled at the very core of my being. Was I looking at what my son might have to face if we lived here? How could he be spared this dismal life? It seemed as though opportunity had skipped over this neighbourhood and that society had forgotten them. My guess was that the standard of living in this town or village might have had a lot to do with the standard of education in the local schools. As I looked at the devastation around me, I could not help but think about the school system. Would as little money be poured into them? If I did not act to improve this dreadful condition, Halim might experience a similar fate as those children.

I had no intention of settling for this type of pathetic lifestyle or simply accepting it as my life, and I had no wish to have depression or anxiety as my constant friends. If a fight were needed, then I would fight with all my might as long as it meant a better life for my child.

Whatever happened in the future, I would be satisfied as long as I know I did my very best. How was I going to achieve my goal of this better life? I had absolutely no idea, but determination was my weapon, and willpower would generate the energy needed to achieve my goal. Now I was fighting for someone much more than myself.

Chapter 27: Finding a Better Life

During the course of my life, I have seen what motivation and passion can do, even in the face of an almost hopeless situation. I was convinced that the right neighbourhood and the right upbringing could improve lives. I wanted to keep moving forward, not backwards. The battle would be tough and the road would be rough, but I was ready to face whatever obstacles lay in my path.

Our quest for housing continued longer than we expected. The choices of accommodations got smaller and so did the available government funding. It seemed to me that the only affordable choice was in those run-down areas of the town. I knew where I would like to live, but the rent was outside of our price range.

We collected the door keys from the housing office and made our way to our new home. Our enthusiasm was soon crushed by what confronted us. The surroundings told the same story of chronic dilapidation—unkempt buildings, broken doors, boarded-up windows, and garbage blowing in the wind.

Cautiously, we walked slowly up the creaky stairs, taking care where we stepped. I pushed the key into the lock, pushed and pushed again. Slowly and grudgingly the rusty creaky hinges cooperated. The door opened. What we saw was simply a vacant room, a room that had not seen new paint in many years. The wallpaper peeling off the walls looked as if reaching out its arm for help. Its badly faded colours made it challenging to tell the original colour. The linoleum curled at the edges making it difficult to walk normally without fear of tripping on the turned-up edges. The windowpanes were cracked, while others were broken or boarded up. There were drapes, but they were so old, dirty and dingy, and if they were to be washed, they would certainly disintegrate into strings.

Where did we go from there? The only furniture we owned was a baby's crib. We needed to find a second-hand store and fast, and this was high on our to-do list. Bright and early the next morning, we found a particular second-hand store, and we were like kids in a candy shop. We shopped, as the saying goes, until we dropped. We bought a bed, a table and chairs, two plates and two cups. In those days, these few items cost a few English pounds, but to us they were expensive items. Regardless of our used furniture, we were pretty happy to have our own beds, table and chairs for the very first time.

The next day our stuff arrived and we put the furniture and other items in their appropriate places. I wondered if this was what my entire life would look like. One part of me was almost grieving, because of the environment in which my child had to start his life. Although my son's present living situation was much better than when I was his age, I was still saddened by my inability to provide something better.

Unwelcome Visitor

Days seemed to hurry by, and months followed almost at the same speed, and the underlying sadness stayed with me for a fairly long time. One day as we were having our meal, I saw something suddenly run across the room. I wasn't sure what it was, but perhaps I was only seeing things. I thought my troubled mind was playing mean tricks on me, or that my weary brain was clouded by simple denial. Days later my thoughts cleared; it was definitely not my weary brain, nor was it denial; my mind was not playing tricks on me. What I saw made me almost jump out of my skin. It was a big fat mouse!

The fright made me shiver. I was scared of that big fat mouse with its two bright eyes that looked at me as though I was invading his space. This rodent was so large, and what first came to mind was whether it would attack the baby.

My imagination went absolutely wild. 'What if' questions started to bombard my brain. What if this creature gnaws at the baby? What kind of disease is it capable of transmitting to a human being? How many others were in the colony? The most outrageous thought was: Could a number of these creatures drag my baby away like in the horror movies? Let me say right now that I certainly was not prepared to wait for any answers. Protecting my child against it, or any other pest, was what I intended to do!

Looking around the outside of the building, I could clearly see why rodents loved this place, the garbage-littered surroundings made for an ideal breeding ground. After that day, my baby's stroller was never placed on the floor.

Although I was surprised at seeing the mouse, other residents found it an everyday occurrence. They had accepted it and were almost to the point of being jovial, but I failed to see the joke in having this unwanted visitor in my room, especially with a relatively new baby. I do believe that mothers are vigilant and watch out for their offspring like hawks, and now my level of alertness was at an all-time high. I was not paranoid, but it was very likely there might be many more mice living in that building.

Most of the residents were young single teenage mothers who were visited by their boyfriends. Certain times these visitors' faces looked as weary as I felt after those long hard hours in the fields in Trinidad. A few visitors arrived wearing old torn clothing which looked in desperate need of a dose of water and laundry detergent. Miraculously, the next day these young men looked different, more alert, rested and, yes, well groomed. Judging by the time and frequency of these visits, meaningful employment would definitely be out of the question.

These young mothers' priority was similar to most young persons, and that was keeping up with the latest fashion, regardless of the type of behaviour needed to get it. There were times when the bobbies (police) visited and handcuffed the accused, and made arrests for shoplifting. How many times were the police involved? I simply did not know, but listening to the conversations, I learned that this behaviour was nothing new or earth shattering. The common opinion was that government benefits were not enough to buy clothing, so they had to get it somehow, even if they did it by stealing.

Even if I had felt like indulging in the same business, I was not polished and experienced enough to make a good job of such a career, so I stuck to my earnest living. Besides, I have heard more horror stories about what happened in jail, and they were much worse than living in that mouse-infested building.

As time went by, the excitement was too much. My husband and I worked on plans to move to better accommodations. We were fortunate enough to qualify for a small government housing loan, similar to a mortgage and, thankfully, for a low interest-rate. Our happiness could never be expressed with mere words.

In those days, the rules of borrowing were not as strict as they are today. Part of the conditions of being accepted for the mortgage was to ensure that the monthly payments did not cause the client to be deprived of life's basic necessities such as food, warmth and the ability to pay bills. And so we waited and waited for the final mortgage decision. This time was another anxiety provoking period for us. We believed that someone was looking after us. Who that person was I simply did not know. This time the assistance received was enough to put our minds at ease. The problem was solved and we were left amazed and speechless.

It reminded me of the time when I was trying to enroll in the Registered Nursing Program, when I was supported and assisted unconditionally by complete strangers. I also looked even further back to that dreadful and sad backstreet abortion, when my life was truly in danger of blood poisoning or even perforation of internal body parts, leading to bleeding, a few of the complications that could have befallen me. To say that I was blessed and being looked after by a power greater than myself is one thing, but to understand why I did not become a fatality was truly baffling to me.

Being Looked After

As I casually flick over the pages of my life, I can see many such situations where I was raised up by the wings of an angel to a place of safety, in spite of problems, trials and roadblocks. In my life, I still seemed to end up in comfortable places. This does not mean that everything has been easy, but as long as I did what was humanly possible and asked for help, and finally handed it over to that Higher Power, I knew that all would be well. Some might just call it determination, a few might say it is the desire to strive for a better life for my child, and even others would agree to the Higher Power concept. Regardless of its name, one would agree that a stronger force was working in my best interest.

Chapter 28: More House Hunting

Another letter came from the building society, requesting an interview about the mortgage. We assumed that a mortgage agreement would be signed at this time and we were right! This particular meeting was longer than the previous one, but eventually we reached the most important part of the meeting, our mortgage approval. We waited anxiously. I was ready to spring over the manager's desk, kiss him and tell him how we thought that he was the very best building society manager in the whole of England, perhaps in the whole wide universe. But we did not kiss this man, because he might have been a stoic straight-laced Englishman and we did not want to scare him. On the other hand, he might have been pleasantly surprised.

Our next task was to go house hunting. When I mentioned house hunting, I truly meant house hunting. The prospective buyers had to find the particular house themselves, arrange the viewing, contact the building society, and have the necessary inspections done by a home inspector of their choice. We knew that purchasing a home through a reputable financial institution was also a good stepping-stone for finding a home in a better-maintained neighbourhood.

Thankfully, we eventually found a suitable house. It was called a 'two-up and two-down' home. It was a small house on two levels that had two main rooms on the ground floor and two bedrooms on the top floor. This house was joined to the next with little space from one front door to the next. The doors were painted in a variety of bright colours, in reds, blues or purples. The colours of some of the doors looked like no other I have seen in any magazine. To me, the owner might have mixed any colour or type of leftover paint he could get to paint his door. We were too happy to bother with colour schemes; our main focus was on leaving that mouse-infested dilapidated place where we were living, before those nasty creatures could hurt our precious baby. I really despised those creatures, especially when they stared at me. I simply could not wait to get out of those surroundings.

The deal was completed and we, the buyers, had no property to sell, so the closing date was quick and easy. The long-awaited moment had arrived. The building manager gave us the keys to our new home, and as we opened the door, we jumped for joy and hugged each other, shedding a few happy tears. I am certain if our son could understand, he might have thought his parents were insane, but happy. This home was not just the building; it was in a much better neighbourhood with peaceful surroundings, and fewer disorderly conducts requiring police visits. This was just another blessed relief. I felt as though I was now in the Promised Land.

Moving into this house was quick since we had only a few belongings. We were happy and comfortable but had to understand the science of looking after a home, from operating the burning coal heating system to finding our way to the local shops and day care centres. We were rather fortunate, because our neighbours were good-hearted people. Thanks to their help, I became a self-proclaimed professional coal-burning expert.

After we moved in, Issah returned to his engineering studies at the university in Essex. Because of the long distance, and the cost of public transportation, the daily journey home was impossible. As we now had a huge financial commitment with our mortgage, we needed to be even more frugal. Economizing was relatively easy, because initially we were forced to look after whatever we had, and there was not much. We never did adapt to the habit of spending money on unnecessary things, or keeping up with the 'Joneses,' in fact we lived simply from one paycheque to the next.

Being deprived has both positive and negative sides. For me, tightening my financial belt was quite easy, because I already lived within my means. Dining out was almost a non-issue; I prepared delicious and nutritious foods at home. Before married life, I ate most of my meals in the hospital cafeteria. The few times I purchased just a few items from the grocery shops, I did not pay attention to the price tags, but now I had to be aware of prices too, because I was feeding a family and did not want to default on the monthly mortgage payments.

During the period my husband was away at school, I took a leave of absence from my job to care for our son. When Issah completed his studies, he returned home and accepted a new job at the University of Liverpool. I took care of Halim when my husband worked Monday to Friday, and then he took over on weekends while I went back to nursing on a part-time basis.

After a short time, I was promoted and my salary increased. Our financial situation looked healthier and so our budget could be revised. I didn't even know what financial planning involved. I have certainly heard about a budget when the Minister of Finance presented it to the nation, but to see it done on paper for personal business was another story. When Issah mentioned this new idea, I eagerly agreed because I thought he would do it. I was wrong; he wanted me to create it. I had never done anything like it before, so how was I expected to do it now? He said that this was exactly the right time to start since I was now co-owner of a house.

My feelings of resistance were similar to when I was challenged while studying for my registered nursing examination. Initially, there was a lot of number crunching and I hated it with a passion, but the more I worked with the figures, the more my comfort level increased. Percentages were a chore and I shunned it as much as possible. If I heard one more thing about percentages, I acted like an ostrich that buries its head in the sand, or in my case, substituting a few pillows to cover my head. I did not wish to incur any brain damage with this new and weird knowledge.

The truth is, if my mind had been a tad more open, I believe that my brain would have been more receptive. I learned old ways of thinking could be difficult to change, because they affect you for a long time, whether positively or negatively.

For me the latter is true. Resistive thoughts show themselves in me dragging my feet or procrastinating. Today, tomorrow, next week or never were some of the stalling tactics I used.

How could I change those self-defeating behaviours? I knew I had to change and see things in an entirely new light.

Still Learning
Another thing I had to learn besides changing my thoughts was to acquire a better command of the English language. I was determined to do just that. Almost all areas of my life were gradually having a facelift. The grammar part was not too difficult as I had my very own English teacher, my husband Issah, to call whenever I needed. But he was away at university at the time.

Thinking back on when he coached me in my studies, I learned he had the patience of a saint and was excited to impart knowledge to me. I felt like a sponge, absorbing as much information as I could. To me the English language seemed as wide as it was deep. There were so many things to learn, including similar sounding words with completely different meanings. And it was a pain, yes, that's what I thought about this language. It was a pain, but a useful one.

Time went by and my love for the English language increased. I learned much more than I realized and asked about the origin of odd words. My husband explained the source of the words—some from Greek—with such delight. His eyes would light up like the brightest stars in the heavens. This, for him, was a clear sign that his student was not only learning, but also interested in acquiring additional knowledge. We had reached an understanding about not overwhelming me with Greek as well as English unless, of course, I asked for an explanation.

Learning for the Sake of My Child
There were many everyday things I had to learn. I am saddened for those years of lost opportunities, however, what

was done was done. The time could not be turned back and lost opportunities could never be regained. I could only, and have been, striving to make my life better. The driving force behind my desire to learn was to help my child. How rewarding it would be if I were able to even understand some of his schoolwork and to be able to advocate for him until he could do it for himself. Yes, the drive was undoubtedly there to learn as much as I could.

I wanted to learn about children's toys and what could stimulate a baby's learning process, and so I began to observe the toys that mothers used for their children. I watched how the children responded with eager facial expressions, the brightness in their eyes, and their little hands, although with poor coordination, trying very hard to grab the toy.

England had its own shop called Mother Care which was famously known for making their customers happy, especially the children. There were lots of toys scattered in a small playroom. Mothers, fathers, or whomever was caring for the child could actually test the toys to see the child's reaction as they played. Never in my entire life have I seen so many new and wonderful playthings. As I looked and played with different items, I was overcome with a stab of astonishment and jealously. How I wish I had at least one of these brightly coloured fascinating models! One toy I distinctly remember was a ball that could rest on any of its many sides, and each side containing four to five different shapes. The trick was to put each shape into its corresponding slot. It was fascinating to see how those tiny fingers placed the shapes where they belonged.

I had to be frugal to get more than a pound's worth of goods out of a pound. I was introduced to thrift shops. In one particular shop, in a well-off district, the rich residents seem to live like they were in a world of disposable items. I am not complaining in the least about how perfectly good usable items were regularly brought to the secondhand shop. I loved them. Whenever we visited this shop, it was like going to a candy store; we loved it so much because items were cheap and of a superior quality. I even purchased that ball with a variety of shapes for my child who spent countless hours sitting on the floor trying to match the right shape into the right slot. Even this toy excited me. Much later another activity was incorporated to add more fun to the game, and that was counting! The little one was now old enough to count to 10. He also tried to fit in as many shapes as quickly as possible. What fun it was see those little fingers at work and play.

I learned when choosing a child's toys, it was not only their language parents had to stimulate, but also to instill confidence in a child through games too. And not just as a child, but throughout his life. It seemed as if learning was imbedded in the subconscious mind and it went on even while asleep. This education was not exclusively for my child; it was, to a large extent, also for me.

Most parents start off knowing a lot, or have some level of understanding, about how to raise their children, but my experience was much different. Others may have learned by observing role models, caring for younger siblings, babysitting in the community or attending babysitting classes, but all these learning opportunities were out of my reach. Childcare at that time was not the same as what I had as a child. My experience was more like fending for yourself and wading through life's deep murky and flowing waters as best as I could. Even as an adult, I never understood the lack of guidance and the severe discipline I had experienced. It was certainly backwards. Maybe my upbringing was an example of things not to do as a parent. There were a few that were good, some were tolerable, but the majority was totally unacceptable.

I felt utterly shameful when I saw the gaping holes in my childhood upbringing and the differences in behaviour that I saw in England compared to what I knew from home. It was then that I started to strip off some of those unhealthy lessons. Replacing these old messages was painfully slow and hard, but

I knew I had to start somewhere, not just for me, but now for my child also.

Chapter 29: Sacrifices

Life's struggles and difficulties continued. My husband continued his electronic engineering studies away from home. I gave up my nursing job again and sacrificed my income staying at home with my son. In my limited way of thinking, it was the right thing to do. How clearly my thoughts raced back to being sad, lonely and deprived of my parents' love. I did not want that to happen to my child.

I remembered when my mother was home, my spirits lifted to a whole new place. It was not about having material things, but simply the presence of an adult, even in her limited way, that made me feel safe. I did not think I was asking for too much.

What a wonderful feeling to be free to stay home with my son. What would my life have been like if I had lived in a safe and secure place as opposed to an unsafe and negatively sheltered life? Would I have ended up being a selfish, uncaring, arrogant individual? The person I am today is due mainly to my personal experiences—the good, bad and the ugly. Those experiences gave me choices. I learned to observe and interpret body language and facial expressions. Given these skills, it's easier for me to choose which paths to travel and the ones to avoid, at all costs.

More Changes

Days turned into weeks, weeks into months, and months into years. Where did the time go? Our focus was to live in a good neighbourhood so that our child could enjoy the programs that both school and the local community offered. Our present home was simply a stepping-stone to something better, and so it was time to move to a different part of the country.

Moving proved physically and emotionally much easier for a few reasons. First, we were more experienced as homeowners, and so navigating through the red tape in the home-buying and selling business was easier. Second, we were faithful mortgage payers; we had even added one or two extra payments along the way that might have brought a smile to the building society manager's face. Third, my husband had graduated from the engineering program and had been accepted as a full-time employee at the Liverpool University. Hooray!

I resumed working, but on a part-time basis. Issah worked during the days from Monday to Friday, and I worked the weekend night shift. Granted, these working hours were not the most conducive to one's marriage and sex life. The only other alternative was to enroll our son in a registered, and expensive, day care centre or send him to a babysitter where the supervision might not have been the best. We decided to make another worthwhile sacrifice, and we did so without regrets.

The process of applying for another mortgage and the sale of our house started, and before long our plans fell into place. The mortgage was granted, our house was sold, employment was secured, and our young man was registered in a new school.

In spite of my weekend 'graveyard shifts,' we still found time to reawaken our intimate relationship. Before we knew it, we were expecting another little Ibrahima. I am still wondering how this little fella squeezed through the birth control pill barrier, but I was a happy mother, and daddy was delighted. Even our young son felt the energy in the air and was happy as well.

I had the usual doctor's visits including routine blood tests. All results were normal, which was good news. One morning after breakfast, I suddenly experienced menstrual-like cramps that increased in intensity. Initially, there was spotting of blood that turned into a heavier flow with a few clots, but in less than 24 hours, all of that had changed. Another blood test proved that the pregnancy, although early, was over. Birth control risks flashed across my mind. I shed tears of sadness and experienced feelings of disappointment. My consolation was that this fetus was conceived under much better circumstances, and with love and affection. No major adjustments were needed. I continued to live a healthy life and let Mother Nature do her work, and she did it quite efficiently, too.

Health Risks and Concerns
Later on, both in the newspapers and on television, there was much talk about the potential risks to mothers taking birth control pills. It seemed to me that, according to the experts, not a single brand of those pills was safe. Possible health risks ranged from unwanted pregnancy to deep vein thrombosis, plus a whole host of more real and imaginary side effects. Even I had a few concerns in my 'medically unqualified' mind.

The funniest part of one's imagination running wild is the irrational thought process that suddenly comes into play. I clearly remember after hearing the possible side effects of the pill, I began to feel every one of them from the life-threatening brain complications, heart disorder, to blood clots in my legs. I was an overnight hypochondriac. Let me tell you, it was not a pleasant place to be. I interpreted a usual mild headache, that did not require even one regular Tylenol, as my brain hemorrhaging, and I viewed simple leg aches as deep vein thrombosis, and anything other than a slow heartbeat was placed in the potential heart attack box. Mind you, by this time, I had discontinued taking my pills for many months prior. Fortunately, those crazy thoughts went away as quickly as they appeared, and I am happy to report that I was not one of those unfortunate ladies to suffer from the side effects of the pill, and for that I have another item to add to my gratitude list. Decision time again.

Tough Choices
We were planning to have another baby, but although we definitely wanted another child, we could not decide on the

time. Our only child at that time was starting to indulge in selfish behaviours, and using "I", "me", "that's mine" and related words, which indicated rather self-centered and selfish tendencies. I did not like what I was seeing. To me, it seemed such people would grab and receive whatever is handed to them, but when the time comes time to give back, that is where the problem begins. So even though he was still very young, and whether we were ready or not, it was time for some serious planning. So we procrastinated, and procrastinated some more.

Outcome
Honestly, it was as though someone or something was saying to us 'if you two adults cannot make up your mind and soon, then I will do it for you!' And so another life began. There was something different with this pregnancy, I conceived easily—too easily. The little bundle was a breeze to carry, and his birth was even easier. I hope his brother is not getting jealous! Also, this pregnancy was totally opposite to my first full term confinement. As they say, no two pregnancies and labours are the same.

Medical staff ordered routine blood tests to rule out anemia, and ultrasounds and other tests to rule out small baby syndrome. Although the baby was small for his gestational age, it did not pose any problems. Sometimes I wondered if he was part of the intrauterine football team. The squirms, acrobatics movements, football and soccer kicks almost took my breath way. We waited for that long-expected moment of delivery. Two emotions washed over me—edginess and excitement—although the baby was thriving as expected. I still had uneasiness about its welfare.

One Saturday morning in May started out bright and sunny. I was happily pegging my laundry on the clothesline at the back of the house. I'd almost forgotten I was pregnant because I felt comfortable and healthy, but these good feelings were soon short-lived.

Gradually I was made aware that my stomach was still there, but then this awareness was replaced by an uncomfortable feeling, yet I reassured myself that it was nothing to worry about. Unnervingly, the pain got stronger.

Thank the heavens that I only had a few clothes remaining to be pegged as I became dizzy with pain. The pain felt less like a drizzle and more like a torrential downpour. This labour was proceeding as quickly as when I conceived, but it was slower and gentler than what I felt with my first child. My first labour, three and a half years before, had seemed much kinder to me; it was slower and certainly gentler. This time it was as if the baby was ready to meet the world to see his big brother and his parents.

I was in established labour and Issah was now the expectant dad turned messenger. He ran to our next-door neighbours, Daisy and Burt, our childcare providers, and made the announcement, then raced back home shaking like a leaf, and followed by two equally quivering middle-aged people.

With shaking hands, Issah picked up the phone and called the ambulance. While waiting for the emergency service to show up, I reminded him to notify the delivery unit. His hands were shaking too much to hold the phone, so Daisy assisted. Issah was usually an excellent pen to paper planner, but that day I was sure his organizational skills were zero. He looked greyish with apprehension and I wondered if the ambulance crew would have two emergencies on their hands, me to the labour ward and him to the heart unit. The laundry was left to fend for itself; we had more important things to do.

While I was in the hospital, our young son would be in the care of our neighbours, Daisy and Burt. Our son was aware about the baby growing in his mother's belly and that Mommy had to go away to the hospital to help the baby out. But I think at that point he was more interested in all the treats they had for him.

Aunty Daisy and Uncle Burt might have endless patience, but mine would soon be at its end. Shortly after contacting the ambulance station, we heard the ear-piercing wailing of the siren. Initially the sound was faint and distant, so I thought maybe it was going to someone else's home, but very soon the sound grew louder and louder, and quickly the ambulance's siren was at an almost deafening pitch.

It was not only the ambulance and attendants at my door, but also other neighbours with their young children, and people with grey or white hair who had abandoned their favourite spot at the front door, ready to relate the comings and goings to all in the neighbourhood.

These seniors could be called the street social services unemployed officers. If you wanted to know what time x, y and z left for work in the morning, just ask these seniors. If you were unsure of who was dating whom, no need to wonder because that information would be voluntarily provided at absolutely no cost. Now they'd arrived at our house to see what was going on with an ambulance arriving.

Imagine how stressful and anxious I was when the ambulance showed up at my door! I am convinced that even some dads or husbands who were supposed to be walking the dogs found an alternative route to the front of my house. It was quite a scene. As I settled myself next to my husband in the ambulance, I could see my dear neighbours were almost sad, or perhaps there was a sense of disappointment that the activity was only due to my labour.

The distance to the local maternity hospital was short and the labour pains continued as before. It seemed to me that each time the driver went over a small bump or uneven surface, the intensity of the contractions increased. At that point, with even a small increase in the contractions, I was not smiling. I did not like being in labour one little bit!

How my dear, dear mother coped with her many pregnancies and labours in those days I would never know.

What suddenly came to my mind though was that two children were more than enough for me, and I intended to make sure of that. I had clearly forgotten what those labour pains felt like; after all, I had been given more than adequate doses of pain medication with my first delivery, so my memory was not as alert as it should have been.

Not this time. This time my mind was clear and alert to what was happening. This labour experience would definitely be the absolute last one, and I would not leave the hospital until what had to be done was done, even if that meant staging a sit-down protest with my baby in hand.

I still remember one woman in my shared room. She said she had decided to stop after giving birth to not one, or two, but three babies, swearing to her husband that there would be no more children. She was back some time later having another baby. I was sure that I would not do the same.

Almost every time I heard a female say that she could not believe she was pregnant, or that she didn't know how it happened, I couldn't help but smile. I am a 100 percent certain that sitting on a particular chair, drinking tap water, or eating a special type of fruit did not contribute to any woman's pregnancy, so I certainly did not want to have to ask myself those foolish questions. I knew how pregnancy occurred, and also how to avoid an oopsy.

Still in labour, the contractions became more wicked. My midwife told me that it would not be too long, but how long was not too long! Even a half an hour seemed far too long to continue in this situation.

Daisy and Burt

Our son, Halim, loved our next-door neighbours, Aunty Daisy and Uncle Burt, who regularly spoiled him rotten. It seemed as though nothing was too good to buy for him. So when we decided that our neighbours would look after our young man while I was in the hospital, he was 'over the moon' with joy. Our son knew that there would be no particular bedtime, meals would be whatever and whenever it pleased him, and his favourite toys would be at his disposal.

And let's not forget those delicious creamy chocolate bars that they always had on hand. With all those wonderful temptations, who would miss mom and dad? Thoughts about the newly expected baby were likely way in the back of his mind while he had his fun with Auntie Daisy and Uncle Burt.

This couple was typical down-to-earth, kind, generous and pleasant. Daisy was an avid baker and excellent homemaker while Burt had a green thumb that showed in his care of his flowers and vegetable gardens. Daisy was never shy of telling her husband what to do, and her husband usually responded with "Yes, dear." His patience seemed almost like that of a saint. Although I admired his patience, personally, it would have been rather trying to say yes so often.

Labour and Delivery
My contractions moved rapidly from one stage to the next. The health care team worked more quickly than usual. Professionals might be correct most of the time, but not always. There were a few surprises as far as labour and delivery of a baby were concerned. My midwife had assessed me and said, "You are not ready yet," which meant that I could rest between my contractions. That was okay with me.

Well, the baby total disagreed with that plan. It was as if baby said, "I would change all this. I want to see what is out there." As soon as the midwife turned her back and left the room, things started to happen. My contractions became more frequent and pressure intensified in my 'tail end' that I scarcely had time to breathe. The baby decided enough was enough.

This baby was behaving as expected in any normal labour, with head presentation and heart rate within normal range. Mother was doing ok, barely coping in spite of those mean contractions. And the father was anxious! Unexpectedly, I felt a change and the baby was ready to make its debut into his new world.

Again, my dear midwife said, "You are not quite ready."

Something funny suddenly happened. The entire mood in the labour room changed from a stressful situation into one of laughter. I had given everyone concerned fair and advance warning that delivery was imminent.

Well, the baby decided to do its own thing and that was that. Ready or not, here I come. Only his head was delivered and what we saw amazed all in that room. This child turned his head, looking up towards the ceiling almost as if to check out the decor and other things in the room to see if his place of birth was satisfactory. One staff member who attended the baby's birth said, "This baby looked as though he has been in this world before." We named him Isif Ibrahima.

During this whole process, Issah presented as a bit paler but much braver expectant father, holding my hands reassuringly.

As far as I was concerned, this child seemed to have set a rather quick pace, from conception to his delivery. The same behaviour seemed to have followed him through his life.

His brother, on the other hand, seemed to be the opposite, with a more laid-back type of personality who knows how to step up and take control of situations when action is needed.

These observations might not be true for everyone, but it holds true for me. I think that I would like to exercise my bragging rights, when I say that mothers—at least most mothers—have good powers of observation. My children might beg to differ, but I am going to stick tightly to what I believe. And so, that is just a small peek at what happened at the delivery of my second son. My sons are from the same parents, meaning same mother and same father. Ha-ha! I know how nosey human beings are; their personalities are as dissimilar as night and day.

Sons
Earlier I mentioned my first son's entry into our great, new and challenging world. The trauma of this birth soon became a thing of the past. When I was in labour, I was concerned

about the safe labour and delivery of my child. In spite of some bumpy times during labour, luckily, I felt that a greater power was on our side and all went well. Miracles started to appear. I called them miracles because I sincerely believed that a child's progress does not happen by coincidence. Words could never capture the gradual change in an infant's life, as there were times when all he seemed to do was sleep and eat, a lot.

Nursing
Some mothers breast-fed their babies. Others used formula. I was grateful because my child knew what to do at feeding time. In fact, feeding time was one of the happiest times for us. He knew what to do and he did it. At times too well. His sucking reflexes were so strong it felt more like a vacuum cleaner sucking up everything in its path.

His little legs worked in rhythm with his sucking motions. He grabbed hold of any object at arm's length, usually one or sometimes two of mom's fingers. I felt that was his way to make sure mom is staying put and not robbing him of this precious moment.

Breastfeeding has benefits, but there may also be difficulties. It may come automatically for some mothers, but not for all. It can be rather frustrating in early stages and even uncomfortable or even painful. At least it was for me some of the time.

During the pre-natal classes, we were taught that people with fair skin and red hair tended to have more delicate breast tissues, causing sore, cracked or even bleeding nipples. I took this teaching as gospel truth. After all, the pre-natal teachers must know what they are telling us rookie mothers.

Imagine what a shock I had when I was confronted with these three maladies. It was no fun. I had never experienced that type of discomfort and pain before. The pain started as soon as the baby latched onto the breast, and continued that way almost throughout his feeding period. I began to dread it because I was having such troubles. After all, I had never breastfed a baby before, so I knew no better.

Somehow I persevered because of the benefit to this little chap. Really, the things parents, in particular, this mother, endured for the sake of their children.

I looked in my old broken bathroom mirror to check if I was fair skinned after all, but nothing had changed. I was still a dark-skinned African woman with jet-black hair. All those features were still present as they were since the day I was born. Thank heaven this breast-feeding business lasted for a short period and not for a lifetime.

At times I wondered if the only activities this baby was capable of performing were timed activities—sleeping, eating and crying. Now I understand this saying, sleep like a baby, more clearly. I felt almost envious. I became mesmerized by the depth of peace, quietness and the 'not a care in the world' facial expression. How truly amazing a baby could sleep, and not even stir, for such a long period. I simply could not resist the temptation. I curled up near this wonderful tiny soul and snatched a nap too. It was simple luxury!

Grabber

We nicknamed Halim 'Grabber.' Anything and everything placed within his reach was good enough to grab. I thought my son was the cleverest baby in the world. He was holding things, including mom or dad's fingers, at such an early age. I was rather disappointed when I learned that what was being displayed was called the Palmar Grasp Reflex.

When I brushed my fingers along Halim's cheeks, he'd turn his head towards the object and interpret this as his feeding time. I learned that this is known as the Shooting reflexes that help him to find the breast, and the sucking reflexes follow.

I must have lived in a world of make believe for a while. I thought that most, if not all parents, liked to see their children as the brightest star in the sky. I had convinced myself these movements were the products of my clever baby and not reflexes. Sometimes it is difficult to convince some mothers, like myself, to be realistic. Refusal to accept or acknowledge behaviour worked only in the short term. Then the naked truth began to stare me straight in the face and I wanted to run fast or find a suitable hiding place.

Learning Curve

Babies don't come with instruction manuals, and having the beginning I had gave me no model to learn positive parenting. It often seemed as though the baby understood a language different from my own. My learning curve was intense.

At times I was so proud of myself that I almost jumped for joy when my response to the cry created a smile on my child's face. Other times, I failed so miserably and wondered if I would ever get it. I felt as though so many other parents were well ahead of me. They seemed to easily cope with their baby's needs.

I wondered sometimes if Halim was taking revenge on me. I'd do it right one day and then the next I felt completely undone. His gaze seemed more like staring, and his smiles like smirks. These two actions, when combined, felt threatening. I wasn't sure what to make of it. How could such a tiny defenseless baby send out such strong, powerful messages? After all, I was a grown woman. Was it my lack of experience or confidence?

That old enemy, shame, seemed to rear its ugly head, again. Feelings of worthlessness and self-doubt showed up again, but less intense. With courage the size of a mustard seed, I asked for help.

I attended moms' and tots' groups conducted by a community health nurse. There were parents with different experiences and knowledge, and from different walks of life.

Some information had to be taken, as the saying goes, 'with a grain of salt.' Some of the opinions offered to me, I had to sift through and use what seemed sensible, practical and also safe, always bearing in mind that our precious little bundles are totally defenseless.

Baby's Smiles

As a new parent I struggled to understand my baby, and I noticed new behaviours. His smiles were no longer intermittent or haphazard. His smiles lit up his face on seeing me, wherever I moved, and I knew that was a real smile, and it made me not only happy, but also rather excited. My son's eyes followed me more intently and focused on my movements.

It reminded me of an optometrist examination when asked to follow the location of the bright narrow spot of light; only thing was, I was that light. He delighted in following and focusing on things and movements close by.

He also responded by turning his head whenever we called his name. His focus was still on being fed, but now he started noticing other things going on. Not only was Halim smiling, focusing and following movements, he was also responding with the rest of his body, with his hands and his feet.

I loved it when he grabbed hold of my fingers and held on. Might it be some need for comfort and warmth in a new and strange world? I guess we'll never know for sure.

Winter Nights

I wished I could avoid the winter months. We did not enjoy the simple luxury of central heating. We had a wood-burning stove. In those days, the owner had to fire them up from scratch on bone chilling mornings. Mornings when the colourful red orange ambers from the precious night's warmth had faded to a dull lifeless grey, we felt the chill.

Each morning we had to remove the spent amber, clean and repack the fireplace, then with fingers crossed and bated breath, we used a small hand-held lighter to get the stove burning. It only needed one flick to get it going, but sometimes that first try didn't work and we had to do it again and again.

Then once it was burning, we'd soon feel the warmth in our home.

I'd start humming the song, "I saw the light" by Todd Rundgren. I coaxed the stove to generate as much heat as possible because a baby's environment required a comfortable temperature.

Those winter nights, in particular, were unforgivingly cold. It showed no mercy whether one was ill or healthy, young or old, and especially when one was recovering from illness or any another life-threatening illness. I felt the cold in my bones.

Gut Feeling

Many people spoke of that 'gut feeling.' Some referred to it as 'the uncomfortable feeling' in the stomach when something was just not right.

When my first-born was just a little bitty baby, I tucked him in his bed one night, and then just before I retired for the night, I peeked in on him. All seemed well. During the early morning, I felt an underlying uneasiness that forced me to get out of bed and check on my son.

What I saw made me speechless. He appeared to be in respiratory distress. From my nursing training, I knew it for what it was. His coughing was severe and almost incessant. He was struggling, as though he were reaching for some invisible object. His colour had changed from a rich, healthy, dark brown to a sickly, greyish, purplish tinge and his little ribs were paying the price. His lungs were working even harder trying to breathe in an attempt to get some oxygen into his lungs.

I rushed Halim to our family doctor's office. We were seen quickly. The doctor diagnosed our son with whooping cough. The medical terminology is acute pertussis which is a highly contagious respiratory infection caused by a bacterial infection that gets into the nose and throat. To prevent the spread of this infection, I kept him away from other babies.

I knew what had to be done and I did it. I kept vigil day and night and saw how quickly this devastating disease affected such a young child. My son was just a shadow of himself. This was no simple run-of-the-mill cough. It was vicious and unrelenting. This cough meant business. The fight for control started—mother vs. whooping cough.

I was equally determined and vigilant. I, too, meant business and cared for this little helpless soul around the clock. My energy felt drained and the effort of being on my feet so much meant they were unsteady, shaky, and my body, weak and achy. My eyelids felt heavy.

Apart from administering the prescribed antibiotics and medication to suppress the cough or to loosen mucus in the lungs, as per the doctor's guidelines, the rest was pretty straightforward. Basically, care included such things as giving him a small amount of expressed breast milk at frequent intervals to prevent dehydration and vomiting, as well as protection from extreme room temperature and draughts or cigarette smoke that could trigger coughing spells. Placing the baby face down on my lap and gently tapping over the lung area was a healthier choice.

Also, the doctor encouraged the use of a vaporizer to moisten room air. I could not afford one so I improvised by using several large saucepans of boiling water, replacing them at intervals. I was careful to keep it at a safe distance away from the baby and was reassured that my son did not need hospitalization, but that choice was there if necessary.

Eventually the violent coughing became less intense. His colour was returning to its healthy brown and his chest movements were returning to normal with a regular rhythm.

The symptoms of whooping cough became less marked, but I was exhausted and my spirits were still low, until I saw him smile and knew that he would be all right. His eyes seemed to smile too. I did not need a nurse or doctor to tell me that my son was well on the road to recovery. What a heartwarming moment! Like the words in an advertisement:

"I want to save this moment and live in it forever." That is how I felt. I wanted to save that smile and remember it forever and ever.

Valuable Lesson

During and after nursing my son back to health, I learned a very important and valuable lesson—that health, especially a baby's health, is not a given and ought not to be taken for granted. It was as the saying goes "you never miss the water until the well runs dry." My dry well experience was missing my healthy child and seeing his bright cheerful face gazing at me.

Our son's strength returned and he gripped my fingers. I was glad even if his grip was a reflex or voluntary action, because something incredible happened during this time. We began to bond.

I felt a calm happy feeling deep down. The joy replaced the sadness I felt when my son was struggling to get his breath. No, it was deeper than that. It was in my soul. I very much doubt that special feeling could ever be compared with anything else in life. Not even when I met my true love. This was truly a special relationship between mother and baby.

Rules

When my children were tiny tots, there were fewer rules for parents than today. Most of them were related to care and safety of the child. I called it the ten commandments of child care. I remembered a few. Parents were encouraged to swaddle babies like a nice comfortable Burrito-like wrap that helped the baby feel secure and, in turn, to settle easier. Babies were expected to be in their own crib, not in their parents' bed. This practice was frowned upon then, and still is today in various countries, but not all. The reasoning, as I remember it, was to avoid injury or suffocate the child.

There were rules for this, rules for that, and rules that confused an already confused mother, like me. I'm not saying all rules are bad. We need them for law and order. Countries, cities and even health organizations have them, but I felt overwhelmed by too many rules at the time.

Was I the only first-time mother breaking that sacred childcare rule of the baby in mom's bed? Well, if I was the sole lawbreaker, I would gladly bear the retribution of my most grievous transgression. When our son had whooping cough, it was a trying time for our family. I needed my sleep too and then he'd be close by, so I did it anyway.

Chapter 30: The Lopsided Sandwich

When my children were in grade school. I used to regularly pack their lunches. On one particular evening when they returned from school, I observed that all was not well with my younger son, Isif. I enquired what was bothering him. The tears started rolling down his cheeks as though the faucets of his emotions were wide open.

He said that he did not like how his sandwiches were cut because they were not cut in two equal halves. I was really surprised by his power of observation. To me it was only a sandwich, made of white bread, or was it a twelve-grain? I was too busy thinking how to solve this grade school child's crisis to remember what type of bread I used. This was a high priority, nearly an emergency. In his mind it was the world's biggest disaster. A solution was needed, right away. We did some problem-solving exercises, and he came up with his own solution. It was very simple. He decided that he could make his own sandwiches and I would do the rest of his lunch. To be truthful, I was happy to be relieved of this important task as bread-cutter.

After settling things with my second born, it was time to ask his brother his opinion about his lunch. Secretly, I was hoping to be completely free of making lunches. I said to my first-born son, "Do you still want me to make your lunches? I might even cut your sandwiches uneven." He said very clearly and with gusto, "Yes, I want you to make it." He didn't care whether they were cut 50-50, 20-70 or not cut at all. That was good enough for him.

Part of me was a bit disappointed because I was expecting a similar answer as his brother. Bad luck for me.

Living was easier and circumstances that used to be difficult now seemed less of an issue than in our previous neighbourhood where we had to deal with rodents and a higher crime rate. My level of comfort increased while I walked along the streets. Gone were the days when I needed to walk backward on a windy day to avoid what I called the garbage storm.

Gratitude

Being from humble—extremely humble—poor and deprived beginnings, I experienced many advantages and disadvantages at different periods of my life. One important quality was being grateful. Don't get me wrong. I was not always grateful. I felt angry and resentful for a long time. In those days, I had absolutely no idea what the word 'gratitude' meant, or for that matter, I had never heard about it. I felt no sense of thankfulness when I first arrived in England, because I was in a state of total despair and in desperate need of someone to stretch out a helping hand. And that helping hand was there for me.

Some people might say gratitude is simply gratitude, but I think that there are different degrees of this attitude. There were times when I was appreciative for simple things in my life, such as being able to get out of the environment in which I was born and having the opportunity to make a better life for myself. As I looked back at my life, there were certainly a lot of times when I should have considered myself fortunate, although this was not always the case. When problems or issues knocked at my door, I felt rather miserable, discontented and often times ungrateful.

Each day, I was learning to appreciate the simplest things in my life. Being able to groom and dress myself appropriately, having two healthy boys, and last, but not least, having a loving husband.

My Children's School

There were times when it seemed as if my whole life, including my shortcomings and inadequacies, seemed to suddenly appear from nowhere. When my children started school, I was well versed with the simplest lessons—reading, writing and math (sums). It was more like addition, subtraction and multiplication and division. That's it! Those things were easy for me to follow in their lower grades, until they progressed to higher levels. Over the years, the learning gap between my children and me gradually widened until I felt simply lost.

Psychologically, it took me back to the early days when I arrived in England and felt lost in the English culture. The difference was that I developed much more confidence in myself. I asked questions and did not feel too ashamed to get help from whatever source available. As I began to ask—a whole lot of questions—I felt empowered instead of embarrassed or ashamed.

Mom's Learning Quest

One day, as usual, I walked my children to school. The bell pealed. The children lined up and marched to their classrooms. Suddenly, a thought came to me. How should I address this huge problem? How could I learn about my sons' schoolwork? What I did might not have been what other parents might have chosen to do, but then, I am not that other parent.

I had only one mission, and it was to get some help so that eventually I could help my sons. There were no children in the playground or in the hallways at this time. My path was clear.

The children were marching towards their classrooms like miniature soldiers. Their little footsteps were almost in time to the beat of an invisible drum—one, two, three, one, two three.

My Opportunity

I walked into the school works office, introduced myself to the secretary and asked for some time to talk to her. What I said completely changed her facial expression. I told her what grades my sons were in and their teachers' names. I said that I would like to follow their school progress, but I found it difficult because I did not know the system very well and that

I would like to learn more about it. Well, I was unsure who was more amazed, the secretary or me.

She looked baffled or even confused about what should be done. I am sure that ideas were jumping around in her head like bingo balls.

I wanted to learn more about the children's schoolwork. Also, I realized how beneficial it would be if I could work with the teachers and my children. I loved my children and wanted to make sure any issues and concerns were addressed early so that problems wouldn't arise later.

It was difficult to approach the school simply to say I needed help so that I could help my kids. It took a lot of courage. I thought I must have been the only mother who was ignorant about the school system, but my worries were soon squashed.

One day, while I was standing among a group of parents waiting to pick up our children from school, I heard their confessions. They, too, had even less idea about what their kids were learning at school. I read between the lines the same sense of shame and fear, as I had felt. Surprisingly, their conversation pushed me even more to learn as much as I could. I met with my children's teachers on a one-to-one basis. They explained some important points to me. I was grateful the meeting was scheduled this way and not with more of the staff. Most grateful of all, I was not made to feel insignificant or stupid.

Initially, our meetings were frequent. They took place at times when the children were engaged in various activities. No little enquiring eyes. Later, as my understanding of the class-work got clearer, the teachers and I used written notes as the mode of communication.

My children were good supplementary advisors, although some of the information I received from them could not have been further from the truth. For instance, the reasons for time out. I knew a lot more about the working of their school system by then. The days when they could 'pull the wool over my eyes' were gone. Game over. They were unhappy about this part—their newly informed mom.

School's Fact or Fiction

There came the days when my children reported how mean their teachers were. I knew otherwise, but I chose to listen to them. I listened intently. Second, I injected a massive load of sympathy. Third—and this is the best part—I saw their little eyes almost bulging out of their sockets in fear, when I said we will be going to see their teachers early tomorrow morning. It is incredible how soon the story changed.

This plan only needed to be executed a few times, then all would be well.

As my dearly departed mother used to say, "No more cock-and-bull stories."

Children are pretty smart in twisting stories to get themselves out of scrapes. Parents need to be even smarter and be a few steps ahead of them to see the truth of the story.

The only thing about my plan was that it had to be carried through to be effective. I did go to the school and met with teachers and heard both sides of the story. And what a story it was! I called it same story with different points of view. Interesting!

Chapter 31: Education

How important is it? When I was growing up in my homeland, Trinidad, I clearly remembered how some parents would do almost anything to give their children a worthwhile education. They would cut back on things like food or clothing to ensure there was enough money to cover their children's expenses.

For many years I did not grasp why being educated was so important, but I found out. Being educated opens the doors to lots of benefits. Had I been educated when I left Trinidad to go to England, would my life have been different? Probably. I found it interesting observing the difference between people who have been educated and those who did not.

Some things stand out clearly in people like myself, who have been educationally deprived. It shows up in the intense fear of reading, especially in the presence of others. It's like our body language screams, "Please, do not ask me to read." Even worse, the expression of utter shame, especially as an adult.

My memories sadly took me back to my childhood days. How I had yearned to go to school. Apart from missing so much schooling and feeling way behind, I envied the children their nice, clean, crisp looking uniform. Or was school meant to spare me the agony of having to face those long, blazing days in the sun? Or might it have been a way to keep the thread of self-respect as a young girl.

Catching Up On My Education

Attending school was like belonging to an elite organization. Similar to an old-boys' network. When one enrolled at school, one automatically became a club member, whether it was at a junior, high school or university level. Regular questions such as what school the person attended were as common as everyday greetings. Asking that simple question seemed to set the stage for further and deeper conversation.

I couldn't have known then how having a worthwhile education enhanced one's life. Might my brain have worked better to receive information? Living in my same limited environment in my community, I could only see what was around me and little more. My eyes almost left their sockets when I saw for myself the difference between the way of life in my culture and those in Britain. It was a brand new experience and a culture shock.

It felt simply frightening. I vividly remembered the thoughts that first came to my mind about going to England and the feelings that accompanied it. I was excited to be free of my troublesome life that felt more like existing. There seemed to be no way out, with no hope. As I had mentioned earlier, I felt like the female village labourer—an unpaid labourer—who was expected to work almost from sunrise to sunset.

Challenge

Having had so little education in my formative years, going to England seemed to me like trying to divide the Red Sea, all alone. Those negative self-limiting thoughts were so strong, so convincing, and so powerful that it could discourage the best thinking or motivated individual. Those feelings worked against me, often discouraging me from moving forward. At the same time, positive elements within me were fighting even harder to keep me safe and alive. I asked myself, "What do I need or want?" And the answer kept me hanging on. There were times when those negative shadows almost pushed me backwards, but I put up a bloody good fight and only hung on some days by a thin flimsy thread. Difficulties, despair, loneliness, feeling of not belonging to any particular group were not enough to put out my pilot light.

Mental Illness

Only much later in my adult life, I learned what mental illness, in particular depression, was truly about. I learned how it gave a feeling of being in a deep, dark hole with slim chances of climbing out without adequate support. It felt like being tightly enclosed in a big heavy black cloak. Because of low motivation and low mood, I found it difficult and at times and almost impossible to function. Everything looked bleak. Questions bombarded my mind. Why was I even alive? What was the use? I felt there was no hope in going on. And there were many more negative voices.

I hoped that one day the wind of change would blow in my direction in a meaningful way. I'm not saying that education is the solution to all of life's woes. What I meant, at least for myself, is that had I been given the opportunity of some formal education, my life might have been easier. Those self-destructive emotions might have been reduced or, at least easier to understand.

Learning from Children
Several years later on a slightly breezy day in October, we had moderate rain showers. Then almost suddenly, there it came, a torrential downpour.

It seemed as though the heavens decided to empty all its water barrels on our earth. People were running for shelter, but the children were more prepared than the adults. They wore their brightly coloured rain boots and coats and joyfully splashed about in the puddles. It was amusing to see how happy these children were playing in something so simple, so ordinary.

Cars and trucks of different makes and sizes drove by, some at normal speed limits, and others as though they were in a race. Water splashed here and there, on anything and everyone in its path. Some pedestrians thought they were safe on the sidewalk. Sadly, they were not spared. Others used their umbrellas in the regular way, to protect themselves from the downpour, while others turned theirs into a shield to protect their entire body from the splashes from traffic.

As I trudged through the rain showers and the breathtaking strong wind, my thoughts went to how simple things in life could bring such joy as what those children were experiencing. Maybe, only maybe, there lies a crucial lesson to be learned.

Those children were unashamed and opened-minded. They were not afraid of falling in the water and getting their clothing not only saturated, but also muddy. They also showed an atmosphere of friendship, such as when a child fell down, they'd run and rescue their buddy to get him back on his feet and into the happy water splashing, slippery, muddy game.

My journey home was fairly long and challenging that day, but in a relatively short time, a new thought came to me. If those kids could enjoy such simple things in their lives, such as water and mud, then I might consider a similar path. I am not exactly referring to the water and mud type of experience, but looking at how to improve my life. The children were loved and supported. They were not feeling ashamed or embarrassed, but they were vulnerable.

I figured that if the children could so easily adapt, I too could do something to improve the quality of my life. I scratched my head and wondered. How could I do this? Was I willing to be as vulnerable as those kids?

Facing My Demons

There were still many shameful unaddressed questions circulating in my mind. Some of them I would much prefer to brush aside. Others I'd revisit occasionally; as for the rest, I'd keep their lids as tightly locked as a high security prison gate. Secrets, silence, and the fear of being judged served only one purpose. They prevented me from being open and honest and in turn kept me as sick, or even sicker, then before.

I had to face those demons so I could move forward. How could I even start addressing these issues? Who could I talk with? Which professional organization would meet my needs? Would I be supported or would I be judged, again? At the end of my sharing, would I feel uplifted? I had questions and needed answers before proceeding to confront those demons.

For some people, facing the demons might be seen as a non-issue, but I saw it differently. How could a mother guide her children when she felt bruised, battered and damaged? She could only pass on what was within her reach. She could not pass on what she had not received or did not know, whether it was education, finances or, even more importantly, instilling good values in the lives of her young impressionable children.

Start of My Healing Quest

I looked closely at many things with which I could possibly identify. I looked at fellow human beings whom I admired. I gauged my comfort level in their company and also whether their words were congruent with their actions. At that particular time of my life, I was not contented with what I observed. It's one thing saying, "I care about you" and another acting them out.

Memories of past experiences flashed back to me like lightning, and those memories did not sit comfortably in my gut.

I felt as if my guardian angel was gently prodding me, saying, "Take heed, and do not let past painful experiences repeat themselves." And so I took notice, and decided on other ways to start my healing process.

Since I had been abused in the name of religion, that awful taste was still bitter in my mouth. I decided against that route. Other ideas were unrealistic, unachievable or just ridiculous. Thoughts continued to turn and turn in my mind, but I was determined to find a way to help myself.

Nature's Healing

Many years ago I read about how simple things in nature have inspired individuals, for example sitting by a river and watching it flow. It helped them to see their lives differently and to make that long, overdue shift. I looked for a long time, and I felt stuck. I could not see a solitary thing in the world to give me that 'Yes! I got it' moment.

I looked at flowers. I looked at abandoned gardens and well-manicured lawns and still that inspiration to change my mindset seemed as far away as the east is from the west. I kept searching and searching. My energy and enthusiasm had started to lag. Discouragement was uninvited company and my search continued.

Honestly, I had absolutely no idea what that "something" was. But I was very certain that when I found that special thing I would recognize it. There would be a comfortable signal deep within my soul, like finding Mr. Right. And what do you know? That signal might show itself as increased pit-a-pat heartbeats or as a rush of adrenaline. Whatever the signal, I was sure I would feel it.

Inspiration

That's what I think I was searching for. I personally experienced inspiring moments years ago when I met my husband. I felt peace, love, connectedness, and a sense of belonging. He had what I was looking for. I would never forget those moments.

He taught me many things: respect for myself and for fellow human beings. Living by those simple principles created a more harmonious relationship. These things were new and foreign to me. I had mixed emotions—of being both excited and equally embarrassed. I felt like a young child in an adult's body. It was a weird feeling and I won't forget it.

The universe seemed so vast, so complex and yet so simple. I needed to break everything down into small manageable bits that I could understand. My brain simply could not cope with any technical theories—such as how the world turns on its axis. Learning new words, new things, however simple, brought joy to my heart.

Resentment
As a child, when I was forced to do gardening and farming work. I became resentful, angry and rebellious. Those feelings had more to do with having no say or choices in my life, moving and acting only at the hand of those selfish handlers.

Later I learned that resentment, whether overt or covert, could be harmful, especially to the person who harboured grudges. I had good—very good reasons—for clutching tightly to my dear unhealthy friend—resentment.

Change
I heard that when deep-seated pain hurts enough, it forces us to make a shift, to take action. It forced me to think about some way to ease my pain. Something had to be done. For the time being, this process seemed too overwhelming to start. On my own, I could not cross this river; it looked far too wide.

Nature's Inspirations
I hadn't enjoyed working in the garden as a child, but I enjoyed it now. It was soothing and forced me to compare it to life. I observed those small black ants going about their business. They seemed to slow down on their journeys. Did they talk to their equally busy friends? Did they encourage each other? But we are not ants; we are human beings, able to reason and believe. I thought about the ants, but I also realized that regardless how busy I was that I should take the time to encourage and appreciate others.

Creatures large and small, from the lowly earthworm to the bee to the high and powerful great white whale, could be valuable teachers. I am human, unable to adapt to the habits of these creatures, but I could widen my search and read about them to expand my knowledge.

I pondered the phrase 'stop and smell the roses' and wondered what it really meant. And so creatures in nature taught me another important lesson. That I should slow down and take some time for myself and appreciate the little things around me.

Inspirational Lesson
The month of October seemed to be playing a teasing game. Some days it seemed as though the heavens opened up and poured all their moisture below. Other days the sun shone warm and brightly in all its splendour. Then, the real October weather presented itself—chilly, cold and windy with unexpected showers.

Autumn put on an amazing show of colour, reminding me of models on a catwalk, sporting garments of various styles and colours. Any one colour of autumn seemed determined to outdo all the others in the whole spectrum. Nature competed for attention and wanted to be noticed and appreciated. And so did I.

Secrets
It was foreign to me to talk about my problems. I learned from the time I was small that our woes were not to be shared with anyone outside the home, and definitely not with strangers. Why would I want to hang my 'dirty laundry' for all to see?

First, I had never heard words such as counsellors, therapists, support groups or self-help of any kind until much later. Second, even if I knew about these services, I would have been too nervous to accept the help. My old unhealthy, uncomfortable way of life was all I knew. It was dreadful to live with, and even worse trying to rid myself of it. So much nonsense had been drilled into my head for so many years.

Initially, I trusted no one but myself because of what I had encountered. After years of not trusting others, I thought I was right to keep my issues close to my chest. On the other side of the coin, there was enough sadness to last more than a lifetime. I felt sad and miserable, and if I were to hang a sign on myself, that's what I would have written on it.

Take Heed

The body has a simple way of forcing an individual to take notice. In my case the mental, emotional and physical pains were pushing me near the edge; they were almost unbearable. Something had to change. There were very few people with whom I felt safe to share my load or parts of it. At that time, I could have easily counted those people on one hand. I was nervous, I was shaking and I was edgy.

What I feared most of all was having judgment, rightly or wrongly, passed on me. I was uncomfortable in my own skin. In spite of a racing heart, I decided to take that damn bull by its horns, and seek help, but I was too scared to approach trained professionals, and so I sought the help of my 'angel'— my husband. I felt this was easier than talking with a counsellor. And yet I could not tolerate any deep, heavy-duty intrusion, because I felt too fragile.

All I wanted at this time was to pour out a little of my pain. Later, I would cope with the rest when I felt strong enough to divulge more.

Breakthrough

I cannot remember how I started to ask my husband for some quality time. He had excelled in his psychology studies at university and reading body language was easy for him. In fact, I did not need to say much. My emotions were so raw that just being asked, "Are you ok?" caused gallons of pent-up, uncontrollable tears to cascade down my cheeks, like a waterfall. I cried and cried for a long time. I felt as though I could not catch my breath, and my head throbbed so much I felt as though my head had reached a point of near explosion. After psyching up myself to share what I considered deep, dark and dirty secrets, my body and thought processes just seemed to completely freeze up.

Memories shifted back to my childhood days when shame, guilt and fear wrapped their tentacles tightly around me. The only thing I could do was to hang my head in shame. I was innocent then, but I could still be accused of something. If I had tried to explain what really happened, I would only add insult to injury. It was like being on trial and unable to speak.

Flashbacks
Unconsciously, I was reliving past traumas. I was confused and perplexed, wondering why my body reacted to similar incidences, even when I was not the victim or abused person.

After more than half a century, I thought I should be fully healed. But I was wrong. In my mind, I thought the same held true for emotional, spiritual, and psychological wounds, when given caring attention. I found this was not true.

I tried to avoid any situation that would take me back to those dreadful days. Fear and pure panic would grip me so tightly, causing a state of almost devastating paralysis.

Not all of these recollections were traumatic. Some times were better than others, with varying degree of emotions. But coping with them was challenging, especially when I heard about sexual abuse towards vulnerable children or adults. It reminded me of my ordeal on the ship as I travelled to England.

Talking About Education
When I felt stronger mentally, I assured myself I would address those issues that have been haunting me for as long as I can remember. I'd start with the least threatening—the limited education that affected my self-esteem. Then I would use the positive results gained from solving one issue to build on others.

This would be my foundation. Eventually I gathered enough courage to talk about it. I shared about how I felt insecure and abnormal and how I was gripped by shame and anxiety when I needed to put pen to paper. I prayed often in an attempt to spare me embarrassment.

Start of Formal Education

My formal education started as a home-schooling project, as mentioned earlier, supervised by my "Angel," my friend, who later became my husband. My first lessons included adding and subtracting, then vocabulary. These lessons came during the time I was working on my nursing training. I felt so embarrassed and overwhelmed by these rudimentary lessons.

At the time I also improved in basic English. Unlearning old habits and poor grammar was harder than learning new vocabulary. Yet as I learned, my self-confidence grew. I had to work hard, but I made progress.

In spite of feeling embarrassed I promised myself I would do whatever it took to improve my education, even if it meant starting where I left off earlier. That learning curve often felt steep and slippery, but I was determined to keep going.

As I picked up where we left off, I found I still loved learning and felt that I could keep up my learning and one day communicate as well as anyone else.

During my learning process, including the lessons Issah taught, I paid attention to people speaking the language and continued to use my dictionary. My vocabulary grew and I kept on making lists of unfamiliar words that I looked up and used in sentences. In time, and I listened to others, I was able to improve my vocabulary and my self-confidence. People told me my smile came from within. If such a small improvement could bring about such a noticeable change, what would happen if I continued my learning quest? I continued. As others craved chocolate, my hunger was for education. Certainly I had a lot of ground to cover. I was fully aware that I would never be able to catch up and close that educational gap with others of my age, so I persevered and made slow but steady progress.

My lessons started to pay handsome results. My English grammar and math became much improved. Sentences, words and numbers that initially seemed strange and confusing became less mysterious and I found myself ready for more advanced lessons.

Sometimes, infrequently, I could even do calculations in my brain, instead of counting on my fingers or with peas or beans as I had initially done. I kept going, held my head high and smiled because I possessed some of those skills that others had. Those feelings of shame and worthlessness seemed weaker. Now I could ask for help when I needed it.

What a wonderful feeling! I was breaking more of the shackles that had held me back. I had never been to any graduation ceremony, so I have no idea how it feels, but in my mind, I was having my own personal graduation ceremony.

Children

As I continued my learning between regular day-to-day chores, I also attended to my sons' needs. While striving towards my best, I wanted to guide them to be the best they could be, while instilling good moral conduct, such as learning right from wrong. I taught them about sharing their toys, being loving to each other, with no biting, no hitting, no name calling, and being good to their extended family and friends.

As the children grew older, moral values became more and more complicated to teach, but it was important to do so. And I needed to teach them that bullying toward others is unacceptable.

My young children needed to know I would support and love them, throughout their lives and reassurance was available. Whatever the issue, I taught them I was there to listen.

Growing Children

While our sons were in school, it became essential to have more money than our budget allowed to meet their needs, especially clothing, and so I went back to work part-time.

Before that, I began to shop at a second-hand store. Hand-me-downs and the second-hand outlets became our saving grace. Clothing was clean and in excellent condition. I came out each time with bags of used, but perfectly good quality clothing. Oh, how grateful I was to affluent fashion conscious followers. There were times, many times, when I secretly thought people were vain or a slave to the fashion world. Since my initial shopping spree at the best shop establishment in the land, the second-hand shop, I vowed never, ever, to pass judgment on rich people. They unknowingly did my family the biggest favour ever. At least at that time, wearing second-hand clothing did not bother our sons.

Patches

My problems started when the boys started to be choosy about their clothing and coming home with holes in the knees of their trousers from rolling in the dirt and try making contact with unforgiving concrete surfaces.

Thank goodness for the person who invented patches. Patches, it seemed, came in a variety of fabric, denim, leather and cotton and were the craze of that time. They were worn by both the young and the old alike. Even the characters on the television children's programs wore them. So my kids were pleading for patches, and they got lots and lots of them. I loved them.

The patch fever was just as this name implies, patchy and short lived. The trend faded. Few people were keen to be patched up. With the downturn of this marvelous invention, the children were no longer a supporter of the 'Patchy-Patch' movement.

We encouraged our children to make choices and decisions, but I soon regretted this. Now that patches were gone, shopping at my precious second-hand shop suffered the same as the patches. I had to think of another money-saving project.

My Next Project

Knitting was my next project. Advice and help were in abundance. It seemed that almost everyone I knew—men, women and children in England—were handy with needles and a ball of wool or synthetic yarn.

I consulted one of the best knitters on our street, Aunty Daisy. She helped me start my new undertaking. Just holding the sweater pattern she'd given to me—V-necked, long sleeved, just below the hips—and pattern and needles, ignited an eagerness and confidence in me, probably too confident. I chose solid moss green wool. I was ready to work on my new project.

I did not go to regular knitting classes, as it was too expensive. However, advice and help were in abundance, but my regular lessons were from Daisy. I still remember the simple knitting stitches of knitting one row, and then purling one row. Oh, I was excited and hot with enthusiasm. I had visions of opening a new knitting franchise in England.

My red-hot project was progressing very well and I completed my first garment, which was a sweater. My pride was almost uncontrollable. The moment of fitting arrived. I was so excited to display my handiwork. My heart rate increased. I am certain my blood pressure followed closely behind, and I spoke faster than usual. I quickly took the prized work out of the plastic bag. My dear son, Halim, took one long look at it. He agreed to try it on. Then he turned this way and that way while I watched his facial expression. I'd seen that look before and knew exactly what it meant. My heart rate slowed. Then he said, "Mom, I like this sweater, but I prefer the ones in the store."

That was it for me! No more patterns. No more needles. No more wool, be it natural or synthetic. My sadness had little to do with the garment and more to do with my trampled ego. I cannot blame my son for rejecting my sweater. You see, there were holes here, there, and everywhere. There were holes where no holes should be. My masterpiece looked less like a masterpiece than the sweater I had worked so hard to make. I felt deflated. I wanted to quit knitting right then and there.

At this time I realized that things had to change because the decisions were not all mine. Little peoples' choices had to be considered too. When I looked at the sweater again, with all its imperfections, I had done my best for my first project. I would satisfy myself with that thought.

I knew it was good for children to learn the value of making choices, apart from my son not wanting to wear the sweater. I had to find another money saving project. No more shopping at second-hand shops. Patches were out. Thank goodness, I kept my special shop to myself. That would have been another issue if a certain little individual knew where his clothing came from. Mom's hand-made sweaters were certainly out of the running.

Gardening

I knew what I'd do next to try to save money. It would be growing vegetables for the family dinner table. That was the most successful hobby ever and turned out to be a family project. The results were fairly quick. The weather was not only mild and favourable, but also cooperative. Seeds seemed to germinate almost overnight. Seedlings developed growth spurts as if they knew that our family was in desperate need of food.

Plants such as tomatoes and lettuce also did their part. One week the seeds would be sowed. Then later we transplanted the seedlings and watered and fertilized the young plants. Before long, the growth amazed us. Then weeks later, small flowers and then miniature tomatoes appeared. Seeing those vegetables flourish was uplifting and rewarding.

Chapter 32: Adjusting to a New Country

Our family arrived in Canada in 1988. Around that time, I was still disturbed by unresolved issues, relating to the death of my first child, a son. It was almost impossible to forget that part of my life. I needed to find solutions to relieve my grief, but I was too scared to approach any professional person, because, in my mind, I thought that I would endure more condemnation. My fragile mind could not have coped with any criticism.

Added to my unresolved problems, we were in a new country that did things differently than what I'd become accustomed to in England. Adjusting in Canada reminded me of the acclimatization I had to make when I arrived in England. It was dotted with its own share of peaks and valleys—some bigger than others. To start with, I had grown familiar with the English way of speaking, but the Canadian vernacular was different in many respects. This was yet another new way of life—the North American way.

I thought some words were weird and frequently when I use the English version, my good-natured friends "took the mickey out of me" meaning they made fun of me. Car boots were now trunks, trolleys were grocery carts and biscuits were now cookies.

As for the weather, I was mesmerized when the light flakes of snow fell from the sky or were blown about by a cold wind. Those monstrous trucks with blades on the front sent vibrations through our home as they drove by scraping and pushing snow off the road.

Another thing I noticed was that Canadians drove on the right hand side of the road, instead of on the left, as in England. When I'd been in Canada for only one year, I enrolled at a driving school, where I took their course and successfully passed the test. What a memorable day that was.

As if those changes were not enough, even the law (I felt) was out to make this new immigrant's life more confounding.

I even had an interaction with the police for not putting my license sticker on my car. That was my first encounter with the boys in blue, and I hoped the last. There was so much to learn.

The First Maple Tree

Once we were in Canada a while, and looking out on a blustery cold day, I observed something that I had never seen before. Our national maple tree. To be honest, I looked at it but I really did not pay it much attention, but this day was different. Was it because I was searching for something? Or was it a sense of urgency to find that 'something?' There it was right under my nose. It was so near, and yet so far. Why did I not see it before?

I saw a strong tree with thick, dark brownish-grey bark that displayed a unique pattern running in an earth to sky direction. Almost all the indentations in the pattern were of similar length and width, while some of the patterns seemed to take on their own styles. About halfway between the earth and up the trunk of the tree, the main branches went off by themselves, as though trying to carve out a life of their own, and not just one branch but many others going in their own direction. On looking more closely, I saw that the tree trunk was damaged. Bruised, battered and perhaps even gouged, and in places it seemed as though the tree tried to heal itself. The scarred areas were like humps on a camel's back. Some branches grew this way and that, as if they are holding out their arms asking for help. Others looked as if they were rejecting their origins. The straighter healthier branches seemed to reach up to the heavens as in sincere prayer and supplication. These abnormally shaped branches varied in size, some much shorter than the others. Some ended abruptly as if broken off by mighty hands. These abnormally shaped parts made me think of my family.

This tree trunk stood firm against the elements: the gentle spring, the hot sweltering summers, the bone-chilling fall and also sub-zero freezing winter temperatures. Further up the tree, the branches again subdivided in different directions. At that level, twigs and bigger branches were much healthier.

Those twisted branches represented, for me, how difficulties might affect people. The healthier and straighter branches might bear some resemblance to the healing process that occurs following difficult experiences. There were other things about this particular tree. The same way that its branches reached towards the sky, its roots spread wide and deep into dear Mother Earth. While inclement weather may affect the trunk and branches, their deep strong roots, which keep this huge tree upright, are not as easily damaged.

Over the years I have observed how much smaller trees came crashing down by moderately strong winds while more mature trees refused to be uprooted in spite of raging storms, except the more violent ones. Of all the lessons I have learned from nature, this is the most profound. I found it meaningful because the tree reminded me of my battered life.

Three main things helped me to bounce back; first, was having a positive attitude. Second, being optimistic. And the third, and possibly most challenging, was being able to regulate emotions and seeing failure as helpful feedback.

Second Maple Tree

On some of my usual daily walks, I paid very close attention to various types of trees, but none of them provided what I was looking for. Finally, I found that special 'something' that I was searching for. The ordinary, extraordinary gift—a little crooked tree. That plant showed me not only how to be resilient but to look at life optimistically. Another lesson learned. I looked in awe at this special beautiful incredible tree, totally surprised and almost mesmerized. Even an artist might find it challenging to reproduce that look. It was so clearly laid out on front of me, by nature's very best artist. It was as if a bright light had shone on the dark patches of my life. Now I saw things in a new way, as viewed through a new looking glass.

There was a time when I was convinced that unfortunate things only happened to me. Surprisingly, the mind and the brain could be helpful in some ways and yet they could be equally destructive in generating twisted unreasonable thoughts. I believe that everyone has, at some time or other, experienced some degree of pain or suffering. Even those maple trees clearly showed signs of damage by their irregular trunk and warped branches. Eventually, I was able to pull my eyes away from looking at them. Resilience! That word jumped out at me, again. There was a good chance that I could be resilient. Could I bounce back in spite of wading through deep murky waters?

Hope, though dim, remained my constant companion. Plus that wee small voice that kept whispering to me, "You have been resilient for many years. You may not have been aware of the word, but you have been practising it throughout your entire life. In spite of being denied simple human rights, such as the provision of food, a safe place to live, freedom to learn and reach your full potential, you did not give up. Yes, it was a difficult road to travel and many negative thoughts entered your mind, prompting you to take a short, easy and final path."

It always boggled my mind when I heard about how those held captive, by whatever the cause, choose suicide. I could empathize with those pushed to the brink, because I have been there. Those negative thoughts were not only persistent but also powerful.

Chapter 33: Meeting the Rabbi

I was not brought up in the Jewish faith. I had never been in a synagogue, and so I had no idea how it looked inside. Yet one day I was driving by a synagogue, in Kitchener, Ontario, and a thought came to me, and I heard a voice say, "Why not go in there and ask to speak with the Rabbi?"

I followed this suggestion, parked my car and went into the synagogue office. I made an appointment with the secretary to see the rabbi. Would such a distinguished person of the Jewish faith consider me worthy of his precious time? I needed to talk with someone.

I'm not sure why I stopped at the synagogue, especially given my views on organized religion. I still believe in a Creator or Higher Power. It's not often that I felt like a valuable and worthy being, but this time was different. At this stage, I needed to start seeing myself as valuable as any other human being who is part of God's creation.

What a reassuring and comforting space to be in. Healing, even if it was to be slow and small steps at a time, had to come from the inside and it could start in this place. I truly believe it, feel it, and ultimately live it. It took me a long time to look into the mirror and like the person looking back. There's no quick fix to healing a battered and wounded body, mind and soul, but thankfully this was the beginning of my new life.

Eventually the secretary introduced me to the rabbi. He was sitting at his desk but came around it, and shook my hand to welcome me. He closed his office door to ensure my privacy and pressed the "off" button on his telephone. He was very pleasant with an easy inviting smile.

He took his seat and said to me, "Grace, I have as much time as you need. I'm here to listen to you."

As soon as the rabbi asked how he could help me, there was absolutely no way of holding back my tears. He placed two boxes of Kleenex at my arm's length. I finally had the opportunity to share my story, issues and problems, but what baffled me was the comfort level I felt in those surroundings, knowing I would not be judged or considered less than human.

I told the rabbi what happened to me on the ship while I was travelling to England, that I was violently seized by a strange man who had forced intercourse, which resulted in an unwanted pregnancy, and finally, a forced abortion. Gripped with pain, shame and guilt, I continued to share.

When I had finished telling him everything, it was only then that the rabbi started to talk. I cannot remember everything he said, but some of his statements remained with me to this day. He paraphrased what I had shared with him. Then in a compassionate tone he asked, "What is your mental and emotional state? Are you financially comfortable? What type of support was available for you? How would you care and provide for a child?"

It was impossible to give any positive answers to show that the pregnancy, if allowed, would have a satisfactory outcome. Although I still felt a sense of sadness, I was convinced I made the best possible decision.

Before the meeting ended, the rabbi encouraged me to write a letter of apology to my deceased child, telling him about the circumstances surrounding his conception.

Feeling Relief

Previously, I had searched and searched, but I could not find a place where I felt safe and at ease sharing my ordeal. But for some unknown reason, it was only when I visited this synagogue that I felt protected to tell everything without fear or the verdict of guilty stamped on my forehead.

Having almost an hour and a half of such a distinguished person's time was quite unexpected. I certainly did not feel rushed. The rabbi had given me his undivided time and attention. No one had ever given me that genuine attention without any expectation of payback. This was a brand-new concept. Someone does care about my welfare. Yet I pinched myself just to be sure I was still in this mean and horrid world, as I knew it. Regardless of life and its reality, a small trickle of faith in the human race started to flow through, but I remained cautious, trusting only a few, because I did not want to go through anymore traumatic experiences.

I named my unborn child Mercy. I chose this name for one main reason, because this was what I badly needed. Mercy, not only from the wagging tongues of others, but most of all from myself.

Prior to this meeting, I would have folded my arms over my chest, stamped my feet and frankly refused such a suggestion, because, emotionally, that issue was seen as a closed box, never ever to be opened until I departed this world.

I did not have to think hard what I should say in the letter; it was as though the words were ready and waiting to be penned. It was the first time in my life I wrote such a heartfelt and healing letter. I shed more tears, but they were different from those at the rabbi's office. These were happy tears. I had a wonderful feeling of inner peace that continued for many years.

A Letter I Wrote to My Unborn Child.

Monday, October 16, 2000

Dear Mercy,

This is one of the most difficult letters I have ever written in my life. Never have I felt so torn to put this pen to paper and to express how I have been feeling for more than 34 years. You have been in my mind all this time; sometimes I wish that I could forget you. I just cannot because you were part of me; maybe you did not feel the same way.

You have good reasons to think that love for someone definitely does not mean getting rid of that person. Yes, I did get rid of you. Yes, you should be alive today to take your rightful place in the rank of the human race, with your brothers, friends, your age groups, society, but most of all, your place as a human being.

On that day when I was travelling up to England to carve out some type of life for myself, the only thing that I could honestly call my own was my body. That body was my prized possession. I was very proud of it. It was as pure as you were when I saw you.

My body was violated, battered. I was not part of this vicious act. The best I could have done, maybe to save my life, was to resist fighting that awful, heartless man off me—that could have easily cost me my life.

The agony of this action lived with me like a black shadow for many years. There were times when I wished I were murdered on that very night. I had nothing, nothing that interested me. Nothing I was happy or proud to call my own. In fact, I did not know the implications of the action until a few weeks later when I felt unwell—morning sickness—when it was suggested to me that I might be pregnant.

Panic. Anxiety. Fear and a feeling of total hopelessness came over me, which lasted for years and years. It was like carrying a great big tank of garbage, which I never felt I could shed. It was like part of me—yet it was not.

I had to make a decision to continue with the pregnancy or to end it. This was a difficult and sad decision. I thought of ways to do things differently. Maybe contact an adoption society. At that time, I did not even know there was such a place where people could have talked to you and looked after you. There were walls that surrounded me. I felt trapped—trapped with a child inside me that I was not part of its making. Added to this, being raped was scarcely a time when I should be happy with the product.

I had no support emotionally, psychologically, physically or spiritually. Alone, that was how I felt. Desperation set in and I had to do something to save my life. After fighting with myself, I decided to have an abortion.

I could not be 100 percent certain of your number of weeks. But I remember you were a lovely little boy with tiny, tiny body parts. A small head, well shaped for your age. Your fingers and toes were so small they looked like beautiful rose buds. Your body was well proportioned and had you lived, I am sure you would have been a person to be proud of. When I looked at your face, although still in a very premature stage, I had nothing but love for you—and still do.

In my mind I see you now as a 34-year adult who still has a place among the human race and in particular a place in my heart. It is impossible to forget you.

When your brothers were born, I saw you in them, even now I could easily figure out what you might have looked like as a 34-year-old man. At times I walk around town and see young men who could possibly fit your image. I'd have to look again because again because they reminded me of you.

To bring this tragic violent issue to some type of closure, the best thing I possibly could do for myself was to write to you. I am unsure if this will reach you wherever you may be. For all I know you may be one of those angels who stood by my side through difficult times, sad times, lonely and isolated moments, happy and grateful times as well. I know that there is certainly someone who cares, loves, supports and guides me throughout my life. Who? I am not sure. Maybe it is you.

So, Mercy, after explaining the reasons for my action to end your life, which was not the best action to take, at that time it was the only one I knew and felt I could have managed. Given the resources I had and the support to bring a child into a world of uncertainties I felt I did the best thing.

You might not agree with me. And, yes you are right to argue about your life cut short. If you could understand what this letter says and how I felt about you through this long ordeal, I am begging only one thing from you. Forgiveness. I hope that you will pardon me.

In fact, I felt that you have already done so, because there have been so many guardian angels looking over me and I believe you are one on them.

Hope one day we will meet again.

Love Mother

After more than forty years, as I document this monstrous act, I can feel my quickened heartbeat not only in my chest, but radiating through my body, leaving me with an overwhelming feeling of nausea. (I wrote the following letter to myself, much later, on August 20, 2000.)

A Letter I Wrote to Myself, Grace Cooper, at age 21

I am now Grace Ibrahima; in 1991, I married the late Issah Ibrahima. In this letter, I wanted you to know my feelings at that time. How I was taken advantage of and robbed of what was rightly mine—the only thing to my name, to call my own.

It was in 1966, when I left Trinidad, West Indies, to seek a better life for myself. I knew that if I had stayed home (in Trinidad), my life would have been a dead-end type of existence. My sister Ruth, who was a nurse in

England, had saved up some of her meager wages for me to pay for my boat fare to go to England. I did not remember the name of the boat, but after doing some research found the name—"The Montserrat."

I was in a cabin of maybe three other passengers. Somehow I was left alone in this cabin. One of the men who was also travelling up to England approached me and forced me to submit to his desire. In fact, at the time I did not know what sex was all about, but what I remembered was this was not right.

At that time, I did not know that that was an offence or I could have asked for help, maybe professional counselling. In fact, I was so afraid that had I disclosed this matter, the result would have been sure deportation—straight back to the West Indies. I did not want to return home to continue the same lifestyle.

The fear was almost unbearable and could have certainly pushed me over the edge to suicide. Being naïve, I believed that by keeping quiet and wishing that bad experience away, nothing would happen and I would be ok! Well, that fear and anxiety went on for months. The only constant companion was morning sickness. Still, I did not have the slightest idea what was the matter with me. When I learned that I was pregnant and it was either the baby or my nurses training, it was such a momentous decision.

And the anger kept building up, and up, to almost boiling point. Many times I blamed everyone and everything I could possibly point fingers at for my dilemma.

If I had been travelling on an airplane this could have been avoided. If my parents did not have so many kids and gave me more attention and guidance, I would better able to protect myself. Maybe travelling on a different boat, date, year or even another time would have averted this awful violent act.

I have become a bit older and certainly a tad wiser about life. I know that anytime was the right time for those cruel people to pounce on whomever they could turn into their easy target. From that day onwards, I had absolutely nothing to call my own. My nursing career was my own, but in a different way. What was my own was my virginity and the baby boy.

I had to battle with many negative feelings, from loss of control over my life to low self-esteem and lack of self-confidence. It happened so many times that I lost count. Honestly, I said to myself, "I am no longer a virgin." I was very proud of my prized possession—my virginity. That was my greatest personal loss. I simply did not care what happened to me at that moment.

Critical Thoughts

The negative thoughts and feelings that used to pester me still come, but they are not powerful enough to cause me pain or uneasiness. This unfortunate part of my life will never disappear, so I have learned to live with it by addressing any negative feelings that surface from time to time.

How different the world has become since making peace with myself. The world presented as a place where all is not dark. I thought the sun had turned its back on me in one of my darkest moments. I was wrong. It still washes me with its friendly warmth. Even the trees are waving and bowing their branches as if to welcome me to this potentially new world. Like music, the various birds are singing in an international choir, which sounds beautiful.

As the inner peace seeped into me, I knew eventually I would be okay. I would survive the raging storms of life, and thus I wrote this letter to my abusers, in particular, the one on the boat, to release those feelings of anger I had carried with me for such a long time.

A Letter I Wrote to My Abusers

Friday, September 29, 2000

At this stage of my life, my policy is to return merchandise to its rightful owner. This is exactly what I am doing.

In 1966 when I left Trinidad at the age of 21 years, I was travelling up to England to carve out a life for myself, but you shattered the dream, hope and the little self-confidence or faith I had in myself.

You were not invited, enticed, encouraged or accepted in my cabin. In fact, you forced your way in. The worst part of all this was I did not know, like or give you a second look—you could well not have been there, it would not have made the least difference to me.

When you invited yourself into my cabin, I remembered what you did. I was forced to lie on the floor, and with brute force—no match for you—you raped me, more than once. At that time I was almost unaware of what was really happening to me. I knew that something was not right. That was definitely not my style of behaviour.

My sexual education was almost nil, but my gut told me that there was something out of place here. This was not good. I had no one to complain to or talk with. I had to live with all that fear, anxiety, pain and emotional turmoil for a long time—34 years.

I want you to know that because of the rape, the result was an unwanted pregnancy, which ended in a back-street abortion. Had I continued with that pregnancy, that child would have been the object of your vicious deeds. Instead, that child was killed at an early age of 12 to 16 weeks old. That was not what I wanted in my life. Not to be a murderer of an infant.

I had no resources to look after myself, never mind a child. I did not see the use of bringing an innocent individual into this horrible world—one that includes people like you. Even for me, it has been a lifetime of sheer hell.

You have occupied a large part in my mind. It was definitely not because I had even a trace of passion or any good feelings about you. I just wanted to get even with you. Something surprising happened to me. I immigrated to Canada. Maybe I was destined to live here in Canada. Maybe this was God's way of protecting me from you. Now the space you lived, rent-free, in my head is gone.

Today, although this was the hardest letter for me to write, it is also the most inspirational piece of work I have and will ever do in my lifetime. I no longer fear, hate, despise or even plan to kill you. Believe me, that was exactly what my plans were. I changed my mind about taking the life of an evil person like you. I felt I could do much better. Instead, I asked myself, "why not use that energy wisely and nurture the person I was born to become?"

Oh, how I pity you. Probably you are still in the same heartless frame of mind, just looking for the next helpless and weak prey who you can pounce on. Like a hungry vulture just waiting to feed on the unprotected. What a way to live!

With professional help, I have moved on in a remarkable way. You have given me a gift—which you would have no idea about. With all the agony that you have caused in my life, instead of me using it to hurt myself, as I did for some years, I have turned them into priceless positive resources to help other human beings learn how to become valuable members of the community.

As for me, that was one of the mental anguishes, the major one that pushed me to make poor choices. If I did not have an understanding husband, your violent action against me could have cost me my marriage—or most importantly, my life. There was always someone who stood by my side—even in the most difficult circumstances. Why did I live? What gave me the energy, hope and willpower to go on? Where did the insight and wisdom come from to show me that I would be wasting my time, energy and life just because of your pitiless act?

My return policy is this. Today, I have sent to you all that pain, hurt, agony, fear, feeling of uselessness, anxiety and any negative thoughts you have caused that occupied my mind. You have sprinkled unbelievable amounts of emotional, mental, social and physical negative seeds in my mind. That was exactly what you did. They belong to you; they are yours to keep—not mine.

Today, I add one more thing to the long strong list of positive qualities that I have been so fortunate and so blessed with, instead of looking for revenge.

Lastly, I want you to know that I am living a happy and peaceful life and no longer chained to the negative emotions you helped to create.

Chapter 34: Soulmate

I was 21 years old when I left Trinidad, I had had enough of instructions and rules about how I should or should not behave to last a generation. I had little or no say in what happened to me, so getting away from an "authoritarian-type" upbringing was liberating. Some individuals, such as my parents and others in my community, dictated what they thought was best for me. Many times I asked myself, "Who am I?" Was I to change my personality to please others? I became confused and doubted even my own name. I was convinced that a new country would be the answer. I could not wait to see this new land.

When I went to England, I had no idea how I ought to look or feel. I desperately sought to find myself. It was about this time that I found something that helped lull me into a false sense of security and belonging. The bottle became my 'friend.' I was ignorant about when that first fertile seed was planted or how it germinated, but by goodness, I knew how it came to fruition. When I consumed alcohol, I found the world did not consume me. For a while it seemed a place where I could hide and not face up to reality. It was in England when the problem first began, then it continued to haunt me when we moved to Canada.

Alcohol became my soulmate. It was a place I could go to drown out all my troubles: in obliviousness to unpleasantness.

I had heard so many tales from die-hard drinkers about what alcohol is or is not. The best scientists in Canada might find it arduous to prove. Others, such as members of my congregation in Trinidad, said that people who drink so much are not Christians.

Another thing I was led to believe was that the substance that triggers addiction is found in our genes. I am swayed by this theory based on the research of The National Centre on Addiction and Substance Abuse (CASA). * It made no reference about being affiliated with any religion.

For me, as the saying goes, "I had been there, bought the t-shirt, and thanked my Creator I am still here." Whatever the reason this complicated situation dragged me into, I felt I was in hell. If that is what that particular place is, excuse me, I really do not want to go there again. That was not what I would call enjoyment.

I have no idea how I got myself in such anguish. I tried to retrace my steps to see if I could come up with my own justification but without any clear answers. As a child or even a young adult, I rarely saw alcohol consumed in our household. Apart from my father having a celebratory drink on payday with our farm employees, the only other occasion that I had remembered was having the tiniest taste of alcohol around Christmastime. The amount that was served, at least to me, was not even enough to make a toddler drowsy, it was just a little sip. That's all. So how did I end up being in the company of this substance that nearly killed me? I am still wondering.

The first time I had any real encounter with alcohol was many years after I arrived in England. When I was doing my nursing training, I learned that risk factors include psychological factors, stress, and environmental influences.

If this is true, then the assessment could apply to me for several reasons. Then again, it could be argued that it might not be the same for everybody. One size does not fit all. Why do some individuals seemingly carry huge burdens, yet not get tangled up in the web of alcohol?

I had problems, but I did not know what to call them, and I had neither the knowledge nor the skills to address these foreign occurrences. Even if I was able to contact a sympathetic counsellor, I had absolutely no idea how to present my problems. Sporadically, questions came and went as quickly as flicking an electric switch on and off. I'd ask myself, "What is my purpose and why am I on this planet?" There were no answers to either, so I continued on my uncontrolled uncertain course with absolutely nothing healthy to comfort me during those cloudy days and long nights.

As early as I could remember, something carried me through difficult times. Whether I called it luck, fluke or chance, I doubted if these things happened on a regular basis. It had to be more—a lot more. What that something or invisible being was, I simply did not know, but whatever it was, it had been working very long hours on my behalf. I had only myself to care for—no family as yet—and that helped to relieve some of the stress weighing heavily on my shoulders.

Triggers

I never knew what this word meant. I did not realize how past hurts could come back and bother me again. The triggers seemed much more subtle and brought back more painful feelings. Oh, how I wished I had someone to confide in then.

What happened to me many years ago, I had to grin and bear it alone. And that was what I did. Instead of grinning, I stuffed it into the back of my mind, hoping the pain would die a sudden death. That hope was far from the truth. Instead of abrupt death, these things seem to thrive like mushrooms pouncing like a ferocious animal. There were times when those negative thoughts felt like a stranglehold. I do not suffer from panic attacks, but the nerve-wracking dreads sent a cold shiver down my spine. Then I found something.

First Real Drink

I was introduced to a posh, golden-coloured, bubbly alcoholic drink sold in slender bottles. It was regarded as a ladies' drink. I did not consume it on a daily basis—only on weekends, mostly Saturdays or when I was off work. In fact, it was almost part of a tradition to enjoy a drink in celebration of my hard work, examination success, to fight frustration or any number of reasons, and there were many.

I heard that any mood-altering substance, including alcohol, could really dim one's judgment, alter perception, and cloud what is real and what is not. For me, I was okay with whatever alcohol was capable of doing to me. At least for that seemingly brief period, I felt liberated. Who would be so silly as to give up that nice, consoling, and 'who-cares' feeling to bother about the effects of booze? Don't get me wrong; I was not in the state of oblivion, just at the contented and mellowed state. Anyway, my rationale was that if it was good for ladies, it was certainly better for me.

In those days, the people I worked with shared stories of their drinking and dodging work, including having no clue how they got back home. These tales were shared with enthusiasm, pride and joviality in our hospital nurses' communal sitting room. How did staff keep track of numerous sick calls? Did they use a shopping list and stroke off excuses used? I thought to myself, "My boozing habits were uninteresting compared to this group." I thought they should take hold and improve their unhealthy habits. I pledged not to become one of those people. While I was finding fault with others, I glimpsed a small part of myself.

While I was living in England, the pub scene was not unusual. It was a place to mingle and have fun. The people who often gave this so-called expert advice desperately needed it themselves. Yet in their minds, rightly or wrongly, they imparted their knowledge with excitement and persuasion. Although I had been to pubs a few times, they were not my 'thing.' I preferred to drink in the comfort of my own home. It was like saying, "Who needs any other human being when I have booze?"

As I look back on those years now, I can easily connect the dots leading to potential problems with far reaching consequences. The same way people build positive habits, the same might be true with negative and unhealthy ones, one pillar at a time, only those might not be as intentional. I had promised myself that I would never be as weak as "those people" who could not control their alcohol consumption. Someone once said to me, "An alcohol abuser was an unkempt, down-and-out, jobless person who has lost almost everything, including her or himself, and in fact, barely hanging on." By comparison, I thought I was okay and in the clear.

Although the amount of alcohol I drank slowly increased, I was still able to function reasonably well to both work and look after my family. I had to pay attention not to give my habits away by indulging too much. There were some small unaccountable gaps in my days. Where did the time go? The days changed to months, and soon the year ended. At times, I was almost convinced that thieves were swiping my time. This could not possibly be the case, since I was functioning, I was not missing days at work, and I was coping with everyday chores and experiencing no vile hangovers. With all those things still intact, I could not possibly be called a heavy drinker. Times were good, but not for too long. Infrequently, for whatever reason, I began to feel too tired to go to work and so I took a well-deserved day off.

University of Essex
After Issah, applied to the University of Essex, Engineering Department in England, we received the long awaited news of his acceptance. We were both pleased and started making plans for his departure. He lived in residence and came home every few weeks because his school was a long way from home. Alcohol helped me to suppress lonely moments while he was away.

By then our first son, Halim, was in junior grade, his brother, Isif, was a little chap of about two years old. Money was tight and we had none to pay for childcare, so I resigned from my regular job to care for the boys. I had spare time, in fact, too much. It was time to find another bigger house for our growing family. I volunteered for the job.

After leaving my younger son in my friend's care, I accompanied his brother to his junior school and set off on my house-hunting quest. The days were long, exhausting and also extremely challenging. I did not mind the sacrifice because Issah and I decided it would benefit our children. Our primary goal was to secure a home free of garbage and infestation by critters. Also, I believed that having a home in a better neighbourhood would give the boys better educational opportunities.

The description stated in the sales office flyer of the first house I visited did not in any way match the property that I viewed. Although our living quarters were less than ideal, I was still in for some surprises. That home I viewed, in my mind, was similar to our present pest-ridden lodging. Although I did not see any creatures, I suspected the condition of the place as perfect for those critters to thrive.

When we bought our first home, the excitement of a cleaner place was too much to keep to myself. Others who had been living in similar circumstances might have thought we were bragging. Truly, this news deserved celebrating, so the only other person, apart from Issah—who was away, to confide in was another form of alcohol. As long as I had alcohol, being alone and looking after the boys did not bother me greatly.

When I was a little girl back in Trinidad, some people in my community had believed that a small amount of this special tonic wine helped warm and strengthen the blood, specifically in the elderly. Now as an adult, I remembered those words and said, "If a small amount of wine is good for older people, surely it should be even better for someone in her 30s." My view about this medicinal 'Holy Grail' was etched and remained in my brain for many years.

Celebration

I cannot recall ever screwing my nose up at the taste of this tonic wine. It was as if we were meant to meet. Something magical happened during my first introduction to that drink. It was impossible to put those inner feelings into words. I felt warm, confident, good—really good—and I thought, "This is it." That huge sack of worries that I had been dragging around for so many years had suddenly shrunk, or perhaps it was that alcohol had started to cloud my thought processes.

This time the irrational part of my brain convinced me that the labelling was wrong, nevertheless, I should buy a bottle to strengthen my weary body, my happy heart, and just in case, my weak blood supply. I recalled feeling an extraordinary pleasure radiating from the top of my head toward the soles of my feet. It felt like pure joy. Whatever it was called, I loved it, and I wanted more of it—forever. We became friends, extremely good friend in a relatively short time, maybe too quickly.

The drink took on a human-like character; it did not judge or ridicule but made me feel unique. Now, the wine was my cure for everything, from physical tiredness, mental woes such as agitation, angry spells, and sleep problems too. In fact, I just had to name the real or imaginary issues and it was the chosen remedy.

Getting the tonic wine safely from shop to home wasn't hard, but the difficulty I encountered was how to fund this practice. My income was low and even though a bottle of wine was cheap, it still made 'a hole in my pocket.'

Contradictory Instructions

I felt torn between two incongruous voices—the realistic thinking one saying, "You do not need alcohol to celebrate your achievements" while the other shouted, "You deserve this modest reward." There's no need to guess the winner of the argument.

Another point that swayed my decision to buy wine was that nice comforting radiance I experienced, years ago, after drinking the tonic wine. I called it my "reward." Yes, that compensation was unquestionably strong. I felt like Maria in "The Sound of Music," singing, skipping, and swinging my bottle, instead of a guitar.

At times, I experienced those marvellous feelings just thinking about alcohol without even having a single sip. On my short walk to shop, innovative ideas came to me, that maybe the manufacturer was wrong about that tonic wine. By the time I stepped into the shop, I was convinced that that company was wrong. I have no scientific evidence to prove it, I just knew it! The only evidence I had were the words "Wine is good to warm and strengthen the blood" that I heard as a young gullible child from local folks.

This was how I finally swayed myself in one long rambling thought. I deserved a celebration; after all, I had endured long, stressful and tiring days of house hunting, and any human being merited encouragement. A pat on the back or some kind words were not enough, I needed a stronger reward, something with a "zip" that would warm my belly and make me say, "Yes, Yes, Yes!"

God, it felt so good, so reassuring and relaxing. Unexpectedly, the whole wide world seemed wonderful and rose coloured. Who cared about troubles? Not me! After my introduction, I thought I ought to behave like a lady, and started having small measures in small glasses, and then larger amounts in bigger glasses, but eventually, pouring drinks into glasses was too time-consuming, so I moved to the bottle-to-the-mouth method, and without realizing it, the amount of booze dwindled significantly.

Start of Behavioural Changes
My brain started acting like two separate parts. One side pushed me to have one more "shot," while the other side was saying "enough." These voices did not initially appear like flashes of lightning but were more subtle and elusive. I asked myself from time to time, "Why was I not taking notice of these warnings?" Before alcohol, I can't remember any 'strange' thoughts. I knew I should stop drinking when I saw one object appearing as a double, or when I had to close one eye to focus. Surely, these were not natural happenings. Or were they? To be brutally honest, I thought everyone encountered something similar. For lack of a proper name, I

called them "peculiar" and so those peculiarities continued with almost every type of alcohol I drank.

Then my brain continued sending me more convincing messages, such as people who were having drinking problems probably needed to change to a better brand, and I did. So naturally, I switched my intoxicating fluid. The 'unusual' feeling was still there.

Was this another way of avoiding the truth, or was I hiding my head in the sand, hoping my unhealthy behaviour would vanish into thin air? To add to what was already going on, I started to find hundreds of reasons to support my habit; you name it and I thought about it. They ranged from raising two boys to illness in the family, working long and stressful hours. The most important reason of all was 'absolutely no good reason.' I just loved the effect and how it made me feel. I knew this fix was only temporary, but it was better than nothing.

I have heard people say they do not like that "tipsy feeling." I didn't agree. I thought those people had to be crazy to utter such words. What's wrong with them? Don't they know they are missing the best part of life?

Since I became an acquaintance with the tonic wine and other alcoholic beverages, other things changed too. I simply could not stop thinking about the fun that alcohol provided. Just as when the three witches in Macbeth asked, "When shall we three meet again?" I too enquired, but there were only two of us. I answered, "Anytime."

Our neighbourhood store was only a short walk from our house. It was not only the walk to the wine shop that excited me, but also visualizing those rich, red and gold bottles of magical fluid. I simply was not concerned whether that was fact or fiction; they were the cure.

During this time, I still managed my role as mother, wife, and employee, in spite of my habit. As alcohol took priority, I pushed other things to 'the back burner.' Although my drinking had picked up, I was totally blind to what I had actually done to myself. Probably I was too busy looking at others to see Grace. I have heard that sometimes when a person is too busy meddling into others' business they completely miss what is going on under their own nose. So, while I was looking at others' circumstances, mine slowly went down the drain. I noticed the misunderstandings, anger and reduced communication that was happening in my own family, and so I felt that I must reduce my consumption for those reasons. My husband never mentioned my drinking and my children were too young to understand.

Searching Questions

I managed to ease off on alcohol for two very important reasons; I was on my own while my husband was away at school, and my two little boys depended on me for protection and care. It was difficult to completely give up drinking, but I did manage to drastically reduce my consumption. Often times the question kept repeating itself, "Why do I have to have alcohol to get through the day?" I wondered if others engaged in similar conduct? I have heard people called derogatory names like "spaced out, wasted and smashed, or under the spell." And these were the better terms. Luckily I was never called those not-very-nice-names, at least not to my face, but in my head I knew, while I drank secretively at home. Just like a small crack in a piece of glass that spreads, so was my alcohol use. Unless I admitted having a problem or was under excessive pressure, why should I change? My mantra was 'no problems,' therefore, no changes needed.

Because I was not the owner of an automobile or legally holding a license, there was no chance of getting in trouble for impaired driving, so in a way I felt indirectly protected and assisted. Another saying I heard was, "God protected the innocent and the fool." Maybe he also kept watch on those who guzzled copious amounts of alcohol, too. Deep in my soul, each time I looked at my supply, a tiny something—my conscience—began to bother me, but to stifle it, I came upon a novel idea. I hid my booze so that I would forget about it. I would not call it clever, but just trying to appease others and myself.

Now my focus was on two things, acquiring and hiding. Also, the same way I had increased the amount I drank, with time, I also increased its potency. Just as children graduate from one grade to another, I also graduated from wine, to a combination of wine and tonic wine to whiskey. Initially, I detested this disgusting stuff and thought How could anyone like this? Within the blink of an eye, I soon acquired a taste for it. I came not to like, but to love it.

I could almost still feel the heat from the "fire water" as it slowly wound its way from my lips to my stomach, and branched out to my entire body. It gave me a happy, carefree, powerful, and 'all-will-be-well' type of self-confidence. Who in his or her own right mind would not want to relish this joy now and forever? What an amazing feeling. The fear of whatever the universe wanted to throw at me was now gone. "Bring it on," I daringly said. It felt as if I was practically changing into a superhuman. This feeling occurred gradually with most types of drinks, but almost always when I consumed whiskey. These changes went on and something else soon added to my puzzling behaviour. Just like a heat-seeking missile searching out its target, my brain was checking out where I could find a 'pick-me-upper.'

Although I was in that same leaky boat, the strange thing was that I started resenting other drinkers who acted out with inappropriate behaviour. While my accusing pointing index finger rested, my brain took over the accusing role using the most demeaning and ludicrous names I knew of. They sounded good, so I used them. Why? I wondered. And so I asked myself what behaviours or characteristics I resented in those individuals?

Years ago, I heard these words, "We dislike others because we see too much of ourselves in their behaviour." I was beginning to think these words might be true. To keep out of disagreements, I had to work hard to keep my thoughts, actions and, yes, my unrestricted speeches under cover.

During my relationship with dear friend, booze, fewer and fewer things bothered me. He was as cool as cucumber, not oppositional. Alcohol did not dictate or boss me about but was simply there to follow my command. I was certain that our budding admiration would be as in a traditional marriage vow, "till death do us part." Tell me, who would not like to be in such company?

Red Flags

I knew nothing about the long-range characteristics of this mood-altering substance. During our courting phase of our relationship, I was seeing the world through "rose coloured glasses"; my glass half–full, when in fact it was nearly empty.

There were red flags—small ones—then within a short time they seemed to change. I paid them no mind and was convinced I was still in charge. Was I living in an authentic or fantasy world? Problems, slowly but surely, were beginning to show their ugly faces, and now shame was added to insecurity in my relationship with others. When I was invited to other peoples' home, the first thing I wanted to know was whether they drank or not. If they drank, then I was certain to have a drink or two to prime myself before leaving home, but the teetotalers were another thing entirely. As far as I was concerned, that was incomprehensible. How could anyone function or even get through the day without a drink.

Most of those times there was no one to stop me. The boys were too small to realize what was happening to their mother, and their dad was far away from the situation. When he came home for short breaks, I would try to smarten up, and tried very hard to behave as "regular people." How were real people supposed to behave? I had no answer. I decided to go cold turkey to prove to myself that I was still in control. Abstinence proved hard; I thought I was going to die. It was as if my brain was saying, "Hurry up woman, I want my fix." I was desperate. Guarding my supply was no easy job either.

While all these things were going on, that tiny voice reminded me to "stay away from the demon." It felt like I needed some supernatural force to help me keep my head above water. If I let my guard down I would surely disappear forever. As a stay-at-home-mom, I'd had a lot of time to indulge in this detrimental but gratifying habit.

I had never had any legal problems and felt quite proud, almost cocky proud of that. Still, I empathized for those unlucky souls who were stopped, arrested, and led to the jailhouse. I used to think they were reckless, ridiculous and should be more responsible to avoid the mighty hands of the law. The same way I looked down on and passed judgment on other drinkers, I was now passing that same ruling on myself. "Me, sent to jail?" Never!

I frequently reminded myself that I would never allow this to happen, and I vowed to be a responsible drinker. But there were more red flags, more odd things to add to the rest. Now I was starting to miss chunks of time. I'd ask myself, "How I got from one room to the other," or occasionally, "How did I get into my night outfit?" Memory loss, no; I was too young to have messed-up memory.

Husband Returned Home

Issah had finished his studies, returned home, and got a permanent full-time job at the University of Liverpool, England. I had mixed feelings about his return, because it would put a huge wrench in my drinking habit. I was worried—no anxious—about my relationship with my comrade, alcohol. What should I do? My drinking plans would need revising, I needed to find a way to work around this problem, and so I made changes to the time, type and amount of alcohol that I consumed.

Planning was key. As long as I consumed a certain amount of alcohol and gave it enough time to work itself out of my system, I believed I would be okay. This was my dilemma. How much is a certain amount? How much time is long enough? I had questions, but no answers.

Dodging the Alcohol Whiff

I recalled my pub lessons on the art of dodging alcohol smell. Some expert drinkers thought some brands of alcohol smelled more than others. I soon realized that the more drinks poured and handed out, and the nearer the clock ticked towards midnight, the lessons became even more ridiculous.

My limited bar knowledge convinced me that what most of those people were talking about was rubbish. That information must have sounded ludicrous when even I could see the foolishness in them. Still, I hung onto their theory about spirits and wine odour. The same way I had learned about the developmental process of the human body from the villagers in Trinidad, so too I was learning about alcohol from the "substance experts"—the pub patrons.

Professional drinkers said that red and white wine reeked less and, stiff drinks, such as whiskey, gin, and vodka, were the real giveaway. I took that part of the pub goers' knowledge as 'gospel truth.' After all, I figured they were knowledgeable in this field and knew what they were saying.

And so I severed ties with spirits and picked up my old romance—a concoction of wine plus the tonic wine. Boy, I had completely forgotten how this combination was a real 'kicker.' I would challenge anyone who said I was not a wine expert; after all, I successfully mixed two different drinks and was able to generate a carefree mood twice as nice. I did not see any angels flapping their white wings, nor did I view the pearly gates, but it might as well be heaven. What a marvellous feeling!

My spouse made no remarks or gave away the slightest clue about my drinking, so I presumed he was still 'in the dark' or perhaps he was collecting data about my drinking to use as ammunition. My husband was not an emotionally driven guy who talked simply to hear his voice; he loved to prove his point with facts and figures. He uttered not a single word, and that worried me because if he were to spread his evidence sheet on the table, I would surely be pinned tightly in the corner unable to talk my way out.

Occasionally, when we bought alcohol, I displayed a nonchalant attitude, but inside I was jumping for joy as if meeting a long lost, loving friend. I had not touched, poured, or put any of their contents to my lips yet; I was only looking at the shiny metal can or the white or red liquid in the bottle. I could genuinely say that not many things gave me such expected happiness. I wished that pesky unsettling voice that said "Be careful" would go away, forever. I had to find a way to avoid it. Those little red flags stood fixed and refused to retreat.

Alcohol was persistently in the forefront of my thoughts, it was impossible to get it out; I focused on it from sunrise to sunset. It took precedence, unfortunately, even over my loved ones. My sons and my husband were forced to take a backseat. I really thought my behaviour was normal, but on assessment nothing about it was normal, not my thoughts, not my words or my actions. I asked myself yet another question, why would someone concentrate so strongly, twenty-four hours a day, seven days a week, on booze? I silenced that thought with another drink. I still did not know how to get off that slippery path.

Chapter 35: Crossing That Invisible Line

In early 1988, I was temporarily distracted from alcohol because we were preparing to immigrate to Canada. Our sons were still in junior school and I did not have a regular job yet. I was grateful to clean my next door neighbour's house for a few dollars which I used partly to supplement my family's grocery bills and the rest for my own use. Alcohol was not too expensive, and even if it was, I was sure to find a way to pay for it.

If the prospect of moving to England from Trinidad was a big step, this move to Canada was far bigger because I now had a husband and children to consider.

After a few months in Canada, Issah reminded me I was a qualified nurse and should consider challenging the Canadian nursing exams. I followed his advice and studied, wrote the exams and was successful. I then applied for a job and was accepted at our local hospital. With my own bank account, I had more money to spend on whatever I chose. I thought I was progressing in the world; I had a paid job and was able to graduate from cheap low-grade wine and imitation champagne to better and more expensive brands.

Liquor brands were new to me, and so I had no idea what I was looking for; the labels made absolutely no sense. My only guide was the price. Looking back, I realize I could have paid top dollars for a bottle of cheap cooking wine and would have been no wiser. I listened carefully to the names other customers were using and used those same names, including French brands that I still cannot pronounce. Nevertheless, just paying for a bottle of fancy wine was exciting. I wanted part of something bigger and those extra dollars made my ego grow so big that I was afraid at any moment it was going to pop like a balloon.

I knew all was not well with me because I had gone beyond that mark that separated social drinking and having a serious problem with drinking. I cannot say exactly when this happened. Was it when I progressed from the wine concoction and then to whiskey? Was it when a few drinks were not enough? Or was it when I was forced to close one eye to focus on the road, since I now had a driver's license too? What I knew for sure was that alcohol had become challenging, controlling, demanding, and it pushed me to increase my consumption.

Negativity
I knew my behaviour was wrong because I felt ashamed. But not enough to make me cut ties with alcohol. I thought it was probably that little voice masquerading as shame. There was no escape. When I started my 'drinking career,' I felt I hurt no one else, not even myself, as though my sense of right and wrong was nonexistent. To me, all I did was have one or two drinks at the end of a long stressful day and who could argue with that?

The only problem was that a drink or two soon became much more, and because I refused to count them, I couldn't tell the exact number. This is the best way I could explain my relationship with alcohol; it felt as though the alcohol was a magnet, and I was the metal. The more I focused on it, the more it seemed to draw me to it. Eventually there came a point when that magnetic pull was so strong, my endurance was no match. Then my commanding brain demanded only one thing: that I bend under its force, and I drink, and drink, and drink some more. Then I'd swear I must say 'no more.'

I could not understand how a relatively small amount of fluid could have such extraordinary power over me. Many times I vowed I would drink maybe at 8 p.m. like "regular" people. But that promise did not last long. I was smashed out of my mind before those words were spoken. Then I tried, and tried, and tried to stop, but the result was always the same. After those disappointing episodes, I felt disgusted and reassured myself that there would be changes next time. I would not give in. I would beat those feelings and win. As the days and years went by, and I changed the lyrics, I still had the same old chorus. I was a nervous wreck living constantly in high gear with a fearful mind. I was frightened of being found out, of having to stop drinking and living without alcohol.

Anxiety sat heavy in the pit of my stomach if my family unknowingly stood near the vicinity of my "stock." I hid my supply in dark-coloured bottles, under folded clothing in my drawers, in the garage, and my favourite place, under my bed, for early morning access. When I thought it was threatened in any way, I panicked.

Lonesome

One of the best and happiest times during my period of drinking was being alone. I used to convince myself that this was simply because I loved my own company. Much later I learned this particular behaviour is called isolation. What do the professionals know? I just wanted to be left alone to enjoy a few shots and drive away any bothersome issues, but that did not materialize, because when I woke up, the things that I thought would vanish were not only still there but were also gigantic and intimidating, taunting me saying, "What are you going to do now?"

Losing Control

I needed more alcohol to generate those same happy, relaxed, and powerful feelings. My control seemed to be quickly slipping away. For a long time, I felt sure I was at the helm and in charge. Not now. Not anymore. Alcohol had become my master and I his servant. It led to drinking more frequently, far more than I wanted to, and in dangerous situations even where it could have dire consequences, and when I really did not want to drink.

I questioned myself if I was gradually, but unquestionably, turning into a die-hard drinker, who might one day end up in the "slammer." I saw those red flags waving faster and higher, a stern warning that I was indeed on a slippery slope. I knew what was happening, but I took no notice and said, "That will never happen to me." Who was I fooling? I may try to fool the whole world, but I knew I could never fool myself. Some people would call this way of living as spiralling out of control, denial or living in a fool's paradise. My unique circle would term it "having a good time." Good time? It was more like slipping into a bottomless pit.

Scheming Habits

Comparing myself to others in the same dismal situation made me felt better for two reasons: I could pity them and say to myself, "I am not that bad." Most importantly it was a way to avoid looking, really looking, at Grace. It was so much easier to judge others and at the same time secretly look for ingenious ways to hide my alcohol, whether in the laundry room, under beds, and the back of drawers to spread my supply for easy access.

I changed supermarkets to have a wider choice of drinks, or so I thought, but the main reason was to avoid running into my neighbours. Covering my tracks was almost like working two full-time jobs together. I knew in my heart that I was not being honest. Then, when Issah and I visited the wine shop together, I would purchase those dark-coloured bottles so that when I poured a measure—a generous measure—it would not be easily missed.

Although strong drinks such as whiskey or gin were easy to dilute, to a certain point, my heart rate still spiked every time I conducted my novel chemistry experiment. I had no recipe so I was concerned about the dilution result. How would I explain my action if I am found out? But my worst fear of all was the snowball effect; one probing question that led to another and another.

I believe that the same voice that comforted and guided me in trying times seemed now to be almost screaming "careful." Maybe I could not truly comprehend that I was travelling down a destructive path. The more I indulged in self-defeating conducts, the more I felt as though I was slowly suffocating.

Why could I not have seen the troubles in the road ahead? Maybe I did, but still wanted that comfort, even if it was false. Even if I wanted to disconnect, this 'thing' was so strong that it rendered me helpless.

Obtaining liquor got easier because I found another shop only a stone's throw from our house and next-door to the local supermarket. In my mind, how much luckier could I be, to have a wine shop almost on my doorstep? At that time no one could have swayed me otherwise. I was positive this wine shop was strategically placed with the grocery shop as my alibi. I was elated, while lacking any deep joy and peace. One side of my brain said one thing, and the other justified why I should drink. If I was not meant to drink, then why would a wine shop be planted nearly in my doorway? On the other hand, it was easy.

Memory Loss
Now I had an added thing to keep tightly under cover, and that was memory recall. I started to forget where I put my keys or what I did a few hours or days ago. The worst thing was wondering if the people around me—family and neighbours—knew about my double standard and my buying and hiding my stock, and then not being able to find the darn things.

What would its replacement be? I did not have to think hard to find the answer. As my drinking continued, I perceived that alcohol did a lot for me; it gave me some power and control I had never known. It helped me to forget hurts, and made me feel grand—almost better than my fellow human beings. Also, it convinced me that as long as we were loyal companions, all would be well and I did not need anyone else. How could I not believe in this stuff? And I did just that—I lived in my own little world. To me, it was as if I was just having some peaceful time. But if I was really having serene times, why should it be punctuated by shame, guilt and conniving activities that felt like a rock in the pit of my stomach? I certainly did not think those feelings were natural.

Perplexed Thinking
One day I sat and said these words, "Truthfully, I do not know what is happening." On one side I wanted to recover from this way of living, but on the other, I was not prepared to relinquish alcohol. Although I knew I was on a critical path, I was too fearful of giving up what I had known for a long time.

After all, I had established a fairly intimate relationship with the substance, and even though it had started becoming problematic, it still helped me, or so I thought. To put it bluntly, I was fearful of failure but more petrified of success. How could I survive without it? I did not want to live with it anymore, but I didn't think I could live without it either. While these words might sound totally insane, in my mind they made absolute sense. This was exactly how I felt driven by alcohol. What a way to live!"

Family Problems
Problems spilled over, and my relationship with Issah was crumbling. I observed a gradual intolerance towards me. "What is the matter with him?" I mumbled under my breath. Probably he was feeling unwell. My husband had a quiet and not easily disturbed temperament. This time he was not only rattled, but also irritated and angry with me. He screwed up his face and wrinkled his forehead before uttering a single word.

Issah was always tender hearted towards the children. Situations that previously did not bother him, such as when the boys were playing and laughing loudly, now got on his nerves. My husband liked to cook, puttering around in the kitchen. Eventually, he served a tasty "no name" dish for dinner. Because of his frustration, saucepan lids would clang; dishes slammed on the counter and with that, no one, certainly not me, would chance entering the kitchen. When I was required to communicate on important family issues, I used words sparingly, but apart from that, I kept to myself.

Bombshell

For a long time, I considered myself an undercover expert, but I was in for a big shock. Once there was peace in our home, but now there was a significant change in family attitudes towards me. I pretended to be happy and reassured myself that I'd be left alone to carry on, but I was wrong.

One evening my husband and the boys prepared a tasty meal—nothing too grand, just ordinary. The atmosphere at the dinner table was so comfortable that I felt uncomfortable. My senses told me that something unusual was about to happen, the 'calm before the storm,' and it was indeed a storm. We sat, ate, talked and laughed casually as a family.

The children delighted in sharing, as usual, about teachers and buddies, and how they spent recess and mealtimes. They asked for new rain boots because it might be muddy on their upcoming trip to the local farmyard.

Family Meeting

After we had eaten our meal and the dishes were cleared away, Issah announced that we were going to have a family meeting. The kitchen countertop was filled with dirty dishes, but we had a more pressing topic. I knew what that meant. In our household, a family meeting was always about very important issues. I was quite sure of the subject matter.

We took our seats. The boys, about age 12 and 15, took up similar positions, one on either side of their dad. The last time we had a similar meeting, we were excited, because it was about us immigrating to Canada. This time was different though; an ominous cloud hovered above, and I did not feel energized. I felt unprotected, tense, and almost nauseous. Even though I knew I was in 'hot water,' still I wished I could sneak out to have some liquid courage. What a crazy thought.

As stated before, my husband worked with facts—plain and simple facts. The meeting started and everyone else seemed calm. In truth, I would have preferred a darn good argument, pitching a few objects through the air in their direction to deflect the subject. But no, my husband was far too skillful to engage in tactics that would only defeat the purpose of the gathering.

As any efficient facilitator, Issah opened the meeting, stating its purpose. My stomach gave an involuntary contraction and I wanted to throw up. He said to me, "We have been concerned about you for a long time." After the statement, there they came, a list of facts.

"We observed how your personality started to change, that your hands appeared to tremble most of the time. You looked very sad, drawn and stressed, and there were visible signs of weight loss, not eating properly and sleeping at night." He continued, "You are not taking care of your personal hygiene as evident by lack of frequent change of clothing and strong body odour."

While all this talk was going on, I was thinking, "Odour? What the hell was that?"

He said, "It was the boys, Isif and Halim, who pressed for the meeting and had also insisted they be present.

I realized then that not only my family, but also possibly more people, knew about my substance abuse. I failed to hear or appreciate their concerns, and their pledges to help me in any way possible as well as their unconditional love. Tears were running down their cheeks, almost enough to fill a bucket.

After our meeting, the only thing I thought about was how appallingly they had treated me, how they flung the doors wide open to my drinking problem. And the comment," I was stinking." That was impossible. [After all, even if I did not bath or shower frequently, I used heavy quantity of my perfume.] I failed to appreciate their pledges to help me in any way possible. Their sadness was as clear as day even though I could not accept those pleas.

Identity

If I gave up drinking, I would have to change my ways, but abstinence? What's that? It meant no liquor at all. Impossible! These words added more uneasiness to an already difficult and complicated situation. Up until that point, I had never met anyone 'hooked' on alcohol who lived long enough to share the story of sobriety. However, I had been to a few funerals where cause of death was reported as alcohol abuse, either by motor vehicle accident, a major health problem, such as cirrhosis of the liver, or by suicide. These funerals partially shifted my thoughts. I understood those things in my head, but I knew I had to feel them in my heart to make a meaningful shift. I desperately wanted independence.

Two obstacles stood before me, the first, no strategic plans on how to unshackle myself, the second and bigger hurdle was trepidation. It felt like I was sitting on one side of a vast ocean and wishing something better on the other side, but how was I to get there? I was a slave fettered to master Alcohol and wishing for freedom.

These two opposing forces sat on my shoulders: an angel with white outstretched wings warning me of imminent pitfalls, the other that black scoundrel—alcohol—beckoning me to come closer, have more alcohol, and ignore the consequences. Unquestionably, I was no match for these forces.

In spite of all that, I continued to drink and I took on an even less compassionate turn. Buying my children's school lunches became the latest excuse. No one would suspect whether my trip was to buy food or wine. I would tell my family and myself that I was going grocery shopping to buy the children's school lunches.

By the time I walked across the parking lot, everything had changed for the worse; I had completely forgotten the main purpose of my trip. Groceries took a backseat; I felt only a tiny stab of guilt, but I simply elbowed it away as if to say "Don't hassle me, and mind your own business." Later, fewer and fewer things bothered me, and alcohol effectively stifled them.

Research

I was not computer savvy, but by some mysterious means I managed to Google the words "alcohol abuse" and this is what I learned. According the National Center on Addiction and Substance Abuse at Columbia University (CASA), "Addiction is a complex disease often chronic in nature and affects the structure of the brain. "

"That's all! Glad it's not fatal" I muttered. That answer did not console me.

I looked at another website link www.helpguide. Org/articles/addiction/drug-abuse and addiction. It talked about the possible signs and symptoms of alcohol abuse—feeling guilty or shameful about drinking, hiding your drinking habits, friends or family members who are worried about your drinking, if you need a drink in order to relax, feel better, and also "black outs," and forgetting what you did when you were drinking.

Chronic brain involvement, again! That worried me. I did not want to end up as a 'vegetable' just able to breathe. These sites could not have described my plight any clearer.

It was written in black and white. I read only a few pages, but even those short readings showed me my behaviour in relationship to alcohol. Although my brain was still stupefied from too much alcohol, a few things jumped out and truly scared me. It basically spoke about how alcohol sometimes slowly strips away almost everything including the deepest part of who you are.

"Nonsense!" I shouted, and clicked off the computer.

I felt that I still had something to protect—the final fragment of unravelling dignity—and even that was rapidly disappearing. Not convinced, a few days later I looked at the third site. In my mind, I thought those two previous sites might have had errors, but how could three separate sites be wrong? Were the people snoozing who were hired to write this report? Wouldn't anyone correct it? Impossible!

When I really had the courage to open my eyes and look more closely at the signs and symptoms of alcohol abuse, I realized all three sites stated the same thing. I had gone too far.

That Invisible Line

Regardless of my belief in the research, somehow I had crossed from social to heavy to abusive drinking. I knew there'd been a shift for the worse. Initially I drank mostly to feel good, relax, and reduce stress; but later I did not need a reason to drink. I just did it. My consumption level could be compared to a run-away train—out of control. It was no longer giving me that gratified "Oh, be joyful feeling." And those darn morning 'heebie-jeebies' made me feel like a baby's rattle, so sitting on my hands was the best way to steady then. Man, I was irritable, jumpy and quivering like an aspen leaf.

Holding a full glass of liquid was out of the question, half or quarter full was barely manageable. My stomach felt like a raging sea determined to turn itself inside out. A short regular rest was vital to preserving my energy.

Suddenly, during those unpleasant symptoms, I remembered the remedy was just an arm's length away. I was too unsteady to just lean over the side of the bed to reach what was under my bed, and so I got out and sat on the floor and grabbed hold of my cool smooth bottle. When the liquid hit my palate, it was like bliss. Or was it sheer ecstasy? I could neither understand nor care about alcohol's damaging effect. For the time being, all I wanted was the shaking, sweating and dry heaves to stop.

I was lost, unable to see any guiding light in that profound, dark maze. I sat down, elbows on knees and hung my head in despair. What would become of my family, in particular my children? The same inconsistent thoughts surfaced again, I do not want to continue drinking, but I cannot live without it. If this is not inner mayhem, then what is? By now alcohol had taken me on a wild goose chase, down the wrong side of the road. It seduced, controlled, and duped me.

Full-blown Family Arguments
While my mind was trying to convince me that things were not so bad, all hell broke loose at home, again.

Issah stop mincing his words and those irritations became full-blown heated arguments. He said, "Grace, you have been drinking for a long time. It has to stop, because you cannot look after yourself or the children."

I was angry. "What are you talking about?"

"You know full well what I am talking about," he said.

"You have been buying and sneaking alcohol into the house. And you seem to focus a lot of your time on it."

He'd found part of my precious stash and banged a bottle down on the kitchen table.

I was tempted to say, "Be careful," but I thought it wise to hold my peace.

Until now I thought I was the world's best squirrel, cautiously hiding my supply, but not anymore. I felt more trapped than during the meeting. Surely, I could find other ways to safely keep my booze hidden from those three sets of interfering eyes.

As expected, our relationship was poor, communications on essential matters were reduced to mere trickles; the laughter we once enjoyed was now only a faded memory.

Closeness
Intimacy and sex, oh that? It was not a topic to dwell on, so I waved it away, just as I did when faced with disquieting situations. I chose alcohol because I simply wanted to stay as far away as possible from others for self-protection. If I drank in the evening, Issah would smell my breath and know. But he had known after all. Could someone tell me how I could be

affectionate when anger, irritation and hangovers occupied most of the day? Thoughts of sex came to my mind, but that seemed like more work than my safeguard, alcohol.

Children's Reaction

My children's reactions were brutal. They understood what was happening and were vocal—even more than their dad. They were the longest sharpest thorn in my side because their words went much deeper into my soul. Those youngsters were determined and ready for another confrontation. They did not buy into my nonsense. They stood strong with no intention of backing down. The unwavering looks, erect body, and staring me square in my eyes while speaking, told me one thing, that they were up for the challenge.

Several times they said, "This is not our mom, you are changing into something else, you do not look or smell good, you smell of alcohol and stale perfume."

Although I felt that my personal hygiene was insignificant, I applied liberal daubs of deodorant, generous squirts of perfume, followed by gulps of mouthwash, completing my body spring-cleaning routine. So how could I be accused of smelling bad? My sons used facts, just as their dad did, to accurately report what they were seeing. Inwardly I was almost screaming for them to turn their words down, but I knew even if I did, the situation would become more explosive. This was one of those times I regretted encouraging them to speak up when they were unhappy about something— and they were doing just that.

The best time to go on a binge was an hour or two after the boys left for school. I reckoned that would be long enough to receive any phone calls from the school.

Initially, my drinking was lady-like, or so I believed, but later I was too impatient to pour the stuff from the bottle to the glass—it took too long—so I tilted my head back and gulped a few mouthfuls straight from the bottle. Yes, gulped!

Consequently, my midmorning was "half in the bag." When I came to my senses I shook my head, stopped, listened and looked up and around to re-orient to the real world of time, place, and date. That was not easy. By the time I salvaged a sliver of composure, my boys were at our front door, key turning in the lock, swinging the door open and they walked into the hallway after school. They'd take one look at me.

They scrutinized me, and their expressions suddenly changed, then came that dreaded question. Almost in unison they yelled, "Mom, have you been drinking, again?"

"No," I said."

"Mom, don't lie, we can see how you look and how you are speaking. That is not you. We knew our mom. You are turning into something else. Mom, you going to drink yourself to death?"

How much clearer could they be? Emotionally, it felt like a blow. For the rest of that evening and next morning, I cowered. I felt like a mischievous dog and kept a low profile until my family left for school and work. Oddly, the more my family pointed out my unhealthy behaviour, the less notice I paid and guzzled more. In my mind, I felt insulted and I completely ignored how my actions were affecting them.

Their words touched only a tiny part of my heart, but even hearing them did not make me try to change my behaviour. By next day, it was as if nothing had happened and no words were spoken about it. It was as if every word, every sad facial expression and every pleading question was forgotten. Then I'd gripe, "If only my family would amend their ways, things might be better."

Turmoil was the most appropriate word I could use to describe what was happening. My family's patience and respect towards me grew thinner, and irritation and anger culminated in numerous heated family arguments, simply looking at what alcohol was doing to me. I couldn't see it.

Son's Prayer
One day my oldest son said to me, "Mom, I have been praying for something bad to happen to you, so that something good will come out of it."

The only thing I could think was, what a bad boy.

Then it happened! As I was driving my son to his football practice, I went the opposite direction on a one-way street. As expected, traffic was heavy at the end of the day with people heading home to their loved ones. My judgement was poor. I had told myself I was okay to drive, even after having drunk for most of the day. We started out, and I had to close one eye to focus on the road. In fact, my vision was blurry. Halim took hold of the steering wheel, trying to steer the car into a nearby garage parking lot, almost hitting anything on wheels. He stopped the car.

He shouted, "Mom, you were going up the wrong way." When I finally looked at him, I saw the fear in his face.

He must have imagined the result. Something went off in my head, "What if...? Vehicles stayed away from me, and others swerved to prevent a pile-up. A cacophony of horns sounded. To this day, I am unsure how we got home. I think my son might have driven. That might have been the supposed answer to my son's prayer, except that once I realized the danger, I knew that I might have hurt or killed both of us.

The second answer to my son's prayer was unlike the first in my memory. Even my short-term memory began to play mischievous tricks on me. When I could not find my drinks, I decided to try abstinence, but I felt as though I was dying. It felt horrid and I vowed never to make another sacrifice like that again.

School Guidance Counsellor
One morning after yet another particularly heated argument, Halim said what was on his mind, "I am going to speak with my school guidance counsellor."

He indeed asked to see a social worker, for the next time he spoke to me, he said, "I want to live elsewhere, but I will not leave my brother here. I will take him with me."

When he said those words "Child and Family Services," I felt as though I had been kicked in my gut by a horse. Perhaps I was getting resistant, because I did not feel as badly as when my son confronted me later that day when he and his brother returned from school.

Bargaining sounded like an easy escape, so I promised if he changed his plan, I would stop. This young man was not going to fall for my bargaining trickery. I had made many promises before that had never materialized. He looked at me as if to say, "Woman, I am no fool."

Secretly, I was hoping that my son's words were simply idle threats. Wrong again. Not too long after that serious row, he came home from school with news I did not care to hear, but listened to anyhow.

His words were strong, precise, and with a stern look. He said, "Mom, this morning I met and spoke with a guidance counsellor. I told her everything that was happening at home; how my dad is ill, you are drinking a lot of alcohol and about all the rows in our family. She told me that she would talk with the principal and get back to me as soon as possible.

This time I called him not bad, but a "wicked boy." On top of the threat of losing my children, had I failed to recognize my husband's illness while I drank and drank?

I can laugh (now), long after the fact because it reminded me of a scene in the movie, "O Brother, Where Art Thou?" As the sheriff's men and their hounds were at the heels of a group of fugitives, one of them decided to repent and be baptized. That was me trying to squirm out of another 'hot seat.'

Chapter 36: Husband Unwell

In 1989, my family situation moved to the worst possible scenario—the fear of losing my sons, and perhaps Issah to a potentially fatal illness, and now, a domineering and demanding "soul mate," alcohol. In spite of the challenges this presented, I continued in my job.

The irregular generalized discomfort Issah had complained of had turned into lower limb pains with general weakness. His favourite activities—walking and running—required more effort. The symptoms were getting so intense that one morning while on his usual trek, he was too weary to walk back home, consequently he had to catch a ride in a horse and buggy with one of our local compassionate Mennonite families. I knew all was not well with my husband for he was in pain, weak, and had started to lose weight, although I knew he was not dieting.

Doctor's Visit

Issah visited our family doctor and told him of his symptoms and pain. The doctor ordered multiple diagnostic tests. We were familiar with some of them, but others I did not recognize.

Our physician was a gentle, caring and diplomatic man, yet his facial expression and body language gave nothing away. He spoke to us for a long time, explained the test results, and answered numerous questions, careful not to put a label on the collective test results. He said, "Mr. Ibrahima, I am concerned with the results and would like to make a referral to the blood specialists."

The appointment to see the expert came much quicker than our family doctor's. I asked myself, Why are these appointments happening so fast? Would Issah need such a referral? No one needed to tell me. I knew. The words, "blood specialist," bounced around in my head like bingo balls. In spite of what was going on in our family, it became clearer that

I needed to continue in my job in case I eventually become the sole breadwinner.

Issah drove to the specialist's office where I met him after my shift. We walked into the lobby, took the elevator up to the third floor and stepped out. I looked around to familiarize myself and did not like the ambince of the room. Was it me, or was it concern about the results? If Issah's blood levels were just low, why did they not try a course of supplementary vitamins and iron? Why was he in a room with others who looked sallow, anemic and so frail?

A handful of individuals sat near the door in all sorts of worrying poses, covering their faces with their hands, grabbing tightly to the chair arms when they stood, and groaning when they tried to stand or walk. This situation stirred something within me. They resembled patients on the palliative unit where I worked. Could determination reverse the progression of whatever this "thing" was? If it took only willpower to halt the tide, then Issah might have a fairly good chance of healing himself. In spite of seeing all these signs, I was still in doubt, or perhaps it was denial.

The most disquieting conversation going on in my head was that maybe not too long ago, these individuals in the waiting room had enjoyed healthy and productive lives, but I wondered how they had reached this point, where they were barely able to stand or walk?

I observed the change in my husband's demeanour after our first doctor's visit. It was as if he was saying, "This illness might well be part, but not all, of me. I am prepared to give it a good fight."

As a health employee, I presumed I would be less saddened by what I saw than my husband, but I was mistaken. I was not only thinking about my husband's diagnosis, but also hundreds of other things—the distance, location of, and transportation to treatment, as well as his body's response to aggressive chemicals and his reduced abilities and reactions if he were unable to fully function as head of our household. I was also concerned how it would affect me.

Patients' Conversation
The conversation in the waiting area took on a common theme of disease outcome. Information was floating fast and freely, with one person trying to outdo the next with their situation, and even comical stories. In spite of their sad situation, these people still saw something to laugh about. While we waited to be called, I tried to dismiss the onslaught of questions circulating in my mind, but it was almost impossible.

At times laughter interrupted my sadness. The subject changed to who was not doing well, passing on, and who would be the next fatality. I wanted to clamp my hands tightly over my ears and shout, "Stop, stop! I do not wish to hear another word about passing, or passing over. When that final moment comes, then we would face it like everyone else." To me, those terms meant only one thing. Just as those villagers turned into "overnight medical professionals" and the pub's regulars posed as "liquor experts," this group was doing the same thing in predicting illness outcomes. It seemed bizarre.

Crossroads
With family discord raging like a storm, and now news of their dad's diagnosis, and later my likely role as head of the household, I thought about how the boys would react. Would they disapprove?

I had to sincerely ask myself, "What was my personal crossroad?" I had to decide for myself what it would be. Was I prepared to go down that desolate byway that would lead me to sure destruction? Although alcohol occupied most of my thoughts, at home and at work, I found it impossible to cut ties and be alone. But was I really alone, or was that my perception? Truth be told, I made a conscious effort to isolate myself, because then I could wallow in my self-indulgence, also there would be fewer people to disturb my drinking.

With a myriad of things swirling around in my head, I felt tightness in my chest, that's all, no other symptoms. I made an instantaneous diagnosis of heart attack. I remembered how strong emotions such as fear and anxiety could mimic a heart ailment, and so I was reassured.

The Trial

We waited and waited. From the moment Issah started to feel unwell to the moment we sat in the doctor's office waiting room, it felt like a trial. The judge—the health professional—would pen his final signature on the bottom of the paper, stamp it in bold black letters, and finally we'd hear the thud of the gavel on the lectern. The final verdict—the diagnosis—would be read. My mind was like a seesaw and I often questioned what I should believe. More importantly, what should I not believe? I still refused to acknowledge our situation.

A tall self-assured gentleman, with jet-black hair and clad in snow-white lab coat, quietly opened the door. A lady, presumably a patient, walked out. Whatever the news, her bright eyes, smiling face and the spring in her step made her look as though she was ready to do 'a happy dance.' I almost hated her for being happy. The same white-coated man called out, "Mr. Ibrahima."

My husband answered, rose cautiously from his seat and we followed the man to his office. He closed the door, shook our hands and introduced himself as Dr. D. We also introduced ourselves.

Dr. D. tried to break the ice, engaging us in conversation about our jobs, the children, and how we were settling in our new country after about fourteen months. I did not care much for all these trivialities; I only wanted to get to the importance of our visit, that of hearing my husband's test results. I felt frustrated and wanted to shout, "Get on with it, man!"

A bulky beige-coloured folder sat on his dark brown shiny desk. My heart gave an uncomfortable flutter. The doctor slowly opened the folder, looked at the first page, probably rechecking personal information, and then he started.

"Mr. Ibrahima, I have received almost all of your tests results. Some were fairly good, others were marginal, but a few gave me cause for concern. The group that was borderline and concerning would need to be treated, if that is your wish."

He briefly discussed the treatment plans.

Perhaps he thought the bad news was enough for us to comprehend. We had ample time to ask questions, receive appropriate answers and to express our thoughts.

My husband's first question was, "What is the significance of the results? Is it cancer?"

The doctor replied, "I am sorry, yes, it is cancer of the bone marrow that negatively affects red blood cell production."

We knew that it was serious and no more questions were as important as this one, but now we needed information about the treatment plan, how the cancer might progress, and what the prognosis might be. I felt dazed and numb. My husband looked shell shocked. The doctor gave us a pile of related literature, a prescription, and detailed instructions on how to use the medication. He also asked us to make an appointment for the following week, which we did, and then we filled the prescription with heavy hearts. We shed some tears and hugged each other, then walked hesitantly to the parking lot, got into our individual vehicles and headed home.

I cannot remember seeing the familiar scenery, the houses, gardens or trees along the way, but what I clearly recalled was a motorist blasting his vehicle horn at me, like the day I drove up the wrong way on that one-way street. I was annoyed and in my head, I scolded the impatient drivers. Then I came to my senses and knew what I had done. I had driven through the red traffic light at a busy intersection.

I was unsure which incident generated the strongest emotion, the news about my husband, or the possibility of being involved in a near fatal accident. I said 'nearly' because the drivers who had the right of way had swerved to prevent injury and possible fatalities. Man, I did not stop at the scene.

Those reprimanding horns told me the drivers were furious for putting them in such a dangerous situation. So just like my father's wayward, bad-tempered bull, back in Trinidad, I, too, hightailed it and drove home trembling and scared. Our family had enough grieving to work through so I kept this incident to myself. It was only when peace and harmony started to return that I related that experience to my family. They were amazed at my reaction but happy I was alive to tell the story.

Living Out the Predicted Time
Later, as I began to write my story, it was two years after Issah's diagnosis. We felt cautiously optimistic that his weekly, then biweekly medical assessments showed slight improvement. It was almost impossible to forget the doctor's words, "Five years maximum." One of the few times I could forget my husband's possible shortened life span was if I kept my body and mind occupied. I could not keep physically and mentally busy all the time; after all, I needed some down time to unwind and rejuvenate, but even though those times were scarce.

During the tumult, words could not describe the exhaustion I felt. Frequently my brain felt saturated as though it were about to explode like an over-inflated balloon. I wished I could have taken my brain out, recharged and replaced it with new wiring like an electrical appliance, to ease the tension in my head. This might sound bizarre, but that was exactly how it felt.

Comparing
I may not be as unique as I thought since most things that happen to us, such as family discord and making unwise or unsafe decisions, happened to others as well as. My circumstances could not have sunk any lower, nevertheless, I

felt good comparing myself to previous drinking associates. I had not been arrested, charged, or handcuffed, and ultimately led to jail. Had I already forgotten my traffic violation, and blaming my compromised behaviours on a tree branch for hiding the road sign?

I have heard two particular sayings, "People in glass houses should not throw stones," and "When you are pointing one finger at others, three more are pointing back at you." Nowadays I do believe these wise words.

Chapter 37: Edge of Possible Change

One day I had reached an absolute breaking point and could not stop. A part of me was saying that I was engaging in risky behaviour and that something would happen, and the other side counteracted that caution by saying, "I had been drinking for a long time and nothing really bad happened." The latter voice won the argument that day, and so I continued on. How could I have envisaged what was to happen? I tried and tried; the more I tried, the more I drank.

Suspicious Thoughts
The wine started to disappear more quickly than before. My suspicious thinking joined forces with previous feelings of shame and guilt. I wondered if the wine bottle had a hole in it, or if the stuff evaporated from their containers. Or, maybe an unseen spirit helped itself to my wine. I never saw any clue to prove my doubt, but I believed that all these things were against me. While the contents of the bottles diminished, my personality continued to change, and I felt like a chameleon that modifies its colour to blend in with its environment. In my case, it was to suit my craving.

All areas of my life were shattered. Mental anguish added to its physical counterpart. I felt like things crawled on and under my skin. I was convinced that I saw creepy-crawlies scrambling up our beige painted walls and that neighbours were chitchatting about me. Was this a sixth sense? I did not know what it meant to be a spiritual person. Was it connected to spirituality or a voodoo medium? I was disinterested. Financially, our budget had been stretched beyond its capacity with no way of cutting back; I had to get money somewhere to support my demanding habit.

Contemplating Easy Money
I was so desperate for money to support my addiction that I even considered entering the sex trade. What was crucial, at

least in my mind, was to keep fighting to hold my tattered dignity together at all cost. After careful consideration, I declined that risky idea.

At that particular demoralizing phase, questions kept surfacing as to how I thought I came into being; was it coincidental or planned? I was convinced that even Mother Earth would be reluctant to receive my lifeless body. How much worse could it get? As I penned these words, I shook my head and smiled in disbelief at my unreasonable perception. I had lost sight of the countless blessings for which I should have been tremendously grateful.

I imagined I was rather a spectacle, looking like death warmed over, binging, with a strong body odour toned down by a lavish portion of perfume and wanting to go in the sex trade. Seriously? What was I thinking? I compared my thoughts and actions to a pendulum, swinging erratically from reasonable to unreasonable. A couple of sunrises and sunsets evaded me during a lengthy binge. When I eventually came to, there was a fleeting moment of lucidness, and I was scheduled to go to work. I showed up, but only in person. On reflection, I saw the working of my muddled unreasonable mind.

According to www.brown.educ/.../alcohol & your body, in general, the liver can process one ounce of liquor (or one standard drink) in one hour. If that was true, then why would I believe if I stopped drinking at 3:00 a.m. that my body would have metabolized all the alcohol by the time I reported for work at 7:00 a.m. I was mistaken. Alcohol had stripped me of almost everything and now it marched shamelessly into my workplace, exposing my last secret.

The eleven to thirteen city traffic lights from our home to my job meant nothing to me. I tried to recall whether they were actually there, or only a figment of my imagination, or if they'd been installed many months later. Later as I drove along the streets, I noticed mature plants and established patches of grass around weather-beaten light poles, indicating they'd been there for years, perhaps before my arrival in Canada.

Planning My Final Farewell

The previous week I had started planning my final exit out of this uncompromising world. I checked schedules, paid special attention to the dose and action of the operating room anaesthetic medications. Dosage was the key factor—I needed to have enough. I did not want an abortive attempt; failure was simply not in my vocabulary. I had a plan to take my own life.

Usually, I loved working on the unit with our clients and listening to their incredible stories. For some unknown reason, my assignment was changed to the triage-assessment area. There were no clients under my care in the obstetrics area, and those who were in active labour were transferred to the appropriate unit, while others were given guidelines and discharged. I was slated for second lunch so I had some spare time.

Slowly, I made my way to the far side of the triage room with high plain glass windows stretched from one end to the other. Even though I was looking through the glass, absolutely nothing interested me; I felt emotionless.

Truthfully, what I was doing was making peace with myself and saying farewell to a harsh world. Then something strange happened. I heard footsteps behind me; maybe I had a new client. I turned around. I was wrong. Our unit Chief followed me, the distance between us was getting shorter.

He said, "Grace," and asked, "How are you doing?"

I tried hard to disguise my sadness, but before I had time to say a hasty "okay," uncontrollable tears flowed down my cheeks like a river. He closed the door, and we sat at the admissions desk, me wailing like a broken-hearted lover, and him watching and patiently waiting until I exhausted my tears. He started a casual conversation inquiring about my job and family. Through this lengthy chat, I still recall his meaningful statement, "Grace, you got to do what you got to do." I thought he was referring to seeking help for my heavy drinking. His words kept repeating in my mind, "Grace, you got to do what you got to do."

Suspension, April 14, 1993
Not too long after that conversation, I "pushed the envelope" a tad too far. My managers confronted me, accused me of alcohol smell on my breath and suspended me from my job. I was convinced that everyone was picking on me, and I told the authority what I was thinking.

It was ugly. Really ugly! It was too late to save what was left of my already skimpy self-respect. I refused to hear or appreciate all the encouragement, including that my job would be kept open, and that I could take whatever time I needed for treatment. Additionally, my employer offered to cover all my expenses to the Homewood Addiction Treatment Centre, and they guaranteed confidentiality and emotional support.

Suspended! That was the only topic I was focusing on. I heard none of the rest and I felt disgraced. Reluctantly, I went home and complained to my dear husband, but he did not buy into my fabricated accusation.

"If you had been drinking, the managers took the appropriate steps to protect the people under your care," he said.

I hated him for speaking the truth. When my husband left for work that day, and the children were at school, I sat on that cozy emotional pity pot and I had, what I believed, to be my last drink. I knew this time I was surrounded, and all four walls came crashing down.

Contemplation
After receiving the suspension, I wondered what to do? Should I or should I not accept my hospital's offer? As I contemplated my decision, I heard the lid of our metallic letterbox closing. I opened the door and peeked, and looked around for the all clear. I didn't want my neighbours to see me now. I dashed out, opened the mailbox and grabbed whatever was there. It

was an envelope bearing the hospital's name and logo. My gut gave an involuntary contraction; I was sure what this was about. I felt as though I'd pass out.

For some mysterious reason, Issah was at home instead of at work. He entered the room and inquired about the envelope I was holding. I opened and quickly perused it then handed it to him. He read it. Our eyes locked, the quietness in the room was deafening.

The letter, dated May 14th, 1993:

Dear Grace,

Further to our meeting of May 3, 1993, this will confirm that we are unable to allow you to continue to work due to the incident on April 18th, 1993, in which you reported to work with alcohol on your breath and subsequently were sent home.

We have considered the extenuating circumstances in your personal life and in consideration of this, we are prepared to defer a final decision on your employment status on condition that you successfully complete a program as outlined below. In recognition of this we are prepared to suspend you without pay.

In order for you to return to work the Hospital requires that you must enter and successfully complete an appropriate treatment program at a facility of the Hospital's choosing. The program will be paid for by the Hospital. Please contact Occupational Health & Safety at any time for a referral.

Should you successfully complete the program, we will be pleased to reinstate you into a part-time position.

We will continue to assess the situation on a monthly basis through Occupational Health &

Safety and will meet with you again in three (3) months to further review your employment status.

In accordance with the Health Disciplines Act R.S.O., 1980, Chapter 196, Section 84 (1) (b), RE: Physical and Mental Incapacity, I will be advising the College of Nurses of my concerns and actions to date. It is my intention to send copies to the College of Nurses of the quarterly reviews. Please contact me if you have any questions,

Sincerely,
Director of Nursing

Issah looked astonished, sad and sorry. And I felt humiliated once more; secretly wishing the earth would open up and swallow me. Later, I carefully read the letter and experienced intense anger.

"They could stick their letter and report me to the college," I said. I did not care. I was prepared to quit my job, so what was there to lose?

Reflection

This time, I used sheer willpower and was free of alcohol for a couple of weeks. During that time, I was less furious with my children, husband, and employer, alcohol, and anything else I could remember. It all started making more sense. My thoughts were much clearer and I could recall recent incidents. Grudgingly, I reread the letter and was petrified by its contents and by the magnitude of my actions while under the influence of alcohol. That incident could have been far worse. What had saved me from killing someone while impaired?

At first alcohol seemed fun; it made me feel happy, carefree, and superior to almost everyone else in this world. Then it turned against me, took me on chilling emotional rollercoaster rides, forced me to live in the isolation of my own mind. At the end it turned into a green-eyed, domineering monster, demanding that I drink even more whether I wanted to or not. I was certain that that quiet voice—whatever it was—still saved me from myself.

The day that I received the letter, I felt that this was just another bad day. I did not know what to do or where to turn. I thought about my two young sons and their ill dad. By this time my sons' role had changed to caregivers. My oldest son, Halim, was not only looking out for his younger brother but also dad and mom too. This realization made me feel incompetent as a mother and useless as a wife. Children should be just that—children—not forced to change to adults overnight. Had living in a dysfunctional home negatively affected all of us, especially the boys? I wondered if our children might have blamed themselves as contributors to our family's turbulence or questioned whether things would have been better had they behaved or acted in a certain way.

Again, I asked myself several questions concerning being created from odds and ends from a junk heap. If that were true, why would some Higher Power safeguard me in such hopeless situations for all those years? God does not make useless, worthless people; he carefully molded and valued all his children, including me. I am incomparable and unique, because no one looks like me, talks like me or walks like me. I am the only Grace.

Hospital Help

Eventually I accepted my hospital's assistance and agreed to an invitation to meet with senior managers from various departments. Those included human resources; occupational health and safety; patient–children and ambulatory services; obstetric chief; and of course, my unit manager. I felt embarrassed and remorseful for all the apprehension I had caused.

The meeting was constructive—much better than I envisioned. I was expecting to be judged and practically crucified, but that did not happen. The focus was on helping me to get back on my feet to start anew, not to humiliate me anymore than I had already done to myself. The best part about what I called the "High Power Meeting" was the kind-heartedness, compassion and unconditional love, plus they offered to help me navigate recovery. I was speechless. Did I feel unworthy to receive them? Yes, I did. I tried hard but was unsuccessful at holding back tears, which were tears of joy. Why had they treated me with such respect in spite of my conduct?

More moments of clarity came and I was convinced that I was not being criticized; it was the illness that they aggressively pursued. Until that time, I used to think that a person and his or her behaviour were the same, just as how I could not separate spirituality from religion. My belief is this: that a person remains pure and good, as at birth, but it is our individual habits that make us feel disgraced. As an example, I will always love my children, but not their obnoxious misbehaviour.

Part 4 ~ Recovery

"If you're walking down the right path and you're willing to keep walking, eventually you'll make progress."

Barack Obama

Chapter 38 - Accepting Help

Before I went to attend the program, the only thing I knew about Homewood was that it was an addiction treatment centre in Guelph. My heart was thumping so fast that I did not know what to do. My mind pictured the absolutely worst scenario. Would they lock me in a secluded room as was sometimes necessary in a mental health facility?

I could not stop the questions that kept going around in my head. In fact, it was only after I was admitted that I learned what the institution was all about. I did not like the mental health part, because I was not mentally ill.

Homewood

Homewood Health Centre, in Guelph, Ontario, offered services for adults who suffer from chemical addiction and concurrent psychiatric disorders. While I attended, the program was divided into three phases. Phase 1 involved assessment and stabilization, and Phase 2 offered recovery, fitness, recreation and spiritual guidance. Phase 3 worked on relapse prevention and problem-solving strategy for the patient to re-integrate into daily life.

The program included groups, lectures, and activities and was geared to achieving a healthy and balanced lifestyle, whether it was introduction to horticulture and getting your hands dirty or to start morning walks or a particular sport. It was almost impossible to be bored; there were so many enjoyable activities. Some of those activities that I started reluctantly during my Homewood stay remained a part of my life.

Preparing for Homewood

The night before I left home to go to Homewood, my family presented me with a beautiful arrangement of flowers. They cried. I cried. It felt like an absolute nightmare with weird and frightening panoramas running through my head. I felt as though I was being pulled in opposite directions, whether to go or not to go.

That evening I had promised an encouraging receptionist that I would come. I could still hear her reassuring voice. The next morning her voice seemed louder, but I desperately tried to convince myself to cancel this plan. I asked myself, "Who am I doing this for: my community, my employer, my family or for myself?" I believed, at the time, that I was forced to do this primarily for my employer and family. I suddenly developed a strong loathing for almost everyone, the hospital (my employer), my community, neighbours, sons, husband, and, yes, even people from my childhood days.

I blamed and despised them all for my sad situation. I hated them; I hated them all. Don't ask me what most of these innocent people had to do with my predicament. All I know was, it felt good to take the onus off myself and park the blame elsewhere.

In spite of the confusion, I woke up at 5:00 a.m. on the morning of my pending admission. I thought that the previous day had been one of the worst of my life. A mother, a wife, registered nurse, and me, a fairly new landed immigrant being admitted to hospital for alcohol abuse. I was strongly denying whether I ought to go. I told myself, "There is nothing wrong with me—at least today."

I thought if I were to use what I called 'distractions,' such as wearing my best clothing, jewelry and make-up that I occasionally used, I would present as a better put together woman. So I packed my suitcase with those items and more—

much more—and lugged it to my car. I was very upset. I went to say goodbye to my boys and my husband. Even though they appeared more distraught than me, I suspected they were comforted that I decided to get help. I could not take all the credit for seeking help; desperation and anguish played a big part.

Could I trust myself to drive safely to Guelph? Could I really concentrate clearly while I was feeling so sad? My biggest test that morning would be focusing on the road. I was not good at reading road maps, and when I looked at maps the four cardinal points appeared in the wrong direction. My family had offered to drive me there, but pride forced me to refuse their help. Surprisingly, I had absolutely no difficulty on my journey apart from trying to see the road through teary vision.

Arrival at Homewood
I arrived at my destination at 8:05 a.m. and parked in the designated space. I dragged myself around the courtyard at the back of a building, luggage and all, turned right and up a concrete paved sidewalk to the front door. And there it was in bold black letters, the Homewood sign.

I reported to the reception office, and guess who welcomed me? Yes, the same receptionist who I spoke with the previous evening. She was beaming as if seeing a long lost friend. After the usual brief pre-admission formality, she made a phone call.

My Nurse
The next person I saw was a pretty, petite, fair-haired, cheerful young lady who came almost bouncing down the hallway.

She introduced herself; "My name is Nurse Jennifer. My colleague, Nurse Carly, works opposite to me, and we will be your nurses for the duration of your stay."

I detested her instantly just because she was so pleasant, so bright, and me, so wretched. Because they worked together, they had to be cut from the same cloth, so I loathed her partner too, even though I had not met her. All the while we walked side by side down the long hallway, she spoke about how the organization did this and that until we came to the stairs. I didn't care about the information she was trying to pass on to me.

She held out her hand, pointing to the stairs on the left. By the time I reached the top of these stairs, plus approximately fifty to sixty before, I was exhausted.

We reached the top of the stairs, turned to the right along a short corridor and entered a room. The nurse continued prattling even while I was mumbling "uh-huh" and at best grunt sounds as when answering between closed lips. I thought, Woman, why don't you shut up?

I looked around and noticed a selection of familiar things as seen in a doctor's office, an examination couch draped with a white sheet, an anemic-looking solid-coloured folded gown, blood pressure machine secured to the wall, a weigh scale and stationery. I guessed that was the admission room. We sat in comfortable chairs.

My Temporary Home

After what seemed like hundreds of questions, we walked to the other side of the hallway and entered another room, number 214. That would be my home for twenty-eight days. I felt like a criminal, number 214.

The room was large, bright and spacious. My bed, neatly dressed in fall colours of orange, red, and brown, was placed just near the door. This was real. I thought I had spent my entire quota of tears, but I was wrong. I could not decide if the warm tears cascading down my cheeks signified relief from my hush-hush behaviours or if they represented plain and simple remorse. Whatever it was, this time the crying felt different, not gloomy, but more like I was releasing something.

My roommate was sitting comfortably on her bed. She smiled, shook my hand and introduced herself. She seemed friendly and willing to help me as much as possible, even though I found out later that her day's program was rather crammed.

My nurse briefly mentioned Homewood's history, geography, rules, and code of conduct including housekeeping business. She bombarded me with stacks and stacks of forms, leaflets, booklets and other information about my unit, Manor 2.

I felt exhausted from information overload and lack of food. It felt as though I had not eaten for years. I was angry at Homewood, all the nursing and medical staff I had met, those I had yet to meet, and anyone else I could think of. I thought of a suitable name for Nurse Jennifer and secretly nicknamed her "Nurse Cheerful."

My brain felt saturated. It was a struggle. I had to blink often to clear my vision as I unpacked my personal belongings and put them in their respective places. Then I flopped onto the bed and sighed.

I was glad to put that admission experience behind me, but just as my body started to relax, Nurse Cheerful came back, asked my roommate to give us privacy, and then she started to ask me more piercing questions related to my drinking. That same body that was calm only a short while ago did a full turn and became as tense as a coil. I answered in abrupt monosyllables "yes" and "no" and more "yes and no," cautiously guarding my intimate secrets. That nurse was a very good interviewer; she knew how to economize on words, asking open-ended and leading questions to gain the most information. She asked what seemed like another hundred questions. I detested her even more for probing to the foundation of my turbulent life. I almost told her to mind her own bloody business and leave me alone. Boy, she was determined to drag those answers right out of me 'by hook or by crook.'

When she had eventually finished her 'interrogation,' I was downright defeated. Now that the inquisition was over, I began to develop what I called an 'I-do-not-mind-you attitude' towards her. A tiny part of me sensed I was in the hands of compassionate professionals.

The wall clock gave one particularly loud tick, and we both looked up. It was already 11:40 a.m. Nurse Cheerful turned to me and said, "It's lunch time. I will accompany you to the dining room and introduce you to a few ladies." And my stomach growled noisily in agreement.

Dining Room

We walked slowly along the corridor, she merrily chatting away while I feeling annoyed and resentful towards her for having such good interviewing skills. As we walked through the door of the dining room, I looked around. On each table sat a beautiful vase of flowers plus some strategically placed around the room. It brought to mind a well-run establishment.

To satisfy my intense inquisitiveness, I felt them, when no one was looking, to be sure they were fresh, and they were. In addition to the blooms, the tables were adorned in fresh white linens, sparkling glasses, shiny cutlery and appealingly patterned crockery. I had never seen anything like it before. The staff members were dressed in crisp black and white uniforms.

The menu selection varied from a light lunch to a full meal. I enjoyed my lunch. Although my appetite was only 50 percent of my usual; it was much better than it had been for a long time.

During my brief 'chinwags' with other women, I learned that although the ladies' circumstances were different than mine, we nevertheless ended up in the same 'boat'—an addiction treatment facility.

I returned to my pleasant room, flopped on my bed hoping to catch a few winks, but I was not so lucky. My nurse was back.

She said, "Your doctor's appointment will be at 2:00 p.m." She added, "Please be prompt."

This doctor, according to the schedule, dealt with addictions. Well, this was the beginning of the end for me, having to cough up my whole life's history from the bottom to the top, plus my deepest darkest secrets, to yet another stranger. The good, the bad and ugly, would, for the first time, be openly placed on the table for all to see.

I felt suspicious of those Homewood folks now, and I formulated a plan deciding what I would tell and what parts I would keep close to my aching heart. If I were to tell all, they would surely judge or condemn me, just as I anticipated when I had to meet with my managers. Even though they didn't condemn me, still I felt that way.

My First Doctor's Meeting

My nurse and I walked down another long winding corridor, up some steep thick-carpeted stairs and into a pleasantly furnished room. The door was open and we walked in, and there I was, overwhelmed by the elegance. I could not help staring at the huge polished desk in the centre of the room, the glow so bright from the sunlight on it that I squinted.

It was like déja-vu, in the presence of a senior health staff, on the 'hot seat' again. I felt like a naughty child having to talk about dos and don'ts, rules and regulations. Our eyes eventually met, but until then I concentrated on the patterned carpet.

The doctor was a pleasant man with an easy smile, and me, I had almost forgotten how to smile. I do not know what was in his head. I certainly knew what was in mine. Don't think you are going to get a lot out of me, Mister, I reassured myself. While I was trying to sort out what I was going to say, I noticed something in this man's face that made me feel all would be well and we could work together for my benefit.

He extended a welcome, and with a firm handshake and smile he said, "Glad to see you, Grace. Please have a seat."

His casual conversation abruptly changed course to deeper and even more probing questions about my drinking history, even deeper than Nurse Cheerful's. I answered them all, not straightforwardly, but kind of, twisting some in my favour, skimmed over others, minimized a few and avoided many point-blank.

The man seemed to carefully listen to my story. While I was inventing my drinking rigmarole, the doctor sat patiently, then he changed position with his chin propped in his hands.

Confronted

The doctor's facial expression and body language plainly said what he was thinking, "Come again, Grace, do you think you're fooling me?" He asked many questions, but the one that detonated the fireworks was this, "Grace, how much and when did you have your last drink?"

I answered with as much conviction as I could muster, "I had a third of a glass of wine on Friday night."

Then he added, "And your breath smelled of alcohol when you reported for work on Sunday morning when you were suspended and sent home?"

"Yes," I said. And then it came, the fireworks.

"If you had that amount of alcohol on Friday night," he said, "there was absolutely no way you should have smelled of alcohol on Sunday morning." He went on to say, "I would encourage you to think about your answers when you see me again in two days. Honesty and open-mindedness are essential in recovery."

I was truly cornered. I was dealing with an addiction specialist who knew his job well. Basically, he implied that I was lying. I preferred using the milder term of denial. I shuffled out of his office, shoulders almost touching my ears, avoiding any interaction, and feeling even more defeated than when I was trampled by alcohol, and more than when I read that wretched hospital letter, or after my husband read it. Humiliation was so strong I wanted to crawl into a deep hole and stay there forever.

I asked myself, "How do I jump so often from the frying pan into the fire?" I was worried and could not relax for the next two days. As for sleep, I had only fitful naps. What was I going to say at my second interview?

What does he mean by honesty and open-mindedness? It had been a long time since I practised those qualities. Does he not know I was too busy acquiring, protecting, and covering up my shameful tracks to come anywhere near truthfulness? As for the latter, that might have been possible depending on what was in it for me. I have heard many times since then that it is difficult for substance users to be honest and open-minded because they usually lived in a state of denial.

Information
While I was stewing over my predicament, I attended the mandatory groups. Gosh, the information I was acquiring was coming so much and so fast that I found it intense. I learned that alcohol was not confined to any particular creed, race, profession, gender, or status, and that alcoholism is an illness, a mental illness. I also heard that if it's not treated, it could be fatal. Mental illness? Fatal? Really?

"But I am not mentally ill, besides, I am too young to die." I reassured myself of these things. I would never forget this extraordinary education.

Medical and Blood Work
The next day while I was nursing my wounded ego, my nurse reminded me, "It's time for your medical and blood work."

I walked down the hallway with her, feeling more shamefaced than before arriving at Homewood. The doctor's words played and replayed in my mind like a broken record. The next meeting would be the next day.

My Second Doctor's Meeting
This meeting generated as much, if not more, anxiety as the first because of the expected blood results in addition to our

unresolved first meeting. Still, I attended my second interview with the doctor, and by this time he had all my tests results. He said, "I am very pleased with your results, especially your liver enzymes. Your hemoglobin level was borderline."

I have heard this report many times, so I was not overly concerned about being marginally anemic. I was more pleased that the organ was working effectively. I almost shouted, "See, my liver analysis proves I was not at a dangerous point."

It was as if the doctor was reading my mind. "Although the other tests are normal, that does not mean that you have not been a heavy drinker," he said. And then he returned almost to the same point where he had stopped two evenings before— the fundamentals of recovery, of being honest and open-minded. "Without a complete history, we cannot prepare a personalized treatment plan for you."

I was even more irritated and wanted to shout at him, "Then just make me a half plan." I could not say that because there was almost no room for negotiating. My next best option was switching off while he was preaching to me. I started my own inner dialogue with the same committee in my brain that had encouraged me to keep drinking. Dude, in which world are you living? "Stop this trustworthiness and broad-mindedness nonsense, right now." I was uneasy. He was digging too deeply and soon he might reach forbidden areas in my life.

First Health Professional Meeting
As if the pressure on me was not enough, on the first day at Homewood, I attended my first mandatory Health Professional meeting. Well, well, well! I did not feel so alone. There were professionals from a cross-section of the health care field: medical, nursing, dental, and other allied groups. The meeting started with the 'Promises.'

The promises are almost a preamble: the benefits of following a 12-step program. Each member gave a brief introduction of how the week went and requested time as needed. This was an eye-opener for me, possibly the start of my new life.

I sat in the second to last row, hoping to be invisible, and praying that Dr. M, the facilitator, would forget I was there. At times I slid down the seat, made myself smaller and hid behind the bigger people in front of me. My request did not go up where I wanted it to go.

Soon after the group's house business had ended, the facilitator said, "This evening I would like us to welcome our newest member to our group, Grace." Until that time I really loved my name.

He looked past my human shields and settled his eyes on me, and so did the 30 to 40 inquisitive other pairs of eyes. He asked me to introduce myself.

Again. I wanted to scream. I am doubtful if repetition was part of the program strategy, but even if it was, I did not like it.

"Please, could you tell the group what crisis brought you to Homewood?"

I had a burning desire to correct him, crises not crisis. I decided against it. I felt nauseous with fright and as naked as a newborn babe. I was really in that 'hot seat' to tell it all from start to finish.

Before that gathering, I found out about the length and structure of these meetings from some old-timers. I also learned that members could and would challenge discrepancies in reported statements. In spite of those tips, my sixth sense said, You better not try to give any ambiguous tales, say it as it was.

My biggest obstacle was to tell the truth. Then I started, "I have been drinking for many years. It started with an occasional celebratory drink, then it continued as a way to relieve stresses, help with sleeplessness, and finally I could not stop. The major crisis came when I drank from Thursday to early Sunday morning. I reported to work at 7 a.m. and was confronted and accused of alcohol odour on my breath and was sent home."

I was too ashamed to say the word suspended. I felt as though some words and phrases were sticking in my throat as if trying to choke me. I paused a couple of times to centre myself and dabbed my eyes. I could see expressions of understanding, friendship, and encouragement directed at me, and I was pleasantly surprised that I was not beaten, judged, or ridiculed for my previous behaviours. This was the first time during my, what I call 'drinking career,' that I was encouraged and accepted for who I was, faults, fiascos, flaws, and all.

When I had finished speaking the facilitator said, "You are no longer alone," and the group joined in the chorus, "You are no longer alone."

While at Homewood, I heard a lot of encouraging words, but these were exceptional because I was profoundly touched. In spite of trepidation, I was glad I had finally done it.

The meeting continued for a couple of hours, as others in the group had told me. At the end, I was hugged—many times—and some members shared snippets of their own rocky journey. At that moment I no longer felt I was alone on life's lonely road, or on the periphery peeking in. As Anne Shirley, from Anne of Green Gables, by L.M. Montgomery would say, "Kindred spirits are not so scarce as I used to think. It's splendid to find out there are so many of them in the world." Would this truly be the start of my new existence? I wondered.

Chapter 39: The Light

After the meeting was over, I experienced contrasting emotions. I felt joyful and relieved for having shared in the group, and at the same time, I was uncomfortable in my own skin, because I was afraid of the success mentioned in the promises. Yes, I wanted a happier life, but this felt like too much too soon.

That evening, I enjoyed something new and extraordinary. It felt as though I was standing on the very pinnacle of the planet, arms flung wide open, and that I was floating on air and shouting, at least at that moment, for all to hear, "I am now walking in the light, no more darkness." Sharing my blackest secrets proved to be exhilarating! I couldn't find suitable words to describe what I felt.

My doctor's appointment was still pending. I was edgy but also excited about what might be in store for me. It had to be downhill from this day forward. What worse could possibly happen? Mind you, this was only my third of the twenty-eight day stay, but I felt so invigorated that I felt anything more would be virtually unbearable.

New Activities

Nurse Cheerful arrived and gave me a list of recommended activities scheduled to start the next morning. Recommended meant mandatory in Homewood's language.

Before being introduced to the Homewood facility, I had only one hobby—and it definitely was not walking. First came the one-mile walk each morning. This distance was marked clearly from point 'A' to point 'B.'

Our punishing walk ended at the peak of a moderately steep hill, where a time clock hung high in a tree. At this time, I was breathless, keeled over, and with my hands on my shin nursing intense fatigue from lack of exercise. I never thought I would make it all the way. We were required to take our radial pulse (at the wrist) for a full one-minute and record it in a special book in the auditorium. Initially, it was an effort completing the task, but after I'd done it a few times, it became a bit easier.

Praying and meditation came next. I was happy that the prayer was not to any particular being. We were encouraged, for the time, to use anything that represented the God of Our Understanding. I loved that concept because, to me, everyone's god is what he or she understands it to be. I called mine a Higher Power. I was comfortable with that choice because I believe that divine being is a power much greater than myself.

Journaling? What's that? I never knew what it was. In my mind I thought it involved writing a book each day. Later I learned it was simply jotting down my thoughts, feelings, actions, and reflecting on them.

"Reflecting? What is it?" I asked my nurse.

She said, "Thinking about what you might want to keep, improve or change in your life."

"Improve or change?" I asked. "Woman, that would involve almost all of me, save my name, the colour of my skin and hair texture."

She stared, as if seeing me for the first time. It was at this point, I believe, I—no we—had our first deep belly laugh. "You have already made a start by coming to Homewood," she said.

I really needed to hear that important reminder. Some of that nurse's words have stuck with me even to this day.

Next came horticulture, which I called gardening. Years ago, when I was required to go to the farm, I detested it, especially because the choice was not mine. Now, I enjoyed 'getting my hands dirty' for two main reasons: I had choices, and I liked being close to nature.

We also had the chance to learn lawn tennis, baseball and other sports. Can you imagine a woman, at the ripe old age of forty-eight, holding a racquet for the first time? I did try my hands at tennis. I felt free, relaxed and enjoyed some pretty good, and-not-so-good, serves and returns. Some returns were so good that the balls ended up in nearby courts, hitting trees and bouncing off in dense bushes.

When we rested between plays, we took the opportunity to appraise the staff and gave our opinion about how the program should be run, but we were careful to keep those views to ourselves.

My Third Doctor's Appointment

Back when I anticipated the first and the second appointment with this doctor, I was almost a nervous wreck. This time the meeting went much better; I felt more confident, probably because I had nothing to hide. I did my regular 'to-do things': morning hike, meditation, shower and ended with a healthy breakfast. With alcohol out of my system, plus the delicious enticing meals, my appetite was improving considerably.

My doctor visited me briefly after breakfast and gave me an appointment to see him that afternoon. My stomach gave another of its awkward flutters but nothing as bad as those knotting types I had experienced the week before.

Pity Party

My mood had fluctuated and continued that way since my encounter with that mind-altering 'stuff.' Sometimes, I felt like a motherless child living in a strange world and having no one to care about me. Then I'd get the 'poor me syndrome' and start feeling sorry for myself, wondering if my family cared about my plight.

I made several collect calls home and eventually spoke with Halim. He was tearful with joy to hear my voice, and then he began relating to me all the things he had been doing. He asked me hundreds of questions about the program, almost as many as those I'd answered during my admission. He said, "Dad is tired and asleep and Isif has gone to his baseball game. They would call me back later."

First 12-Step Meeting

The next day I phoned home again, but no one answered. That evening I walked with a group of clients to my first 12-step meeting at Delhi Recreation Centre. We talked about our individual circumstances that brought us to Homewood. I was surprised to hear that some individuals had been to more than one treatment facility. I thought this one was more than enough. Besides, I very much in doubt that my generous employer would dip into their pockets a second time. I also heard reasons for seeking treatment—to pacify others (family and employers) or to keep a relationship together.

The more stories I listened to, the more I could identify, because I had experienced most of what they shared and believed that I was in the right place.

The speaker's message was slightly different than mine; the bottom line was the same heart-tugging, shameful, hopeless feeling. A sliver of paranoid thinking came to me. Was the speaker talking about me? Have they been planting electronic eavesdropping devices in my mind and in our home? If not, how could they know these feelings? I needed an answer, and soon.

The next day I went about my business at Homewood, feeling disappointed that my family had not returned my call. I went to play tennis to occupy my mind and scored a few decent points. I slumped on my bed afterwards for a minute, to rest my fatigued muscles.

Phone Call

There was an insistent tap, tap, tap on my bedroom door. The messenger eagerly said, "Grace, telephone for you."

I thanked her and raced along the hallway, grabbed the phone and said, "Hello." An excited male voice at the other end said, "Hello, Mom."

It was my son Isif. He said, "Mom, my dad, my brother and me, have been trying to phone you and we could not get through. Success at last."

I thanked him and then said, "Isif, how did you find me?"

"Mom, I am good at finding things and phone numbers, especially when I want to speak with my mother."

I felt both sad and happy. Sad for thinking my family might not care about me, and happy they still continued to support and love me in spite of having putting them through the 'emotional wringer.' And then more good news, tomorrow they would be visiting me between 3:00 and 3:30 p.m.

Family Visit

Because I was so excited, I thought they might come earlier. I wished I had more patience. I stood about an hour earlier at the front entrance the next afternoon waiting, and waiting, with the same mixed emotion as when I spoke with Isif the previous day. I recalled their expected time because he repeated it, but for whatever reason, I concluded that they would arrive an hour earlier. I was antsy. Then my mind was at work predicting what type of reception I would receive. Suddenly I felt sad and anxious. Would they drag up all the garbage of my past behaviours? Would they be angry? And a lot more questions kept bombarding me.

I hurried to the washroom. I had never emptied my bladder in such record time. I rushed back to pick up my post at the door. And there they were—my family—standing in the lobby. They were grinning from ear to ear, eyes as bright as the sun. The boys raced up, trying to hug me and almost knocking me off my already unsteady feet. Hugs and kisses flowed liberally. Initially, in their excitement, they had forgotten about the bouquet of flowers and the treats—fruit and chocolate—that they brought. The chocolates were still safe inside their protective container. As for the flowers, they needed some first aid to treat their injuries—broken leaves and stems barely attached to the beautiful blossoms.

What my family wanted to know, more than anything else, was how I was feeling and what the program was like. The boys held my hands, one on each side of me, as we strolled (it was more like skipping) along the hallway.

I looked at my husband's face and read a sense of joy and peace. The screwed-up forehead and facial tension I had last seen were replaced by his adoring, radiant smile. The most important thing I thought about that visit was that Issah seemed to have forgotten about his illness, at least for the moment. It was as if he had a new lease on life.

Before my family left, they reminded me of their unconditional love and support. If only I could have predicted the future, I would've saved myself unnecessary worry.

Another Meeting with the Doctor

This meeting with Dr. M. was the opposite of the others, but I did not like the first part. He talked about alcoholism and then said, "You drank, not because of your home situation, but because you are an alcoholic and your body processes alcohol differently than non-alcoholics."

"Alcoholic," I replied. I wanted to yell, "Wait a minute here, and mind your mouth, mister. Don't you dare call me that repulsive degrading name. I did not end up homeless or living on the streets, I still have some money, and I still had a well-paying job." I remembered that even my job was hanging in limbo. I had conveniently forgotten that the negative effects of this disease on my life included those around me, such as ignoring my responsibilities, drinking in unsafe amounts or driving while impaired. Another thing that slipped my mind was this: I was not living on the streets, but I was heading for somewhere far worse.

The rest of our talk was much better. I felt happier because I was straightforward with him and the other staff who were trying to help me, but mainly with myself.

At this point he informed me, "You will be promoted to recovery."

"I thought I was already there."

He looked at me, smiled, just as at our first meeting and replied, "You were only in assessment."

I wanted to say that was a lot of work to reach that level. I resisted and for good reason. This advancement was not a reward, but having a load of emotional junk lifted off my mind was a reward in itself.

Financial Assistance

I was convinced that my life would be perfect once I took care of booze. My life was like an onion with many layers, and drinking was only the outer peel. The next layer requiring fine-tuning was our finances. My absence from work was classified as sick leave. I registered, completed the necessary forms with Employment and Immigration Canada.

As requested by the department, I attended an interview. I sat in the room on a hard shiny brown molded plastic chair with other hopefuls, waiting for the next available clerk. I felt a stab of embarrassment for being there.

A couple of weeks after my interview, I received a small brown envelope with a cheque and a letter stating the conditions for my continuing payments. Although I was very appreciative, I was even happier signing my last unemployment slip.

As a Landed Immigrant and being relatively new to the Canadian system, I was surprised that the government would help. What type of system is this? Ever since I was a little girl, I had always loved Canada, but now I loved her even more.

Feelings

While in treatment, the topic of feelings came up in our group discussion. The group leader handed us sheets of paper with an example of some types of emotions. I shook my head because I had no idea there were so many. Luckily, it was not too late for me to learn about them. I took a chance and spoke for the first time, not superficially but profoundly, with the counsellor's help, about this mysterious entity. I did not realize how these negative feelings were slowly killing me.

I felt nervous, ashamed, and dirty speaking openly about my life to a group of strangers, but later I became more relaxed, especially when other supporters began sharing too.

Another gift I received during my therapy was the reassurance that what occurred at certain chapters of my life was not my fault. It was freeing and so much more. Those words helped me to unchain myself from the burden of self-blame. This small but crucial step showed me the power of honest sharing in the right time and environment.

Plans for Weekend Pass

At Homewood, there was a procedure for almost everything. I called it 'making sure things do not slide unnoticed.' I was disappointed to learn that passes were not granted on the first weekend, but when the opportunity was open for me, I presented a plan on how I intended to spend my weekend, not to my nurse, but to the complete team, and it was accepted.

"Don't they trust me," I mumbled to myself. Later I learned that was how the program operated and those decisions were made by the team input.

In the meantime, I continued to attend support groups as recommended. That night, as I listened to another speaker share about his life's ups and mostly downs—how he lost almost everything, job, family but most of all himself, was arrested and ended up in front of judges, and finally sent to the 'slammer' not once but three times. He spoke also of how he worked the "simple, but challenging, suggested program and was now experiencing a fulfilling life."

The inspiring message I got was this, "We are not completely hopeless cases, and that we could be healed only if we believe in a greater power and allow it to help us." I was all fired up and determined to get better and strive to stay that way.

First Weekend Pass

I packed my personal belongings, a recovery group schedule and recovery plan, including what I nicknamed my 'textbook'–commonly termed 'The Big Book' in the 12-step program. It was worth waiting for my pass. I arrived safely home in Waterloo for my first weekend on June 11. What a homecoming that was! My family was excited to see me and to know all about my treatment. My emotions fluctuated mainly because I had been away and could see that household chores were a little bit more than my family could cope with. Yet I was grateful to be alive and mindful of those feelings.

The following morning, I got up bright and early and followed my Homewood routine. My husband and I chatted as we enjoyed our early morning stroll, something we'd never done together before. I attended a midmorning support meeting and was fortunate to find a sponsor. A sponsor is someone who has been following the suggested program for some time, in this case for 14 years. As if that was not enough, there was more to come. I attended church and listened closely to the sermon as it related to a few aspects of my recovery plan. Surprisingly, I did not look, not even once, at my watch. Although I had gone to church until the time I was 21, I had become angry and resentful. Then when we came to Canada we attended church for a while. This marked a fresh start for me after my treatment began.

Shortly after I returned home, I heard the ding-dong of the doorbell. I opened the front door, and there stood one of my coworkers and her teenage daughter who was holding a huge bouquet of flowers. I was astounded but delighted that they thought of me. I invited them in and we chatted for a long time. Their visit lifted my spirits.

Returning to Guelph

Then it was time for me to say a sad goodbye to a seemingly short, nonetheless gratifying, weekend. This sadness was in sharp contrasting to the first time I headed off to Homewood.

For instance, the first time I felt a low-spirited sadness, but now I felt happier and more hopeful.

I arrived at Homewood within the required time, at 6:00 p.m., and was warmly welcomed by both fellow 'guests' and staff. Even though I was a little sad leaving home, it was nevertheless motivating to be back to complete my treatment. More beautiful flowers, blazing red and snow-white roses, greeted me. I opened the tiny envelope. My husband had sent the flowers. I felt neither happy nor sad, but pensive.

As I stared at those blooms, something remarkable happened. I reckoned, in spite of my husband's health struggles, he still took the time and some of his limited reserve of energy to think of me, and with that in mind, I became more committed and determined to be successful.

Additional Knowledge

So far, the program had been an eye-opener in many ways. I had never thought there was so much to learn about the effects of alcohol on the entire body. I could not understand how it could be described as cunning, baffling and powerful. It terrified me to think what could have happened, and if I neglected to follow the suggested program. I could only think of three places where I might end: prison, a mental institution or the grave.

That day's workshop discussion emphasized two things—the first, that alcohol addiction should not be taken flippantly, because it is a lasting and potentially deadly disease; and the second equally enlightening session, about anger management, and how the emotion stays with us all our lives, how to keep it in check instead of giving it free rein. On contemplation, I realized that I would have to work twice as hard—first, to delete old beliefs and second, to replace them with healthy sensible ones.

Chapter 40: Recovery—A Family Concern

After sharing in the Health group, Dr. M. and I had a candid conversation, then another one, about the effects of addiction on folks nearest to us. He said, "The same way serious illness and healing process affects the family, the same is true with addictions." He continued, "If Issah agrees, I would like to meet with him at the family meeting on Tuesday, June 22, 1993." My husband quickly agreed.

Second Weekend Home
Friday, June 18, I arrived home at 4:45 p.m. and I was overwhelmed by the welcome as soon as I drove into the garage. Before I had time to turn off the engine, the boys said,
"We have a surprise for you, Mom." Isif reminded Halim, "Surprises."

I said, "I am excited, why not tell me about it?"

"Mom, it is top-secret, we agreed not to tell," they said. And that was the end of that classified information.

The boys jostled each other for the privilege of opening the car door. One got my stuff from the back of the car while the other took my hand, escorting me inside. This time their dad was standing at the entrance between the house and the garage smiling—no, grinning. I didn't ask why he was beaming. Was it was because of the boys' actions or seeing his family healing? I will never know. The excitement brought tears— happy tears—to my eyes.

Culinary Geniuses
No one had told me that my sons were culinary geniuses. I was starving, surprised, and simply could not wait to dine. The table was set, ready for dinner. My heart was about ready to burst with pride in my youngsters. I had to smile watching these 12- and 15-year-old 'chefs.' You should have seen the expression on their faces. Pleasant and very businesslike and

focused on pleasing their 'customers'—Mom and Dad. The only item to complete their professional appearance was the towel draped over their arms and a toque blanche.

Then they announced the menu. Halim prepared rice, minced beef, sweet corn and tomato. For dessert, Isif had made strawberry pie. It would be served with ice cream. We took our seats, blessed the meal and started to eat. I was famished and did not take much time to chew or relish the taste. That was the yummiest meal I have had for a long time.

During our meals, the most important virtues our family held dear—harmony, communication, and laughter—were creeping back slowly, but nevertheless returning.

Mixed News

I returned to Guelph enjoying more inner peace than the previous week. My days were quiet. No major emotional peaks and valleys. I was feeling healthier and also getting impatient for a discharge date. The next day I received both good and bad news. The good one was that I would be discharged Tuesday or Wednesday of the next week. The choice was mine. I felt happy and proud of what the staff helped me to accomplish.

The social worker informed me that my son, Halim, couldn't attend tomorrow's family meeting with his dad because he had to be 18 years old. That was the bad news. I was disappointed but accepted the rules. As usual, I continued to attend my groups, picking up additional skills to cope with the real world of jobs, family, health and so on.

Family Meeting

I met Issah at the side entrance. We hugged and kissed and strolled, hand in hand, along the hallway. It brought back memories of the first day we first met in the Valley Garden in England. I accompanied him to the prearranged Family Meeting Room. Tardiness was frowned upon, unless in unavoidable circumstances. So I hastened to my own meeting.

Issah's Health

I had seen Issah only three days before and was rather surprised how his health had changed for the worse. He looked pale and seemed tired with a lack of spring in his steps. His proper fitting shirt collar now seemed too large, the seat of his pants sagged and his belt was tightened two belt holes from the original spot.

It saddened me but at the end of our meeting, I was left with something valuable. I figured if Issah could make this journey, in spite of his illness, then I must show appreciation for his effort and fully embrace the program. That was and still is my gift to him.

End of Treatment

That was a memorable day. My treatment was drawing to an end; my doctor was satisfied with my progress and encouraged me to present my recovery plan to the team. I did, and was given the 'green light' to return home. When I was introduced to Homewood, I was furious with almost everyone I could possibly think of. Now that I had a definite discharge date, I almost wanted to grab my nurse's hand and scream, "Don't make me go, let me stay for another twenty-eight days, please." I felt protected while under the establishment's roof. The time had come for me to apply the skills of recovery into all facets of my life and to continue a safe and meaningful existence.

With each tick of the clock, part of me felt as uncertain as when I left Trinidad for the first time. I was not given a food hamper, an iMac or any fashionable wardrobe; instead, they had given me relevant information that would serve as my lifeline. The other part of me was pumped-up with unbelievable incentive to go out and fulfill my promise—to make a success of my life. In spite of mixed feelings, I could not wait to go home and see my family.

Farewell to Homewood, June 29, 1993

I felt sorry leaving my friends of twenty-eight days but pleased that I had successfully completed the program. Now it was my task to face that perplexing world out there, a world that had seemed unforgiving. The world I had detested and the world that seemed to go out of its way to 'get me.' Or so I believed.

As I sat opposite the nurses' office and waited for my prescription, I could not stop smiling. It was as though anyone from staff to patients to visitors were paying homage to me.

I felt like Queen Grace, gracefully bowing my head in acknowledgement and wondering if I should also add the royal wave. My roommate even took my belongings to my car. The first and last time I had felt this way was receiving an envelope from England plastered with colourful British stamps and passing my nursing exams. I could not recall any better send-off. I bade goodbye to Homewood and headed for the highway.

Back Home

When I arrived home the boys were doing a modified version of 'Jumping Jack'—too happy and excited to stay quiet. As soon as my husband came home from work and saw me, he smiled and his eyes lit up, and it looked as though he was about to shed joyful tears.

Reflection

I realized our universe would go on turning with me or in spite of me. I had decided that my best approach of attaining harmony with the world and myself was to be a positive thinker and a valuable member of society, instead of being at war with it. Also, I believed in the power of attraction—whatever I thought and sent out, that is what I would get back. If that was true, then I'd better be mindful about what frequency I sent out. Before my treatment, my thoughts had been mostly negative, and guess what? Heaps of negativity were dumped on my head. Like attracts like. My life changed from that point. I became optimistic that a better life was possible with a change of attitude, the 12-step program and the use of constructive problem-solving skills.

Canada's 126th Anniversary

Red and whites dominated our land in celebration of our nation's birthday. Our family celebrated with other proud and excited Canadians by watching the fireworks display on the sports ground of the University of Waterloo. I, too, was having my own party in my heart, in honour of my first day home from Homewood.

Chapter 41: Insecurity about Recovery

Initially I felt unsure of myself, as shown by my over-cautious behaviours. Truthfully, I really wanted to keep going forward. I still heard that familiar little voice whispering to me, again, as when I could not resist the alcohol. It said, "You are completely cured. You do not need meetings." Was this the persuasive voice of that chronic, potentially fatal, cunning, baffling and powerful disease? Uneasiness suddenly spread through my body, indicating my need to exercise caution.

At one meeting I heard accounts about what happened to people who claimed themselves cured. I recalled the characteristics of alcohol, how it affects the brain; the possibility of relapse is almost always present. Was that why I could not get off that alcoholic treadmill?

I thought the twelve-step program—a gathering of like-minded people sharing with others in similar situations, what life was like, what helped and their hopes for the future—was a non-compulsory take-it-or-leave-it package, but not anymore. With extra resolve, I continued to not only attend, but also to unload ambiguous thoughts and perplexing feelings.

Life's new normal, for me, included driving my children to music lessons, sports events and Issah to his numerous medical appointments.

Notified Employer

The idea of informing my employer of my discharge from Homewood kept going around in my head many times, but I hesitated. Somehow, some time, either before or when I returned to my job, I would have to face both employer and colleagues. One way or another it had to be done. I glanced at the telephone a couple of times. My heart rate quickened, but I picked up the receiver. It seemed as heavy as lead. I quickly replaced it in its cradle. I couldn't do it.

After a few failed attempts, I decided to try again and this time I would finish what I started. I quickly grabbed the handset and dialed the secretary's number, but as soon as I heard, "Hello," I put down the phone again.

Embarrassed by my failure, a few days later I made that call. I was unsure who was happier, my director or me. She was interested in the program I'd been through and asked many questions. We mutually agreed to have a face-to-face, managers' only meeting. I was comfortable with that, because I could only cope with a few people at a time.

After our lengthy conversation she said, "Grace, I will transfer you to the Occupational Health and Safety, because that department needs to start the process for your return to work."

And she did. I felt as though another massive weight had been taken off my back. I felt hopeful because these two conversations went much better than I had expected. In spite of my earlier conduct, I was astounded by the empathy. Again I asked, "Why are people so kind-hearted?" Maybe I should quit asking why and simply start enjoying these positive gifts.

The Power of Partnership
Before my discharge from Homewood, staff had strongly encouraged me to continue to attend the Health Professional Groups and also to register for Phase 3: Aftercare Relapse Prevention. These groups were held every Tuesday afternoon for at least a year. I wondered how I was going to get all that time off. I did not have to worry long; it was automatically offered to me. My transition from Homewood and back to work was pretty easy. I was fortunate to have two supportive organizations—Homewood Health Centre and Kitchener-Waterloo Hospital*—on my side.

Attempt to Reconnect with Work
As the weeks flew by, my cognitive abilities became much clearer. There were additional work hurdles to clear. The first

was a meeting with departmental managers, and the second, with my colleagues. I could only manage one at a time, so I decided to see these people on different days.

It would take me some time to build up the nerve to look them in the eye. One day I picked up the phone to arrange a meeting, but fear overtook me and I 'chickened out.' Another time I plucked up courage, picked up the phone and dialed the number. When someone—probably that same secretary—picked up the phone and said, "Kitchener-Waterloo..." I became tongue-tied and lost my courage. I kept reminding myself, I have to do it. I have to do this sometime soon before returning to work. I finally became braver and made that phone call to my managers' secretary. I asked, "Could I arrange a time to meet with them."

She asked, "Could I tell her what it is about?"

Those words freaked me out. I tried hard to restrain myself from shouting, "No, this is none of your business." I calmly said, "It is a personal matter." I thought that was a far easier route. The appointment was easily arranged. Due to unforeseen circumstances, I waited fifteen minutes longer, when I arrived at the manager's office. Those few minutes seemed like infinity, but it gave me time to unwind.

First Face-to-Face Managers' Meeting (Part 1)
The managers of the department approached me with unpretentious smiles and an enthusiastic "Welcome back, Grace." Their level of interest during our phone conversation matched what they said in person. They genuinely wanted to hear all about my treatment. The casual chat broke the ground for what was to come next. Then I said, "Before I begin to share my experience, I want to say I am sorry for all the unnecessary troubles and stresses that I have caused. Thank you for all your support." My apology was warmly accepted.

"We really want to hear about the treatment model," someone said, "because the information might be useful in helping others."

Then I started to tell them what really happened. "I was ambivalent, humiliated and despondent about going to Homewood." I shared how I tried to tell the doctor only what I wanted him to know, and that he simply did not believe me. How he gave two days to think about my answer before our next meeting. Those days were nightmarish; I could not sleep because I was so worried. Eventually I let down my barrier and said what really happened.

I told them, too, how I had tried sitting in the back row behind some bigger people, thinking I was invisible and so I wouldn't be called on, but that the facilitator called on me anyway. He called my name, introduced me as "our new member" and, suddenly, I was the focus of all 30 to 40 pairs of eyes. And I added how I nearly collapsed when asked to tell the group what crisis brought me here. I said, "The most important part of my experience was learning about the characteristics of alcoholism, that it is cunning, baffling and powerful, how it affects the brain, and that it is chronic and can be fatal." I took a breath and continued, "And, relapse is possible if the suggested 12-step treatment plans are not closely followed. I was reluctant to admit it, but this description was exactly what happened to me. By the time I started realizing how unmanageable my life had become, I was completely defenseless."

Meeting (Part 2): My Views
During the second part of our discussion, I was granted the chance to say how I felt about the incident. And I did. I said, "I felt disgraced and angry with all those who were involved because I was certain the organization just wanted to get rid of me, because I was black." Some gasped.

I continued, "I could not believe I was so blind and saw that dreadful situation in such a negative light."

Managers' Summary

Then it was the managers' turn to speak, while I listened. Both managers spoke individually and basically said that they acknowledged my extenuating situation and thought I needed help. They felt that often staff is responsible for the safety of not one, but two individuals, the mother and her baby. Their biggest dread on that particular morning, when I was caught with alcohol on my breath, was of something going horribly wrong.

My evaluation letter from my Homewood physician was read. They asked about my home situation. I was straightforward and said, "Sometimes I found it extremely challenging to balance work and family commitments."

The managers reinforced their support and encouraged me to ask for help earlier rather than later.

Reflection

It did not take me long to reflect on those positive statements made by the managers. As I contemplated what happened, I agreed that the organization had made the right decision on my behalf, although I could not have seen it at the time. I appreciated the safe place, in a Senior Manager's office, to freely verbalize and express my emotions, in my early recovery and for a long time before and after Issah's death.

July 7, 1993

I paid an impromptu visit to my unit. As expected, I felt worried about my colleagues' possible reactions. Instead I received hugs, kisses and encouraging words. I was pleasantly surprised by their kind and friendly response. I was feeling light-hearted with joy as if my feet were not securely planted on the ground. I would not fret about yesterday's events. I could have saved myself needless uneasiness had I been able to predict my mangers' reactions.

Return to Work

After almost three and a half months, it was time to return to my job. It did not excite me. My sleep was disturbed by unanswered questions: Would my brain be able to comprehend and apply policies and procedures? Would I be able to cope in emotionally challenging situations? How about my working relationship with others I had yet to meet?

I know that the 'Higher Power' that guided me almost all my life would still be empathetic and supportive. I appealed for strength, courage, patience, and whatever guidance I would need to travel this brand new segment in my life.

I set off early for work and drove as nervously as a newly qualified driver. On arrival at my unit, a small group of girls who had just finished their night shift welcomed me warmly. Somehow, I felt sad because my colleagues welcomed me back in spite of what I had put them through. Probably the feelings of sadness were due to remorse and guilt. My regular group arrived a few minutes later and the response was even better. I heard comments such as, "You were always in my prayers", "You were always in my thoughts", "I phoned but there was no reply" and "I left a message on your phone." I totally believed my colleagues because their facial expressions and body language were congruent with their words. It was like music to my ears to hear these simple, but to me, powerful words, "Grace, we are on the same shift and I'm willing to help as needed." Even after all these years, I can still recollect where my co-workers stood as they uttered those reassuring words.

Naturally, not everyone supported me. I realized that reactions to a particular situation would not be the same for everybody. However, I thank those gracious individuals for their ongoing encouragement.

At the end of what seemed like a long four-hour shift, I was exceptionally appreciative for many things, that my shift went well and my co-workers were friendly and caring, that I was given a second chance and the gift of seeing things in a completely different light, and most importantly, contrary to my distorted thoughts, my employers' mission was to help an employee (me) return to health rather than trying to push me out.

Here is the letter I received regarding permission to return to work:

Dear Grace,

Due to the successful completion of your program at Homewood Health Centre Inc., we are pleased to reinstate you to work on August 2nd (0700-1500) and will work August 3rd (0700-1300), August 7 (0700-1900) then you will sort out your schedule starting August 13th.

You will be required to meet with Occupational Health and Safety on a weekly basis...I am delighted to welcome you back to work and am confident that you will continue to succeed.

Post-Acute Withdrawal Symptoms

According to Addictions and Recovery.org, Post-Acute Withdrawal Symptoms (PAWS), occurs because your brain chemistry is gradually returning to normal. Although I'd been alcohol-free for more than eighteen months, my body went through similar withdrawal symptoms as when I was recovering from a binge—the moodiness and impatience about trivial things, disturbed sleep, intense fatigue, variable concentration and the temptation to abandon all chores and crawl into bed. Only this time the symptoms were milder and less troublesome.

Two simple things made these uncomfortable symptoms easier to tolerate: recognizing they were symptoms of the addiction and knowing they would soon diminish. Knowing this helped me to focus more on others and less on myself and continue to follow the 12-step recommended program. The steps may seem simple, but, for me, life's demanding schedules made it challenging.

These recommendations served as the blueprint to my daily survival. As I look back, I can see how circumstances could've easily derailed me into relapse. It was a very trying time, but I am glad I stayed motivated and kept moving forward.

The Ultimate Gift

The months went by and I noticed an unusual phenomenon. The health scale for my husband and I started to tip in opposite directions. Although I was recovering, my husband's health was slowly deteriorating. It was as though he was saying that he might not make it and he was giving me all his energy to add to mine, so that I might use it more efficiently.

I noticed how the sparkle in his eyes was growing dim. He looked sad, and his healthy mocha-coloured skin was taking on a greyish hue. I did not like what I saw. Appointments, medical tests, family doctor and long emergency department visits became more frequent and overtaxed our time and particularly Issah's limited energy. Those drawn-out evening emergency stays that turn into early mornings were the worst.

Relationship Building

I was encouraged that our relationship was heading in the right direction; communication, both serious and jovial, became easier. Finances were tight, but we still treated ourselves to Tim Hortons lunches and, occasionally, a meal at a pleasant and inexpensive restaurant. The boys might have been slightly jealous, because they were not always invited, but they were happy because their parents were rekindling their relationship. We did the everyday family things such as talking and laughing at silly things, went for short walks, and addressed any relevant issues such as school, work or finances.

We chatted about a well-deserved and overdue family vacation in Jamaica, to celebrate Issah's 53rd birthday. To be truthful, everyone was excited, except me. While I was driving to and from my Homewood group, I thought long and hard about the idea. I considered it from various angles, and each time two things came up—doubt and uneasiness. Would my main concerns—Issah's failing health and my early fragile sobriety—stand this arduous journey? Still, I chanced it because I did not know if this might be our last family vacation. Inspired by Issah's brave efforts and almost perpetual smile, I knew better—all was not well with him.

My husband never gave up easily. He was determined to enjoy our holiday. Probably some of that enthusiasm and excitement rubbed off on the boys and me. At times, I could still hear his famous words resounding clearly in my head:

"There is no such word as quitting." In his case, it may have meant that he wasn't ready to give up his fight.

On our holiday in Jamaica, we enjoyed the peace and serenity of being among the gentle nodding and waving trees, the breathtaking tropical flowers and plants, the cheerfulness, the flair and the islanders' unique traditions. I especially enjoyed the mollycoddling: no cooking, no shopping, and yes, no house cleaning. After seven days of what felt like a taste of paradise, we returned home, rested, relaxed and revitalized.

Nurturing the Caregiver

We returned to our diverse lifestyles, school, work, and medical check-ups. To assist my family, I needed to be physically, mentally, emotionally and spiritually strong. This was achievable only if I continued seeking help for myself, since I could not give what I did not have.

I stayed close to my support groups. We discussed topics most people encounter in their life: sickness and losses, relationships, employment and finances.

Pleasant Surprises June 1994.

What a year it was! Surprises gradually started to trickle my way, and I was able to start collecting the shattered pieces of my life. The same way builders plan and construct a house in stages from the foundation up, I did something similar; the only thing was, it was real life and not a physical structure. I put my shoulders to the wheel, used pieces of whatever worked, one bit at a time, to slowly reconstruct my life.

At this point, it had been almost a year to the day since my return to work. I could not believe what happened next. I received a letter from my employer that a client had sent to her, congratulating me on a job well done. The letter took me back to those overindulging days. Days when I was so drunk that I could not see clearly. Days when everything seemed to be gloomy and hopeless. Days when I felt that I was on thin ice, and any moment I would fall through it. And days when I never thought I would live to see another. In my head, I suddenly started puffing out my emotional feathers like a proud peacock and taking all the credit for this success. Almost as quickly, I stopped and reminded myself that I could not have done such a good job alone. I am convinced that some strong force helped. What other reason could there possibly be?

Commendations for a job well done from the Vice-President-Patient Services, Judith Skelton-Green, on May 17, 1994

I received the following compliments from Debra Hawkins on May 4th in which she expressed her utmost appreciation for the excellent care and support that was provided to her while she was a patient in the Delivery Room:

"Without the assistance from Grace during labour and delivery, I honestly do not think I could have completed the task. She was everything I heard of the obstetrical staff: professional, compassionate, firm and always in control. She guided me through humour and grace—she is truly amazing. My baby and I will remain her red-headed friends forever. Thank you and bless you, Grace."

"I would like to add my own personal commendation for your caring attitude and support to this patient. It is obvious that your high standards and quality care meant a great deal to her. You are an asset to the hospital and your profession."

I desperately needed that 'pick-me-upper.' I tried as hard as possible to do my best, not only because I felt I was on probation and the full beam of the spotlight was on me, but because I wanted to prove to myself that I could be back where I belonged, as a competent person. But there were more pleasant surprises waiting for me.

Cognitive Changes

A bigger surprise was the day my husband asked for my time to help him to problem solve. Not too long before, this situation would have been virtually impossible, because just my appearance would be sufficient to generate hostility. Something else had happened. The dark fog of anger, mental and physical weariness that had dogged me for years was gradually dissipating. My thinking seemed clearer and sharper than it had been for a very long time.

During our planning and problem-solving sessions, I noticed that my husband's decision-making skills were slower as compared to only a few months before. He seemed to hesitate as if searching for words, and periodically seemed exasperated when he could not find them. I encouraged him to take his time and sometimes said that we could resume our discussion later.

"Oh no! Let us continue," he would say. I admired and congratulated him for his perseverance. The planning activity was challenging, even for me.

Meticulous Plans

Armed with pen and his black notebook, Issah used his neat penmanship to write even the smallest point. His favourite saying was "It is easy to reference." These everyday ideas, such as putting funds aside to pay for our younger son's driving education, to important financial business, gave my heart several uncomfortable unnerving beats. I wondered if this signified something important.

Taking a Chance

I ask myself, "Why should such an ill person be so thorough putting his business in order?" I came up with a single answer. I did not want to believe it was true, just as I had done numerous times before. The thing was, denial was beneficial for only so long, until the reality of the situation became as clear as crystal.

The truth was that those strong treatments Issah had received, that had shown signs of improvement, were now less effective. Issah was visibly frail; he had lost a significant amount of weight, and he had much less energy. His job presented challenges too. His employer offered him an optional schedule that meant he could choose when and how many hours he wanted and was able to work.

In spite of Issah's deteriorating health, he still encouraged us to carry on with our lives. He might have been thinking that regardless of what happened, that we could not and should not lose hope.

Chapter 42: Making Amends

During one of my group sessions at Homewood, I learned many things, such as how my addiction affected others, and the importance of making amends.

"Amends? What's that," I'd asked the counsellor.

She said, "It is a way of acknowledging wrongs and sincerely apologizing for them. In addition to this action, the other important thing is to continue with changed behaviours."

Amends sat uncomfortably in the pit of my stomach, but I realized it was important to achieve peace of mind in my continuing recovery. So I started with what I thought was the easiest—my family.

Making Amends to My Family

After fretting and procrastinating how to accomplish this mammoth task, I decided to call a family meeting. This one was unlike the others because it had two new healthier components—behavioural change and healing as a stepping-stone to re-establishing family relationships.

We took our seats around the table. Before uttering a single word, I paused, looked each member in the eye, indicating the importance of their presence. This was even more difficult than I realized because my head was clear, so there was no room for excuses.

To my entire family I said, "This process is important to me, because in order to continue recovery and be at peace with myself, I have to clean up my side of the street, meaning, acknowledge without reservation what happened while I was drinking. How deeply sorry I am for all those horrid moments that generated fear and anger. I remembered some, but I am certain there were many I do not recall, and for those, I humbly apologize."

Next, I looked at my teenagers. "I am particularly saddened for cheating you of your youth and forcing you to turn into premature adults. I am very sorry for that too."

Lastly, I turned and spoke candidly to my dear husband. "Issah, I have fallen short, in fact, very short as a spouse, a friend and a mother. You had more than enough to endure and should not have been subjected to unnecessary additional stresses. I am truly sorry."

The floor was opened to allow them to verbalize opinions and feelings. And boy, those two young men did just that. They said, "We felt very angry, sad and frightened because we thought we were going to lose both of you, Dad to his illness, and you through alcohol, leaving us as orphans. Mom, we knew that that was not you. You have been very good to us before you started to drink, then you changed. If it had not been for people at our school who loved us, we would have gone hungry a lot of times. Mom, we are glad to have our real mother back with us."

I was astonished, but happy, how those two young chaps separated my behaviour from the real me. It took me forty-eight long years to understand that concept. They said they were not angry with me, but with what alcohol was doing to me.

My husband, on the other hand, was more diplomatic in his choice of words. I was not sure which one of us was more emotional at the end of this meeting, but now another massive emotional load was gone and it felt freeing to me.

Had I known the result of our gathering would have been so wonderful, would I have taken this step earlier? Probably not, because I was too scared of repercussions. Still, as there is a time for everything, I think that I had chosen the right moment.

Filling the Void

After clearing those enormous hurdles, the family was in a very receptive mood, so I seized the opportunity to talk about another topic—fun things that could fill the void, as recommended by Homewood. First, I was thinking of enrolling in voice lessons, and second, to face one of my fears—water—and learn to swim. They unanimously supported my ideas.

I chose only one. I enrolled for my first nine voice lessons with The Beckett School of Music, in Kitchener. I arrived early and was ecstatic and determined to learn. I met my teacher, and we chatted about my objectives. I said, "I only want to learn to sing "Amazing Grace" because I am planning to sing at my husband, Issah's, funeral."

She looked puzzled for what appeared a long time. She repeated, "You want to sing at your husband's funeral?"

I said, "Yes."

I knew nothing—whether a musical note was whole, half dotted or quarter. Honestly, I was not interested in knowing about them either. Before I realized what was happening, my experienced teacher gradually and gently incorporated them into my voice exercises. Not only was I using them but also enjoying my newfound knowledge. It still baffles me how I expected to sing without learning at least the basic notes.

Life Continued as Before
Our family life, although stressful, went on the best we could manage. The boys attended school, took part in extracurricular activities and spent time with their pals. Issah continued in his regular job and did whatever his energy level allowed. I tried to keep the wheels of our family life running smoothly.

A Change in Treatment Methods
Early in Issah's illness, our family physician had recommended certain treatments that were effective, to a degree, but as the disease progressed, Issah required much more. We were instructed to use our local hospital emergency unit for future medical concerns. Initially, Issah's visits were infrequent, and then more regular, such as once or twice

weekly, eventually requiring assessment, admission and stabilization, depending on the symptoms.

Previously bearable discomforts quickly became virtually unbearable. Issah was never a 'pill man.' I cannot remember ever seeing my husband swallowing any type of analgesics (pain medicines). Nothing had changed; in spite of discomfort, he rejected them before and refused them now. The treatment team held mini workshops in our home, explaining the benefit of being ahead of the pain to ensure maximum comfort.

As Issah's pain became out of control, his emotions started getting the better of him. It was almost impossible to offer simple suggestions or even ask what he needed. For instance, asking if he needed something triggered annoyance, and not asking generated even more irritation. He'd say, "No one cares about me." It became a regular refrain.

Accusations such as this stirred up unpleasant memories in me. When I was immersed in my alcoholism, I too repeated, "No one cares." I knew a lot of people cared about me, but I benefited from saying those words, because, at the time, it gave me more reason to feel sorry for myself and eventually indulge. I wondered if Issah felt the same way.

Amends at Work
I took a chance, perhaps one of the greatest so far. I shillyshallied about making amends to colleagues who my actions had negatively affected. How am I going to do this? How should I start? Well, I made a list that stretched down the page.

Hesitantly, I drove to the hospital, into the parking area, turned off the engine, opened the car door and stepped out, feeling immobilized. After a few seconds, I gathered some courage, headed for the health office, where I might find the director.

Deep within I was wishing she would be tied up in an important meeting, but to my astonishment, there she was standing in the hallway conversing with her colleague. Was she meant to be there?

She acknowledged my presence, excused herself, turned and walked towards me. She started talking while we strode to her office. I was undecided. Am I taking the right action? I handed over my list before waiting for a reply. She flicked pages of her diary and chose a date, time and a place for us to meet all eight staff members. I was relieved that she selected a room far from where I was working. I could not believe what I was about to do. Not so long ago, this action would have been foreign to me.

This is the Moment

The day came for our meeting. While waiting with the Director for the group to arrive, I was petrified and suddenly felt an inner chill. If I were completely honest, I hoped the people with whom I wanted to meet would be absent, but they all arrived. They offered more smiles and hugged me.

It was awkward for me to acknowledge my wrongs to these people and to say how sorry I was for the circumstances I had pushed them into. I spoke with them with a sense of humility—not arrogant pride. Their reactions were encouraging.

Additional Assistance

Following a short admission for assessment and stabilization, Issah was discharged on Halim's 17th birthday. Halim invited a few of his friends and we had a low-key celebration.

The doctor had predicted a time line for Issah. "Three to five years" kept flashing in my mind like a beacon on a lighthouse. This was his fifth year.

As with most serious illnesses, the oncologist suggested a case manager and a team of health care staff to assess, supervise medication, and to assist with light household chores. The next morning, after his release, the doorbell chimed, I opened the door and greeted a young woman with smiling eyes and a compassionate demeanour. She held out her name badge, introduced herself as the case manager and I invited her in. She was easy to speak with. We sat and listened while she explained, in detail, a well thought-out plan.

Her patience and eagerness to use almost anything from conventional pain medication to a 'granny type' remedy, that was new to me, impressed me greatly. I was grateful for her willingness to work towards Issah's comfort. Both boys felt like adults, because they were included in the meeting and were encouraged to ask questions. And they did. Naturally, they asked about their dad's health, if he would get better and, yes, would he die? She addressed each question separately in an empathetic manner using language they could easily understand. And it was our turn to listen.

The boys' expressions went through a spectrum of emotions from smiles to pleasant to sadness to heartbreaking tears. I felt the same, as though I were in the eye of a tornado, hoping to arrive in a friendly land with effective pain management. My emotions were on rollercoaster rides too, from happy, sad and angry, to denial, and feeling no emotion.

Reality was staring at me; it could not be refuted any longer. I had to pause and consider life's other side, as painful as that might be.

The main hurdle was whether Issah would accept the recommendations. I could only encourage him and reinforce the benefits. By early afternoon our local pharmacy promptly delivered medications with guidelines. Issah rejected them. Our only option was waiting, hoping he would change his mind.

I often wondered if there were a connection between his early military training and receiving help. Would it be that he felt he had to be strong to set a good example for the boys? Or was he having concerns about adding chemicals to his already compromised body?

In my case, when I was ill, for some unknown ridiculous reason, I felt strong enough to manage on my own, but truth be told, I simply felt unworthy and undeserving accepting this kind of help.

Issah's illness affected everyone, especially the boys. But regardless of what was going on, they were encouraged to do fun things such as sports and stay connected with their loyal friends who were a big part of their life.

First Recital: Preparing for the Inevitable
By this time, I had been taking voice lessons for about eighteen months, and the time had come to show what I had learned. I invited family and friends to the recital. I felt happy about the concert, then panicky and scared about performing. In the days leading up to the concert, my mind raced this way and that. Sometimes I felt ready to perform, and then there'd be uncertainties. Would I remember the words? Would I come in at the right time to keep up with the piano? After talking about it with my teacher, we decided I'd sing accapella. I totally agreed, but I had another problem.

"Accapella?" I repeated.

"Singing without any musical instrument accompaniment," she said.

That decision pleased me very much because I did not have to bother about those 'weird train tracks with black dots on them'—what the teacher called musical notes. I practised and practised before the final day. The event was held at our local church. Dressed in my best outfit and with my hair freshly done, I felt elegant, but nervous. When my family and I drove to the building and we parked our car, I'd never seen so many cars crammed in such a small parking lot. People were chatting, smiling, strolling hand in hand towards the hall. The other performers looked as uncomfortable as I felt with their body hunched forward and shoulders drawn up, nearly touching their ears. I knew my feelings were normal.

We walked through the doors, and I checked in with my instructor. With all students present, my teacher welcomed everyone and gave her short introduction to the audience, stressing how hard the students had worked to reach this point and to perform this evening, and then she asked for applause to welcome the performers.

Determined not to miss a single note of mom's debut, my sons chose front row seats, with their dad sitting between them. The boys were grinning and dad was smiling.

Would you believe it? The first name the teacher announced was "Grace Ibrahima." I nearly passed out just as I had when I heard my name at that Health Professional Group. We were asked to state our favourite piece or pieces. I strode up on the stage with great self-assurance, at least on the outside, smiled, and said, "I will be singing 'Amazing Grace' by John Newton, 1725–1807."

I took a deep breath, felt the cool air at the base of my lungs, then let it out slowly. With another small breath, I started. Rightly or wrongly, I belted out those notes. At the end I bowed and relished the applause for a couple of seconds.

Having more confidence, I scanned the audience and saw one of my neighbours with red eyes and unusually rosy cheeks. "Oh no," I thought. Had this action happened prior to my performance, I would have surely joined her with the tears.

One by one the vocalists performed their pieces. The last, and by far the most experienced soloist, choose a classical Italian piece. I could not comprehend the words but I loved it anyway.

My main reason for taking voice lessons was sitting in the front row. He winked at me. We smiled. It excited me seeing Issah at my first singing recital. If I had nothing but his contented facial expression imprinted in my mind, it would have been worth my effort. I continued my lessons with even more determination. The teacher introduced me to various types of music, however, I found my choices almost always led me back to timeless, soul-soothing gospel pieces.

Two Years Sobriety: April 18, 1995
It had been two years since I began my membership in the 'world's elite club'—the 12-step program. What a difference it made to my thoughts, words, and actions, and more importantly, my emotions—opposite to those days gone by. I was not preoccupied about alcohol; however, I have remained vigilant and have kept a healthy respect for it. It's been hard for me to forget the faces of alcohol—its calculating, puzzling, and yes, commanding character. I've been grateful for and enjoyed all those positive modifications in my life. In spite of what life tossed at me, my days since then have been the happiest as far as I could recall.

May 8, 1995 My 50th birthday
That day was one of my best birthdays. I made a quick list of changes in my life: head clear, no hangover, body physically healthy, and my mind serene, alert and receptive. Plus, there have been many understanding and helpful people in my life, which has been a big thing for me. I've willingly accepted any help and know also that I have been guided and protected by a supreme being that I call a Higher Power. The material things have been important, but not as much as the above-mentioned ones.

Reflection
In celebration of my special day, I went for an early morning walk and reflected on things. As I stepped outside, I felt the sun in all its splendour, as if it were saying to me, "Welcome to this new and wonderful day. Enjoy it."

I answered from the bottom of my heart, "Thank you, I will." These words are important to me, because only years before, I remembered how I felt when I had that abortion, as though the sun had turned its back on me. I felt so horrible about myself, convinced that had I died, no one or few people would attend my memorial.

In the past, practically anything, including some people, places and things triggered me, giving me reasons to keep drinking and remain very ill. Not anymore! I needed to learn about the wonderful things in my world, explore nature, meet interesting people and visit breathtaking places. I did not want to think about those agonizing family meetings when I needed 'liquid courage' to pacify gut-wringing anxiety. The teamwork of dedicated professionals, including mutual respect, tolerance, and helpful contributions amazed me.

I am sure issues will surface from time to time, but they will be appropriately addressed. I refuse to count the missed family celebrations, that being said, I intend to keep looking forward and not dwell on regrets.

As I walked, I thought how much my life had turned around, although it is not where I would like to be, but thank goodness, it is definitely not where it used to be.

At times our family life continued to be topsy-turvy, nevertheless, I felt overjoyed for several reasons. First, being present—not only in person, but also in spirit for Isif's 14th birthday that we celebrated together. Second, Isif attended a summer camp at the Centre in The Square—our local live theatre and performing arts facility in Kitchener. With permission from his program supervisor, Isif invited and gave me a tour of the building to see what they were doing. He explained things to me, in his businesslike approach.

He said to me, "Mom, we will be putting on a show at the end of the camp for the public. I will be operating the light system. I will say hello to you when you see a bright light." I sat waiting and waiting. Then there it came, the biggest and brightest light beamed and swept from one end to the other across the stage (three times), and I knew it was for me.

The third, being able to listen to family concerns, opinions and reacting appropriately, especially when Halim voiced his concerns about his reduced allowance.

He said, "Mom, you did not act fairly and reasonably. Although my room was not always tidy, I do a lot of other things in the house."

He was right, so from that day forward, I returned the full amount of his pocket money. We were equally happy!

Chapter 43: Issah's Failing Health

The cancer in Issah became more active from early summer and continued into late fall. I encouraged Issah to give up his full-time job and think of a part-time position, but he refused. At the end of his day, he'd look emotionally and physically exhausted. The final decision would be entirely how best to conserve his energy.

Issah's health was causing additional concerns compared to only one week before. His overall test results were poor, his pain control medication less effective and his blood hemoglobin level plunged. He experienced general weakness that intensified when he attempted to rise from a sitting position.

The specialist said, "If Issah's blood level falls any further, we might have to consider blood replacement therapy."

I did not like what I had heard. To me, it signified his life was slowly ebbing away. Even through these tough times, he refused help. This was a difficult situation because he was alert enough to make his own decision but not enough to realize the benefits of additional medication.

This situation felt similar to when I was pulled between those two opposing views, to drink or not to drink. Undoubtedly now was even worse, because my brain was sharper. I could see the bigger picture and realized how agonizing it must have been for him and the children. I felt powerless. I just waited and waited, in case he changed his mind and accepted assistance.

I thanked Mr. Reinhold Niebuhr (1892–1971) for the "Serenity Prayer." * I must have used it hundreds of times to keep me in check in periods of uncertainty. I wondered how I would have coped with all those things otherwise. To start with, my thoughts were so puzzling that I found it extremely hard to care for myself, or anyone else. Over the last two years, a part of me constantly felt sad and heavy hearted. Sometimes when my brain felt overloaded, and I felt that I was unsafe to work, I asked for days off.

My Question
Might my husband's comfort and energy level have improved had he taken the medication earlier and in sufficient amounts? I had no answer. As I look back on those days, I wonder if we were seeing things differently, or if Issah thought, as a male, that he should be brave and strong and try to cope.

Broken Record Technique
I used a modified version of the 'broken-record' method to reassure Issah that "I am here to assist." I felt he responded in small but meaningful ways. One of the things that bothered me about the progression of this unforgiving disease was how it negatively affected the entire family. I felt as though my hands were tied behind my back.

We continued to attend oncology outpatient appointments. His body was unquestionably in the clutch of this affliction. His face looked sickly gray, his body more frail, and he had lost a significant amount of weight and appeared less alert. One day when we went to the clinic, Issah's doctor asked about his health and what my husband reported was incongruent with visible symptoms. Then the doctor asked me a similar question so I reported what I had observed. Needless to say, my report did not sit well with my husband.

Oncology Admission
Admission to the oncology ward became necessary. I felt as if a noose was always around my neck and the tightness varied depending on Issah's health status. The only time I could have relaxed and breathed a little easier, for a little while, was when his concerns were addressed while he was in the hospital.

On my regular visits, I saw an extremely ill man. His thoughts were illogical and his speech slurred; he grimaced when trying to lift his head off the pillow, and it was progressively getting worse. Could the medication be causing these symptoms? Although he still seemed uncomfortable and agitated, overall he appeared marginally brighter.

I felt disappointed, angry and resentful, not towards Issah, but with what the illness was doing to him. It had sucked almost all the good things from him: his smiles, his joy, his jovial attitude and now he seemed only a shadow of his former self. I hated the illness.

More Unanswered Questions

Issah's calm, gentle personality had changed considerably. Was it due to fearfulness of what was happening, or might happen? Had the illnesses started to affect his brain? I wanted to know. The medical staff said "these extreme mood swings, ranging from anger to calmness to blaming to expression of rejection was not my husband's personality, but a part of the disease process." These changing emotions, nevertheless, pushed our patience to the limit. Although I have cared for individuals diagnosed with critical illnesses, this was quite different. It was much more than caring for a person; this situation touched every fibre in our entire family.

Physician Consultation

On the fourth day of Issah's hospitalization, we had another consultation with the primary physician. I did not like what I heard.

He said, "Mrs. Ibrahima, Issah's disease progression has now involved the third and fourth cervical vertebrae—the neck bones. In fact, they are unusually thin, almost at breaking point."

Something in, my brain clicked. Then I asked, "Would it possibly be the reason my husband is struggling to lift his head?"

The doctor replied, "Yes, we have already contacted the appropriate department to fit a neck collar to prevent further damage or severing of the spinal cord."

Again, I thought five years. I did not know what to do and didn't want to hear anything more. I felt like clamping my hands tightly over my ears, just as when I learned of Issah's diagnosis. It was as though I had enough to last more than a lifetime. I suppose my family might have felt that way when they saw, earlier, how alcohol had steadily drained the life from a mother and wife.

In spite of life's ups and downs, I still had to be grateful for good memories—for a caring husband, two handsome, loving and healthy sons, my health and sobriety, my supportive family, helpful friends and my belief in 'Something' beyond me.

The specialized treatment that once helped to control Issah's symptoms had become ineffective. The medications appeared to be no match for the rampant disease. Aggressive therapy was needed to treat this equally aggressive malady.

Untested Therapy

Another family meeting was arranged, and this time the clinician suggested an experimental medication. We tried to listen with an open mind, and then our younger son, Isif, said that he would like to say something.

"Doctor, when my dad was able to think for himself, he said that he did not want any experimental medication; he preferred to have a good short life rather that a long miserable one. My mom and brother have to decide for themselves, but I do not want my dad to have any of these drugs."

Before any conclusive decisions were made, there were three significant points to consider. The first, I did not want to dishonour their father's wishes. Second, I was not the only decision maker and was obligated to consider the children's opinion too. Third, what would Issah benefit from this questionable treatment?

Even though we were asked to think about it, we did not have to consider for long. After careful sifting through the information, we concluded that the disadvantages were far greater than the benefits. We unanimously honoured Issah's wishes. I felt comfortable with our decision then, and even today.

London, Ontario, August 6, 1995
The trial drug was ruled out and another treatment was suggested. The nurse said, "Tomorrow Issah will be taken by ambulance to London Cancer Unit for radiation treatments."

What we experienced during our daily visits was as perplexing as it was foreign. New symptoms and irrational behaviour ran parallel with the advancement of the disease. Frequently, when things became heart-rending, I felt like 'throwing in the towel' and backing out for good.

I have a better understanding now and more compassion for what loved ones in comparable positions go through. On second thought, I could never abandon Issah, because I know that these character deviations were uncontrollable. I had to keep reminding myself about a few significant things—this was not the same thoughtful, rational thinking man I met that bright sunny day in England; this was not the person I had married, and this was definitely not the same affectionate father of my boys. He has been my unwavering supporter throughout my turbulent life. Simply, that was not my nature to disregard those points, and I would support him regardless of the changes.

Solace
My consolation was believing that the same small voice that had guided me to safety through those past dark and dismal years would be with us still. I was not saying that I was happy and shouting for joy. Oh no! What I was saying is that I knew it would not be easy, but that I would accept things I could not change and work through them. I knew all would be well with us. It was a precarious situation, living week to week, rather was more like one day to the next, or even one hour at a time.

As the ailment advanced, Issah's decision-making became not only illogical but also equally unsafe. One evening while a colleague was visiting my husband in our home, I was puttering around, doing a few chores. Their conversation continued and then the tone of voice changed. The voices became quieter—as if saying something confidential. I became curious, and my ears perked up. Then I heard my husband's words.

He said, calling the person's name, "I want you to look after all my business, including the house, because everything would be left for you."

I could not believe what I was hearing. I voiced my concerns in the family's interest, about following these irrational requests. I said to this person, "Issah has family. I overheard the conversation; this is my first and only warning to you. If you were to honour these wishes, I would hold you totally accountable for any consequences."

In the meantime, I rechecked that our will was still legal and also I sought and received reassuring [legal] advice that put my mind at ease. Whether or not Issah thought he was talking to me, I was satisfied that my concerns were taken seriously and the issues were resolved.

During these tumultuous times, I continued to pray for our family. Often I felt angry and impatient, as though no one was listening to my plea, but I was wrong, yet again. I might not have received results as quickly or as often as I would have wished, nevertheless, they came at the right time.

One day I felt as though there was a huge breakthrough. For the first time in many months, Issah gave me the chance to help him with his personal hygiene. Yes, it was simple, but my request was answered, nonetheless. It was not only that, but also our interaction before, during and afterwards. We had quality time to make jokes, and just chitchat about nothing in particular. I had planned to go for my customary morning walk, but this was as good, if not better, than my stroll.

Issah's moods changed from partial compliance to aggression, and again, I did what worked before—I kept offering necessary help.

Conversation with Sons

After assessing the entire situation, I started to brace myself for the inevitable. I sat and spoke with my sons in detail about their dad. I interpreted the medical language that the doctor used and only gave them small amounts of information, but enough to understand the gravity of the situation.

"The doctor said that the cancer cells have reached almost all parts of your dad's body. Baby-like cells have spread to his head. They were most likely causing his short temper and his inability to think clearly or make good decisions. We will keep him as pain free and as comfortable as possible." I stopped to let them think on this much.

The boys bowed their heads, and then looked up through the large glass patio door, way beyond skyline as if expecting something. I waited through a long silence to let them absorb the news. What were they thinking? There were tears, lots of tears, then more silence. When the tears stopped trickling down their cheeks and they became more composed, I knew what the next question would be.

"Mom, does that mean my dad is going to die soon?"

"Yes," I said. "No one knows how long your dad will be with us, but I think you might want to always keep in your memories what a good dad he was to you. Furthermore, whatever he did, he did for your benefit and that was not easy, such as living on three continents."

A fresh wave of grief-stricken tears started. I was helpless in consoling them, but I allowed ample time to weep as hard and as long as they wanted. It was the hardest answer I had ever given.

September 1995
Because of demands on my time with my work, my family and Issah's failing health, I had taken a break from my singing lessons. I phoned my voice teacher because something deep within prodded me to double up my singing efforts.

The next Tuesday, I resumed my lessons. Singing has done wonderful things for me, such as releasing stress, but not only that. Singing brought me comfort, reassurance and was, overall, a good pick-me-upper. Now I had experienced what my Homewood counsellor meant by a "healthy self-reward."

I felt comfortable speaking to my teacher. I said, "I do not think I might have a long time to practise my singing. My husband's life is quickly ebbing away as indicated by his latest tests, the doctor's reports, and his general condition. I would like to focus only on "Amazing Grace." That is all I can cope with right now."

I do not know who looked sadder, her or me. I am not quite sure how to describe what I saw in her facial expression. Was it sadness, compassion, trepidation or a combination of all three?

It was tough to get through that one piece of music. I wish I could erase the images from my mind, but they kept recurring. The trick was trying to sing without choking up. I had to stop often, but in spite of how I felt, I intended to learn it as best I could. This was my only chance to express my sentiments. It was now or never.

Chapter 44: October 1995—Like a Tornado

October whirled in like a tornado, determined to turn our lives upside down. And it did. My expectations were this new month would be kinder to us, but that was just wishful thinking. My new hopes were dashed by the beginnings of Issah's declining in health. I needed something to cheer me up. And it happened.

Visitor

One afternoon, while I was at work, one of my colleagues said, "Grace, there is someone here to see you." My heart fluttered uneasily. Lately, unexpected hospital guests incited fear in me. My first thought was that maybe someone from emergency might come bearing terrible news. I tried to replace that assumption with something rational. Maybe my children dropped in to say hello, as they sometimes did.

I asked a colleague, "Could you keep an eye on my clients while I head to the sitting room?" I walked to the waiting room. There, standing with the one of the biggest smiles I have ever seen, was a family—my former patient, her husband, and their baby. I cannot say who was happier; I think all of us were equally excited. We exchanged hugs and more hugs. I last saw the baby when she was only couple of minutes old. Now she had grown into a stronger, brighter and more beautiful child. I lovingly held the baby and gently rocked her. We chatted for a few minutes about their lives as new parents, then I returned to my tasks, feeling uplifted. Other staff and expectant parents were also admiring and smiling, oohing and aahing over the little one, too.

This visit got me thinking. Several times, in fact, for many years, I noticed that just when I was feeling downhearted or needing help or somebody to talk with, that help was usually at hand. And that happened as recently as in the last two days when I was talking with my colleagues about my feelings of loneliness, especially while attending the youngsters' school sports or parent-teacher meetings.

She responded, "Grace, even though my husband died more than 13 years ago, I still feel lonely."

Her words of wisdom were not only encouraging, but it also showed me the power of communicating and asking for help.

Home Care Services
October brought more changes. After a detailed assessment and consideration of our situation, we were offered home care services and accepted them. I was extremely happy, but on the other side I asked myself, shouldn't I be able to cope with the equivalent of two full-time jobs?

I said to our health worker, "I still think that I should be able to manage without outside help."

She said, "Grace you are doing much more than two full-time jobs. You have to accept the help and take care of yourself to prevent burn-out. You have lots of major decisions to make on behalf of your entire family." Then she hesitated, as if giving me a chance to process her wise words that made complete sense to me. And she was absolutely correct.

She worked certain scheduled hours and helped with the general household chores. It was gratifying to come home to a clean house, freshly folded and pressed laundry, and a tasty meal. Homecare gave me the opportunity to spend more quality time with my family.

Issah's relatively pain-free movements were accompanied by his equally amiable moods. It appeared as though pain control and elevated mood went hand in hand, or was it a shift in the disease process? Whatever the reason, I would accept and enjoy this rare moment. These brief optimistic moments afforded us the time to communicate, laugh, and share ideas. It was like old times. We shared suggestions and made tangible plans. If I could only carve these precious moments in the pages of my heart, I would gladly do it. This good feeling made me want to skip with joy, forget about life and do other things, if only for a short period. And I did.

I attended the boys' sports games. Although I was now used to doing these things alone, it still hurt, especially seeing couples supporting their children. I knew if Issah could, he would be there with us. Painful as those moments may be, I still had to carry on because our youngsters needed my support more than ever before.

Even though I did not understand much about tackle football, I still went for two main reasons. The first was to support my son, Halim, and his teammates, and the second, to observe his performance on the field.

Halim had been experiencing knee discomfort. An orthopaedic specialist, who assessed his knee, recommended resting the knee if he felt any discomfort during or after the games. So, my being present enabled me to observe Halim. Thankfully, I did not observe any sign of limping or acute injury.

We had an enjoyable conversation to and from the game. We talked about life's general issues, our feelings relating to Issah's illness and safety at home. We shared some sound suggestions, but we laughed and cried too.

Safety
Issah was feeling a bit better so he decided to try his culinary skills. We had concerns that he might forget things, like turning off the stove or even the electric fan heater. How could I address this concern, yet not dampen his enthusiasm to feel useful, appreciated and yet in control? I treaded cautiously. We were extra vigilant.

Another Hospital Visit
In spite of having good days, the unpredictability of the illness meant further hospital visits. Issah's plummeting health meant another admission. I got news that I did not care to hear. The treatment team could not do anything further for Issah. I

understood that I had to accept things, but this was the most difficult of all. I felt numb, like I was firmly fastened where I was standing, and shocked.

This news felt worse than learning about his diagnosis, and worse than when my son, Halim, announced he was going to see his guidance counsellor and did not want to live at home anymore.

Oncologist meeting

After Issah's pain and concerns were addressed and he was sleeping comfortably, the attendant physician asked to meet with me. I followed him into a private room that looked like an office. He offered me a seat. I sat on a brown patterned padded chair. Then he asked if I would like a cup of tea, coffee or a glass of water. My stomach could not manage anything stronger than water. He chose coffee and sat down behind his cluttered desk and started speaking.

He began by speaking casually then asked how the boys and I were managing. I answered politely, yet I felt as edgy as that day when we sat in our family physician's office waiting for the initial blood test results. I just wanted to know the real reason for this meeting.

Then he started, "Mrs. Ibrahima." He paused, as if trying hard to suppress his own emotions. "Your husband's illness has progressed to a stage that it has almost affected his whole body. The X-ray results indicated his bones have been affected, and blood tests showed his inability to manufacture enough blood cells to support his health."

He paused before his next words. He went on, "I am very sorry. There is not much we can do for him apart from keeping him comfortable and as pain-free as possible. We have contacted the VON[7].

---

[7] Victorian Order of Nurses

Issah was discharged a few days later with a plan for further assistance at home.

I knew this day was near, but not this close. I understood that I'd have to accept many things beyond my control. But this? I saw how Issah's life had been steadily taken away, piece by piece. Again, as difficult as it was, I realized that this phase is part of living.

Had I not believed in a Higher Power, having the support from my family and friends, colleagues and 12-step support groups, heaven knows how I would have coped. They were my lifesavers.

During my short time on this earth, life has shown me its opposing poles—some of which were wonderful times, bringing joy and happiness. The other extreme presented us with sickness, grief, sorrow, and now, impending death.

October 8, 1995
Isif and I went to church, but Halim stayed at home while his dad was sleeping soundly. It was a lovely service. We skipped the social time in favour of heading home to make sure all was okay. I went straight to Issah's room to see how he was doing.

"How are you feeling?" I asked.

He replied, "Okay."

Later that afternoon, I prepared scrambled eggs and a cup of tea as he had requested. It took him more than three quarters of an hour to eat half an egg, but he refused the tea. I doubted if such a small meal had satisfied him. And even eating that was visibly exhausting for him. I was uncomfortable with what I was observing and I needed more help.

I made a call to the VON office. The nurse came promptly and did a full physical assessment. She requested that I call the ambulance while she hurriedly phoned the appropriate unit, 5D South, at Kitchener-Waterloo Hospital. The specialist had given us a direct admission standing order to the unit where Issah had previously been admitted.

So, in a very short time, the emergency vehicle came screeching up our street with lights flashing. Ambulance workers took Issah to where I believed he should be, lying in a hospital bed. We followed behind him.

We stayed in the waiting room while the attending health team further assessed my husband. The nurse gave us regular updates. When they had completed their work, we were invited into his room to see him. I was surprised how quickly and efficiently procedures were done. Initially, my eyes settled on Issah's face; he was resting, no sleeping. Then I looked around the room. I was familiar with the intravenous monitor attached to lines and plastic tubing that held a clear bag of fluid that was, in turn, inserted into Issah's fragile veins. Another thinner and shorter type was "piggy backed" into the primary line.

The boys asked the nurse, "What are all the tubes for? She gently placed her fingertips on the thicker tube and replied, "This one is for maintaining his nutritional and hydration level." She gently touched the short thinner line, and said, "This is a morphine pump that delivers the prescribed amount of medication to control pain." Reassuring us, she said, "We are trying to keep him as pain-free as possible." At this point we had not been asked about final treatment wishes. That might be the next question they'd ask.

The Question
Another meeting and this time the physician wanted to know our final treatment wishes. Our family had decided Issah's comfort was the priority. We were satisfied that the doctor's thinking was similar to ours. And so, over the next few weeks, we were essentially calling 5D South, Room 18, our temporary home.

Precious Moments
Most of the time Issah was either drowsy or sound asleep, but there were also small windows of clarity when he responded

to his name. We wisely used those precious moments. The boys were afforded private time with their dad to say what they most wanted to share with him. I also had my time.

At this stage, I believed that we said what we needed him to know. It was more like underscoring the things he already knew. We reminded him that we loved him and that his life was meaningful.

We also wanted him to know that we really would be okay. I promised to look after the boys. I told him, no matter what, we would not crumble. But the last, the most important words that tugged the hardest at our hearts strings, was saying, "Good-bye," and stepping aside and leaving the room. My throat felt suddenly parched as I kept repeating those words.

Although saying "Goodbye" was a way, I believe, of releasing him from the cares of this world, nevertheless it made me feel as though I was hurrying him to his final destination.

My Thoughts
These moments prompted me to contemplate on this thing called death. Then I whispered, "I do not understand this part of life." It seemed like the boys were having their individual reflections, because Isif added, "I think if God wanted us to know the secret of death, he would have made it known to us." But before I had time to comment, Halim said, "Death is part of the process of living.

We may never be comfortable with this stage of life, may never be able to really understand it, even how much we may want to." I had nothing to add except to say, "It's a mystery of nature."

How I Understand It
I am seeing death as a phenomenon of rebirth. When we were born, we knew nothing. At the end, we are probably oblivious of this life. We came into the world with nothing. We leave with nothing. I called it 'a time of impartiality,' meaning,

regardless of our ethnic background, status or financial background, it makes no difference. When we got to go, we got to go. In spite of these considerations, I still felt sad, cheated, abandoned, hollow and certainly angry. Why me? Probably this question has been asked since the beginning of human existence without any clear answer.

Intuition
Something was urging me, so I stayed close to the hospital. It reminded me of that voice that warned me against alcohol and I obeyed this time. Later that evening, the boys went home.

I did not want to be away for too long. I kept in close contact with the unit whenever I went home for a short break—to check on the boys, refresh myself, and to look after essential business like leaving and returning numerous messages.

My revisit to our local funeral home, to update the final arrangements, was not as difficult as I had expected because Issah and I had already made most of the arrangements.

What Do I See?
As I kept vigil, it seemed like our entire life was playing in front of me as on a movie screen. It took me back in time to when we first met in that breathtaking garden, in England; our first genuine smiles; our first kiss and embrace, and as my first tutor helping me with my studies and the children's upbringing.

Even in my darkest days, I could never forget his determination in supporting me to return to health, while fighting his own affliction.

More Family Conversations
Isif, Halim and I continued with our frequent conversations. Tonight, it was different—longer, much longer and more difficult. As painful as it was, transparency was key because I believed that they were entitled to know exactly what was happening with their dad.

I said to them, "We already know that your dad is only having comfort level of care and the health team is doing an excellent job to keep him as pain-free as possible. That means that we do not know how much longer he will be with us. I was glad we had said to him what we most wanted him to know." I continued, "Is there anything else that you wanted to say to him?"

Between a continuous river of tears, they said," We have told our dad many times how much we loved him. What we said recently was just a reminder."

I also took a moment to reinforce my appreciation for their love and support in these difficult days.

New Changes

I recognized changes on my visits to Issah. His condition continued to slip. It seemed to slide even lower, especially when we were away from his bedside. It was as though he wanted to protect us from the grief. Perhaps that is not true for all patients, but that was how it appeared to me.

I observed the occasional Cheyne-Stoke respiration—rapid breaths followed by no breathing, sometimes for as long as forty seconds. I tried to hold my breath as in sympathy, but I was eventually forced to breathe. I have observed this pattern in individuals on the palliative unit. It's a discouraging sign that made me more uncomfortable. Whether he could hear or understand us, still we kept chatting.

A Surprise

I was amazed at the hospital staff's vigilance at addressing these changes. Many times they acted even before I spoke. As expected, infrequently his breathing became irregular. We were surprised and cautiously optimistic when Issah was alert and talking to the staff, family and minister. We loved it, but even that joy was short lived. Why this burst of energy?

Our minister, Brooke Ashfield's visits could not have been more timely. He prayed and offered words of comfort.

We were surprised and thrilled by Issah's positive response, although it looked as though it took his last iota of energy.

These things may seem small to some people, but for us, any reaction was heart-warming.

After this short but meaningful session, I followed it by playing Issah's favourite hymn, "The Old Rugged Cross" by Ray Price, on my cassette player. Much later, as I was listening to a recorded church service, I realize how preoccupied I was, because I could not remember portions of the sermon. I supposed I subconsciously remembered that which was most important.

Days passed slowly. Issah muttered inaudible words and drifted from semi-consciousness into unconsciousness. His once healthy rich chocolate–brown complexion was now replaced by a sickly grayish tinge. Erratic breathing and irregular pulse became the pattern more frequently than before.

Naturally the boys became upset seeing their dad in this condition and maybe because he could not talk with them. They had taken the opportunity earlier to talk with him so at least that was something positive for them to keep in their memories for the rest of their lives.

Mystified

As I sat there, more thoughts welled up in me like a spring. Some happy, some sad, and others, I had totally forgotten. To stop my mind from wandering into deep unfamiliar territory and to pass the time, I looked closely at his wristband, and what I saw nearly took my breath away. I was astounded. I squeezed my forehead, opened my eyes wider and took another look. This is what I saw. There were three groups of double numbers.

The first number was the current date, next came the year of my birth, then the number of years we were married. These numbers were germane to both of us and easy to remember. In spite of my grief, I shook my head from side to side and squeezed out a little smile. The significance? Even to his end, Issah's connection with facts and figures reflected on his wristband, just as he had encouraged me to do during my initial educational times.

Cognizance

Discomfort often pushes me to improve my learning. During this time, I had to force myself to stop, look, and listen, observe very closely what was going on. I have gained valuable insight into life's humblest and simplest form—one without any biases or preconceived ideas, simply only that which was present at birth.

The situation remained critical. Issah slept for most of the time, maybe from the effect of medication or as a way to conserve what little energy remained.

The oncologist issued the second, and probably what would be Issah's last disability certificate. It stated that Issah was in the terminal stage of the disease. I did not wish to see those words either. Just like the 'verdict' of his diagnosis, this one felt like the 'final' sentence. I knew it, but seeing it in black and white was something new. Truthfully, I was hoping against all hope that, by some miraculous process, the situation would turn around for the better. That was not happening. Regardless of what was on the form, the clock of time continued its unceasing countdown, and it was going fast.

Time Taker

It had been approximately six years since the initial diagnosis. I saw this situation as a timepiece—not a regular twenty-four-hour type, but one with a huge face that represented three to five years that now operated on borrowed time. This thief took more than time.

It was impossible to mistake this shadowy, awe-inspiring power showing its dreadful, pitiless face by stealing Issah's capability to function physically and mentally. Had I the opportunity to negotiate or stop this clock, I would gladly have given it a try. There were absolutely no direct avenues to connect, nor contract, or to offer choices. When our time has come to leave this world, as we know it, we have to go.

Angels of Compassion
Another thing that made it more bearable for me was the care that Issah was receiving. I was very happy with the high level of know-how and professionalism. No particular staff member was better than another. They were all excellent, not only as health professionals, but also as individuals. I called them 'Angels of Compassion' because of their kind-heartedness, dedication and empathy. Watching the entire team made my eyes tear up. I felt reassured that all would be well whenever I needed to leave the unit.

I visited during different times, during the day, at night, and frequently in the early morning, too. It might have been more for my benefit to survive with those fitful nights when sleep evaded me, but the peace and serenity on Issah's face consoled me.

The next morning, I felt resentful and I did not want to open my eyes. But I did anyway. I fluctuated from thankfulness to thanklessness. It was as if the world was saying, "Good morning Grace, and what a brand-new day!" My immediate response was, "What's so good about it?" As quickly as I responded, again, I stopped, listened and looked about me. I thought for a while, a short while.

I had completely forgotten about the amazing things in my life: the availability of good health care, a peaceful home, my healthy and caring children who created no unnecessary stresses, and that I was healthy and able to get daily chores done effortlessly, plus, having my support system.

Keeping in Touch
Reluctantly, I set off for Homewood, the panoramas in my head kept whizzing by just like the scenery along the road. I tried to push them aside, but like a pendulum, they kept

coming back. I'd promised to keep in touch with my weekly Health Professional group. Suddenly I felt something that jarred me out of my thoughts. Bang! Another vehicle rear ended me.

I was not only late, but felt more tense the nearer I got to Homewood. Why, I really do not know. Is it because I realized I would have to relive some sadness I had locked in that emotional box? It felt almost as intense as my first time sharing in that group. At the end I realized my baseless worry and I felt calm enough to talk about my no-injury fender-bender incident and how I stayed at the scene, and how the other driver said, "I have to go to work," and he high-tailed it on his way. The police completed the usual motor vehicle accident procedure and I was free to continue on my journey. Luckily, I was not charged. This incident gave me another reason to be grateful.

Had I continued on my earlier destructive path, this accident might have ended far worse than when I drove in the wrong direction with my son, Halim, a long time before. But now I could act appropriately and the ending was better.

On my way back home I visited my husband. I did not stay long because he was sleeping peacefully. I needed to make some basic practical preparations.

Special Attire
The previous evening my children and I talked about what we would say when the day came, and decided which clothing we would wear. The boys each chose their dark two-piece suits, white shirts and one of their Dad's matching ties. I thought it was fitting to wear my mid-calf black and white polka dot dress that I wore when Issah attended my first recital. Next morning, we dropped off the bundle at our local cleaner's and collected the fresh clothing that evening.

Supports

Many people came and went and offered much appreciated support. Most of those folks were our long-time friends who were there with us through thick and thin, but there were relatively new ones too.

Sometimes, I fully accepted the seriousness of the situation, but other times I shut it out as if it were a bad dream. In spite of what I chose to believe or not believe, that tiny inner voice knew the facts. So I asked myself, why did the specialist call that meeting informing us that they could only provide comfort level of treatment? Why did I visit and update the funeral home? Why the appointment with our minister? And, what was the reason for taking our outfits to the cleaners? In spite of these fluctuating thoughts, I needed a quick way to monitor Issah's condition.

Gauge

For many days, dread spread its black shroud in our hearts and around our home, the same way it did in my most disheartening imbibing spells. I developed my own barometer. My finest and most reliable method was looking at the staff's facial expressions. Bright eyes and the usual easy smiles meant little or no changes, whereas false pleasantness indicated concern, but on the other hand, forced or little or no smiles indicated sad news. The boys requested and were allowed to go to school that particular morning, maybe more for a break and to be with their supportive buddies than to do class work. I guessed that I might need to call them sooner than expected.

Later that afternoon, as previously arranged, our sons were brought by their teacher to the unit. I glanced at Issah's monitor. Its green-bluish lights were flashing, and then it started beep beeping. My heart felt as though it was about to stop. Although faint, we thought we detected odd responses. Was it my imagination? I was amazed by how comfortable and peaceful Issah appeared in spite of these abnormal signs. As the saying goes 'going with the flow,' I felt he was indeed going with the flow of his life.

Halim described his Dad's appearance as 'motionless.' We took our cue and continued talking softly, almost whispering.

Something within me asked, "Might he be waiting to hear something?" Was it to hear that his life was meaningful? That we would always love him? Was it to hear we would be all okay? Or, was it the reassurance that I would look after the boys' interests? Or, was he waiting for the final encouragement and permission to go on and cross over, to a better place? I would never know if those thoughts or the answers were freeing, but I believed and said it anyway.

The Calm

Issah's powerfully beating heart seemed out of place for his frail body. I held and gently stroked his hands and at the same time repeated, "We love you, go on, cross over, I will look after the boys." While all this was going on, the lyrics from a hymn written in 1873* played in my mind.

> Seems the light is swiftly fading
> Brighter scenes they do now show
> I am standing by the river
> Angels wait to take me home…

The song played over and over in my mind during this time of our lives. I found it comforting.

It felt as if Issah's hands gradually grew heavier and heavier, until eventually their full weight was resting entirely in mine. The monitor patterns were just greenish horizontal lines. And then again, just like the scenes of our lives, just like those along the roads to and from Homewood, his life had also changed, for the final time.

Even the staff could not believe what had happened, even though they were present. His nurse said, "Issah looked as if he is still smiling." To me, it appeared as though he was waiting for his prize in the presence of a One greater than himself. If that was true, I would willingly make my recommendations.

Grieving friends and co-workers, staff and family changed the ambience in the room. Our family was glad for the huge support, but we also needed time to ourselves.

Special Time

I looked at Issah and a barrage of thoughts flooded my mind, but the main one was about his exceptional personality, especially as a father and a husband.

The saying, 'Once a man, twice a child,' flashed across my mind, because, like babies, I believe that we are unaware of our entrance into the world, and I also believe, perhaps, the same is true at the time of passing. Issah might not be aware of what was happening in his immediate surroundings, but he knew that we would always love him. Was that his reason to smile?

Words could never describe my feelings, but to me, it felt like my heart was empty and shattered. I never truly understood the phrase, 'Broken hearted.' Now I knew.

That evening I felt unwell. I chastised those flu-like symptoms (in my head) saying, "I had the mammoth job to complete so I had neither the time nor the energy to nurse them." So I continued to focus on the task at hand.

Final Farewell

I wanted this final goodbye to be as meaningful as the life my husband led. In spite of our grief, at the end of the day, I wanted that moment to be uplifting, to last forever. Such as the time I saw my child's first smile as he was recovering from whooping cough, when my family first visited me at Homewood, and just like Issah's response, even when he was critically ill.

Getting dressed is a relatively easy activity for most folks, but not for us that morning. Even though our clothing was laid out on the bed in the spare room, I was in a state of inertia. It reminded me of the indifference I had felt when Homewood was initially mentioned to me, even though I believed it was my best option. This time I had absolutely no choice. I was his wife and the celebration of Issah's life had to be done—today.

We dressed reluctantly. I mused as I stood at the window, staring into space, seeing nothing and hearing nothing, but thinking a lot. I felt disconnected from my surroundings until my attention was interrupted by a soft rumbling noise. Looking in that direction, we saw what we had expected, but what we preferred not to have seen—the funeral vehicle.

My stomach rolled and gave in to nausea and the deluge of tears that the boys and I had been able to control until now, gave way. My legs felt inadequate and didn't want to perform properly. I did not notice much scenery along the way.

When we arrived at the church, it was as I had imagined those days at my voice lessons. A long jet-black shiny vehicle stood like a soldier, in front of the church, waiting.

What I did notice was a crammed parking lot, people in mostly dark clothing walking solemnly towards the front door. Even the plants seemed to hang their leaves in sympathy. I do not know how I really felt seeing the casket with a photo of our early days in Canada resting on it. I wished I could have aroused Issah right then and said, "Do not leave me alone," but it was too late for that.

Our ministers prayed with our family in Issah's presence. Then we began greeting the mourners. Our neighbours, friends and colleagues walked in first, then a group of my children's buddies, classmates and many others followed, from janitorial to secretarial and teaching staff.

What touched me the most was the overwhelming support the boys received. I never asked, but I was sure that school might have taken an impromptu holiday. It was not until we walked into the church that I realized how much people cared. I was amazed and shocked at the same time.

The service started. The choir led the mourners in a couple of familiar gospel pieces. Next came the tributes, one from Issah's friends, one of my friends and the other from Halim, on behalf of him and his brother, Isif. Halim had people clapping and laughing, sitting and standing, wiping their tears—all in one speech.

My teacher and I were next. I walked up to the altar almost as brave as at my first recital. I quickly scanned the room and took a deep breath to centre myself. Then I thought, "Grace, you must have been completely off your 'rocker' to do this." Anyhow, it was far too late to change my mind; also, this was the only chance to honour my husband. This was it!

Softly—almost inaudibly—my teacher started playing the piano. She winked at me, which was my cue. Then I began singing "Amazing Grace" by John Newton.

As I continued, I took two steps down and placed my hand on his casket. Then I felt something amazing that I couldn't put into words. I knew! I knew that all would be well with us. And with that, my self-confidence and my voice soared. At that time, I was unsure if the mourners' extra tears were in sympathy for our dearly departed, for the children, for me, or simply relief, as if to say, "We are glad you are up there and not us."

The service ended. The choir sang "Spirit, Spirit of Gentleness" by J. M. Manley, as the casket was rolled out and all the mourners following.

Looking back on that celebratory day, I was pretty sure Issah would have said, as he frequently did, "Yes, in my day, I would've had it exactly this way." And we would look at each other and smile.

A Seesaw

Those last months, Issah's health and mine felt like we were at opposite ends. Like a seesaw, his was nearer the ground, and mine at the opposite end. The sicker he got, his end sunk lower to the ground, and simultaneously, as my health improved, my end rose higher. I could never tell what it would be from one day to the next.

I found it practically impossible to grasp these changes. I am convinced it was daunting and incomprehensible for our sons. They not only had to cope with hormonal changes that go along with the transition from teens to early adulthood, but also losing their father. I did not see it as trying to make up for lost time, because I knew that was impossible, but I certainly used my newfound strength to help them.

Grieving Came with Many Faces
I remembered how, a few months after Issah's funeral, I struggled to come to terms with the loss. For these two teenagers, it must have been more perplexing having to not only grieve for their dad, but also to make sense of their hormonal changes too.

I observed how they slammed objects against surfaces. Isif totally ignored home rules, such as coming home at a certain time to complete his schoolwork. Consequently, academic performances were poor with grades of 40 out of 100. And even that was tough.

Another time, my son Halim decided to assign himself as 'head of our family.' He decided that rules would apply to everyone but him. So when he realized that I had downgraded his status to Halim the student, Halim the child in the home, he became annoyed, defiant and refused to listen to reasoning. I thought this was strange because this 'head of the house' had no formal education, no money, and no dwelling that he owned.

Looking back, I had to smile and admired him for stepping up to the plate. Maybe he was right to take on the role of head of the family, just as he did when his parents could not look after themselves. Still, I could not allow it at this time because he had done enough, and I was well enough to perform that role.

I knew this situation was far beyond me and felt inadequate to fully support my children because we were all hurting. With the help of community therapy, school counselling and other support systems, we were able to get back on track.

Reflection

Had I still been in my active addiction, I cringe thinking what could have happened. Most likely, someone else would have done the preparation for Issah's final farewell. Although it was heart-wrenching to stand and sing in the presence of his casket, I simply do not know how I managed to do it. It was only after I sang my last word, and my teacher played her final note, that the inconsolable dam broke. I felt drained, but satisfied, that as a team we did what we had planned to do.

Conclusion: Peace at Last

The unhealthy way I viewed my life in my earlier years generated too many unnecessary problems. I realized that the only person that I was harming was myself. I was determined to prove to myself that I was, and still am, a worthy and valuable person. Although my life was studded with emotional potholes, they are only a tiny part of who I am. So, I have learned to accept myself, faults and all. I may never eradicate all my issues, but at least I can chop them down to a controllable size.

Along with the despondent and weary times, there were also triumphant ones too. During those arduous times, when I was physically, mentally, and sexually abused, I never thought this day would come—a day when I would be unashamed to let you peek into my life's stories.

It is in looking back and comprehending where I've been that I can now see life differently. I try walking in my abuser's shoes. I tried to understand that way of thinking and why that person did what he did. Also, I have to come to terms with those stolen tender years, to understand the past for what it was and my parents for whom they were.

This is what I came up with—that one couldn't give what one has not received. The individuals who treated me inhumanely knew no better. That being said, I cannot fully blame them.

These sad situations taught me many things. To start with, as a new mother, I started to treat my children as I had been treated. Fortunately, I came to my senses. I was determined, at all cost, not to let history repeat itself, whether with my family or any other individuals. By observing and imitating other loving parents, I was able to change the course of that unhealthy behaviour. Also, as a result of some of that behaviour, I had the opportunity to see life through completely new and different lenses.

I'm sure that my earlier circumstances pointed me to my destiny of meeting a unique man who loved and guided me unconditionally. He introduced me to new and wonderful things, a world of education, and to learning how to start loving, nurturing and respecting myself, which was something completely new for me.

In spite of difficulties and almost impossible times—when I felt I was truly trampled and when the going seemed especially bleak—still, I marched forward like a warrior.

Forgiveness

After writing letters to my unborn child, my younger self and abusers, I thought that was enough to bring closure to that chapter of my life, but I was wrong.

I was convinced that to pardon an accuser meant to free those individuals of their transgressions. I was wrong again. Years later, I learned that the act of forgiving does not, in any way, condone, accept or clear individuals of their behaviour and the consequences. On the contrary, it is a way of letting go of those toxic feelings such as intense anger, resentment and the appetite for revenge that had shackled me.

What I had never done was to forgive others, including myself. Early in my life, I repeated many negative messages I'd heard, such as, "You are not worth it." These words were etched deeply in my mind. Had I still been in my active addiction, would I still believe those self-defeating statements?

I still must address issues that pop up from time to time, but I've managed to change most of them to be able to respect, nurture, and love myself. I am part of the universe, not on the periphery peeking in.

It feels unnatural for me to think of fully forgiving others and myself, because I never thought I would heal enough to reach this stage.

As I penned these last few words, I write them for you—for all the individuals who have experienced similar injustices, regardless of their names. I believe that my purpose now is to encourage you, as others have inspired me in so many ways.

These changes did not come easily; they came with a price and with effort, but that effort is well worth the time and energy.

I have been given many gifts. The gift of peace, to stop myself from fighting with the world and myself. The gift of time to share my story with you. The gift to continue singing as comfort in both happy and sad times. And the insight to know that I am truly blessed, because, I believe, that our Creator, whatsoever yours may be, made everyone—even me—to perfection.

About the Author

Grace Ibrahima grew up in Trinidad, with very little formal education. As a young woman, she applied, and was accepted to a nursing program in England. She graduated from both Nursing and Midwifery school. While there, she met and married a man who would help her to change the course of her life.

They later immigrated to Canada with their two sons, and she continued her nursing career.

Years after arriving in Canada, she enrolled at McMaster University in the Addiction Studies program and was the recipient of the 1998-1999 (MAPS) McMaster Part-time Student Centennial Award. She invested her monetary prize and partnered with the university to educate students from Eastern Europe about the devastating effects of addiction.

Grace's turbulent life's journey was featured in the Waterloo Region Record, Waterloo Chronicle, Financial Post, CTV and Vision TV.

~